Interactions 2

Listening/Speaking

4th Edition

Judith Tanka
University of California, Los Angeles
Lida R. Baker
University of California, Los Angeles

McGraw-Hill Contemporary

McGraw-Hill/Contemporary

A Division of The ***McGraw-Hill*** *Companies*

Interactions 2 Listening/Speaking, 4th Edition

Published by McGraw-Hill/Contemporary, a business unit of The McGraw-Hill Companies, Inc., 1221 Avenue of the Americas, New York, NY 10020.

This book is printed on recycled, acid-free paper containing 10% postconsumer waste.

7 8 9 0 QPD/QPD 0 9 8 7 6 5

ISBN 0–07–233109–7
ISBN 0–07–118015–X (ISE)

Editorial director: *Tina B. Carver*
Series editor: *Annie Sullivan*
Developmental editor: *Annie Sullivan*
Director of marketing and sales: *Thomas P. Dare*
Project manager: *Rose Koos*
Production supervisor: *Laura Fuller*
Coordinator of freelance design: *David W. Hash*
Interior designer: *Michael Warrell, Design Solutions*
Photo research coordinator: *John C. Leland*
Photo research: *Amelia Ames Hill Associates/Amy Bethea*
Supplement coordinator: *Genevieve Kelley*
Compositor: *David Corona Design*
Typeface: *10.5/12 Times Roman*
Printer: *Quebecor World Dubuque, IA*

The credits section for this book begins on page 353 and is considered an extension of the copyright page.

INTERNATIONAL EDITION ISBN 0–07–118015–X

www.mhcontemporary.com/interactionsmosaic

Interactions 2
Listening/Speaking

Interactions 2 **Listening/Speaking**

Boost your students' academic success!

Interactions Mosaic, 4th edition is the newly revised five-level, four-skill comprehensive ESL/EFL series designed to prepare students for academic content. The themes are integrated across proficiency levels and the levels are articulated across skill strands. The series combines communicative activities with skill-building exercises to boost students' academic success.

Interactions Mosaic, 4th edition features

- updated content
- five videos of authentic news broadcasts
- expansion opportunities through the Website
- new audio programs for the listening/speaking and reading books
- an appealing fresh design
- user-friendly instructor's manuals with placement tests and chapter quizzes

Chapter 11

The Media

IN THIS CHAPTER

Lecture: Marketing and Advertising
Note-Taking Focus: Taking Notes on Advantages and Disadvantages
Focused Listening: Stress in Noun/Verb Pairs
Using Language: Arguing and Conceding
Summarizing and Concluding

In This Chapter gives students a preview of the upcoming material.

114 **Interactions 2** Listening/Speaking

Did You Know?

- The world's population officially reached 6 billion on July 19, 1999.
- The smallest nations in the world are:
  - Vatican City 17 square miles
  - Monaco 75 square miles
  - Nauru 8.2 square miles
- Number of online users worldwide: 257.5 million[1]
- The World Wide Web now contains some 1.2 billion pages and doubles in size each year.[2]
- Language use online:[1]

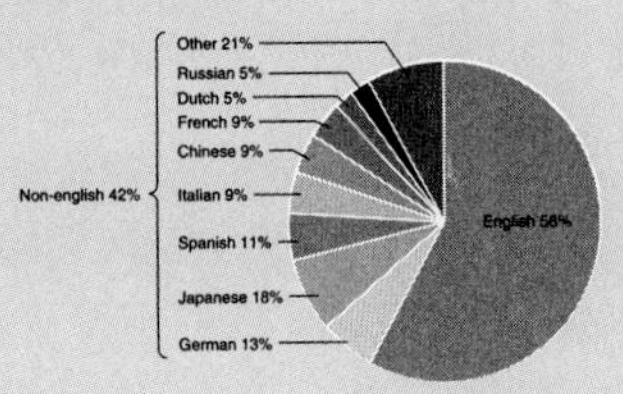

PART 1

Listening to Conversations

Before You Listen

In the following conversation, Jeff helps Anna make a decision about buying a computer.

BIZARRO By DAN PIRARO

BIZARRO © by Dan Piraro. Reprin… UNIVERSAL PRESS SYNDICATE. …

[1] *Los Angeles Times*, January 25, 2000.

[2] *Newsweek*, August 9, 1999, p. 51

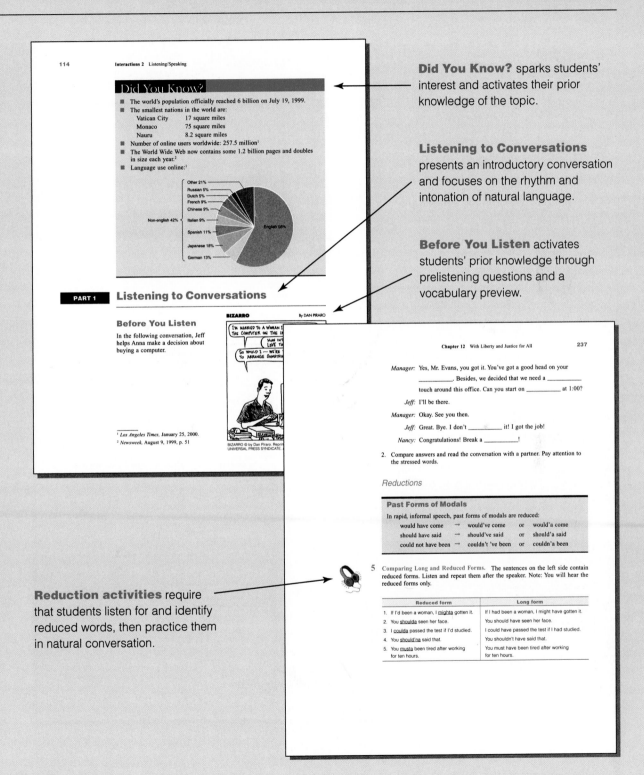

Did You Know? sparks students' interest and activates their prior knowledge of the topic.

Listening to Conversations presents an introductory conversation and focuses on the rhythm and intonation of natural language.

Before You Listen activates students' prior knowledge through prelistening questions and a vocabulary preview.

Chapter 12 With Liberty and Justice for All 237

Manager: Yes, Mr. Evans, you got it. You've got a good head on your __________. Besides, we decided that we need a __________ touch around this office. Can you start on __________ at 1:00?

Jeff: I'll be there.

Manager: Okay. See you then.

Jeff: Great. Bye. I don't __________ it! I got the job!

Nancy: Congratulations! Break a __________!

2. Compare answers and read the conversation with a partner. Pay attention to the stressed words.

Reductions

Past Forms of Modals

In rapid, informal speech, past forms of modals are reduced:

would have come	→	would've come	or	would'a come
should have said	→	should've said	or	should'a said
could not have been	→	couldn't 've been	or	couldn'a been

5 Comparing Long and Reduced Forms. The sentences on the left side contain reduced forms. Listen and repeat them after the speaker. Note: You will hear the reduced forms only.

Reduced form	Long form
1. If I'd been a woman, I mighta gotten it.	If I had been a woman, I might have gotten it.
2. You shoulda seen her face.	You should have seen her face.
3. I coulda passed the test if I'd studied.	I could have passed the test if I had studied.
4. You should'na said that.	You shouldn't have said that.
5. You musta been tired after working for ten hours.	You must have been tired after working for ten hours.

Reduction activities require that students listen for and identify reduced words, then practice them in natural conversation.

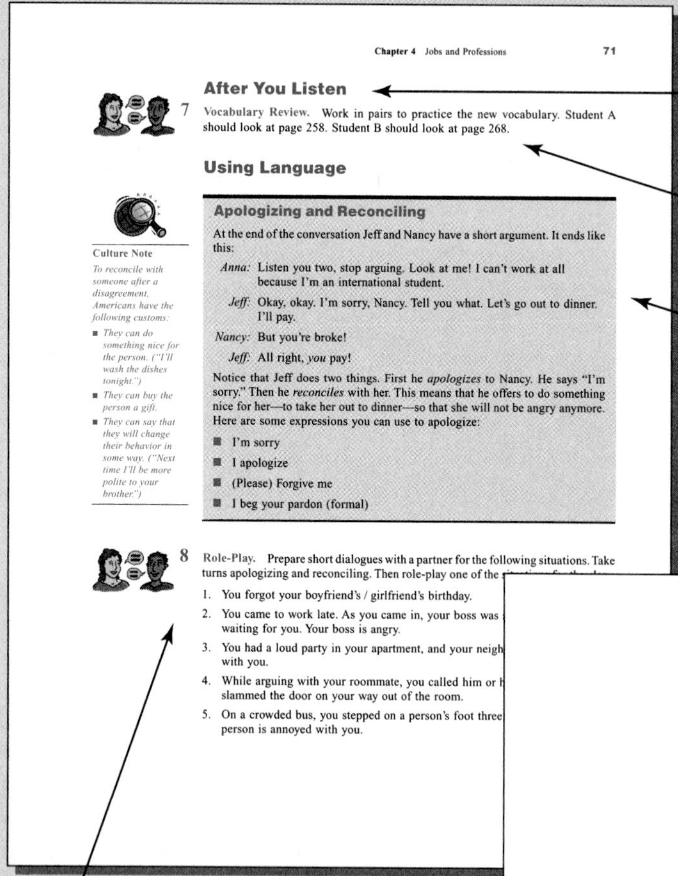

After You Listen

7 Vocabulary Review. Work in pairs to practice the new vocabulary. Student A should look at page 258. Student B should look at page 268.

Using Language

Apologizing and Reconciling

At the end of the conversation Jeff and Nancy have a short argument. It ends like this:

Anna: Listen you two, stop arguing. Look at me! I can't work at all because I'm an international student.

Jeff: Okay, okay. I'm sorry, Nancy. Tell you what. Let's go out to dinner. I'll pay.

Nancy: But you're broke!

Jeff: All right, *you* pay!

Notice that Jeff does two things. First he *apologizes* to Nancy. He says "I'm sorry." Then he *reconciles* with her. This means that he offers to do something nice for her—to take her out to dinner—so that she will not be angry anymore. Here are some expressions you can use to apologize:

- I'm sorry
- I apologize
- (Please) Forgive me
- I beg your pardon (formal)

Culture Note

To reconcile with someone after a disagreement, Americans have the following customs:

- *They can do something nice for the person. ("I'll wash the dishes tonight.")*
- *They can buy the person a gift.*
- *They can say that they will change their behavior in some way. ("Next time I'll be more polite to your brother.")*

8 Role-Play. Prepare short dialogues with a partner for the following situations. Take turns apologizing and reconciling. Then role-play one of the

1. You forgot your boyfriend's / girlfriend's birthday.
2. You came to work late. As you came in, your boss was waiting for you. Your boss is angry.
3. You had a loud party in your apartment, and your neigh with you.
4. While arguing with your roommate, you called him or slammed the door on your way out of the room.
5. On a crowded bus, you stepped on a person's foot three person is annoyed with you.

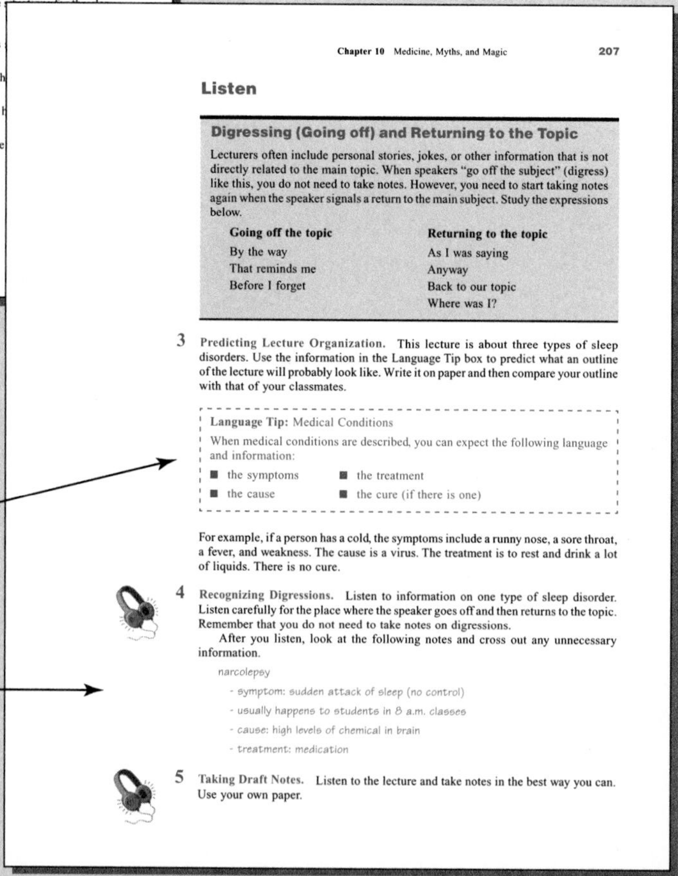

Listen

Digressing (Going off) and Returning to the Topic

Lecturers often include personal stories, jokes, or other information that is not directly related to the main topic. When speakers "go off the subject" (digress) like this, you do not need to take notes. However, you need to start taking notes again when the speaker signals a return to the main subject. Study the expressions below.

Going off the topic	Returning to the topic
By the way	As I was saying
That reminds me	Anyway
Before I forget	Back to our topic
	Where was I?

3 Predicting Lecture Organization. This lecture is about three types of sleep disorders. Use the information in the Language Tip box to predict what an outline of the lecture will probably look like. Write it on paper and then compare your outline with that of your classmates.

Language Tip: Medical Conditions

When medical conditions are described, you can expect the following language and information:

- the symptoms
- the cause
- the treatment
- the cure (if there is one)

For example, if a person has a cold, the symptoms include a runny nose, a sore throat, a fever, and weakness. The cause is a virus. The treatment is to rest and drink a lot of liquids. There is no cure.

4 Recognizing Digressions. Listen to information on one type of sleep disorder. Listen carefully for the place where the speaker goes off and then returns to the topic. Remember that you do not need to take notes on digressions.

After you listen, look at the following notes and cross out any unnecessary information.

narcolepsy

- symptom: sudden attack of sleep (no control)
- usually happens to students in 8 a.m. classes
- cause: high levels of chemical in brain
- treatment: medication

5 Taking Draft Notes. Listen to the lecture and take notes in the best way you can. Use your own paper.

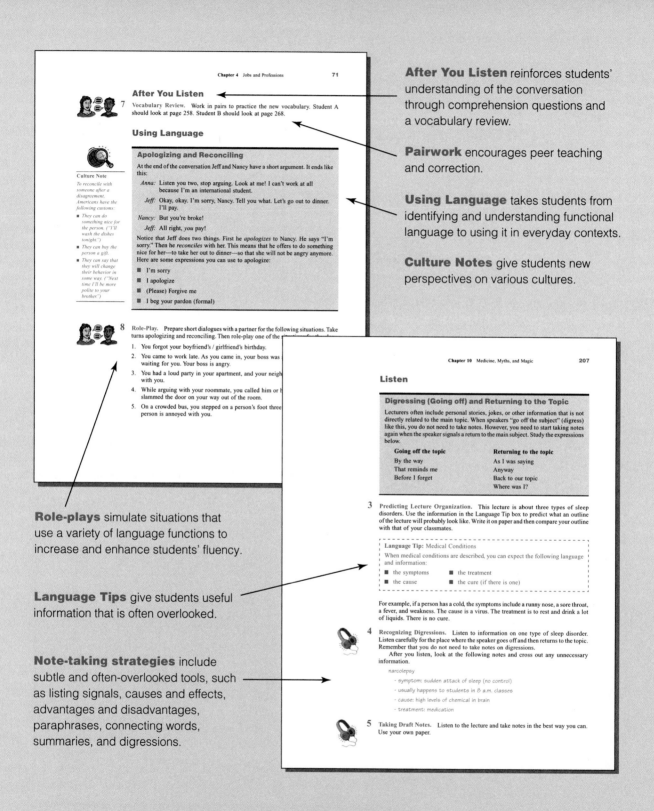

After You Listen reinforces students' understanding of the conversation through comprehension questions and a vocabulary review.

Pairwork encourages peer teaching and correction.

Using Language takes students from identifying and understanding functional language to using it in everyday contexts.

Culture Notes give students new perspectives on various cultures.

Role-plays simulate situations that use a variety of language functions to increase and enhance students' fluency.

Language Tips give students useful information that is often overlooked.

Note-taking strategies include subtle and often-overlooked tools, such as listing signals, causes and effects, advantages and disadvantages, paraphrases, connecting words, summaries, and digressions.

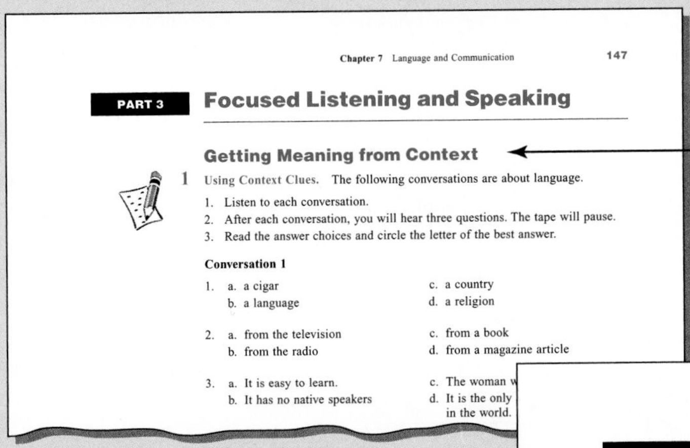

Chapter 7 Language and Communication 147

PART 3 **Focused Listening and Speaking**

Getting Meaning from Context

1 Using Context Clues. The following conversations are about language.

1. Listen to each conversation.
2. After each conversation, you will hear three questions. The tape will pause.
3. Read the answer choices and circle the letter of the best answer.

Conversation 1

1. a. a cigar
   b. a language
   c. a country
   d. a religion
2. a. from the television
   b. from the radio
   c. from a book
   d. from a magazine article
3. a. It is easy to learn.
   b. It has no native speakers
   c. The woman w
   d. It is the only in the world.

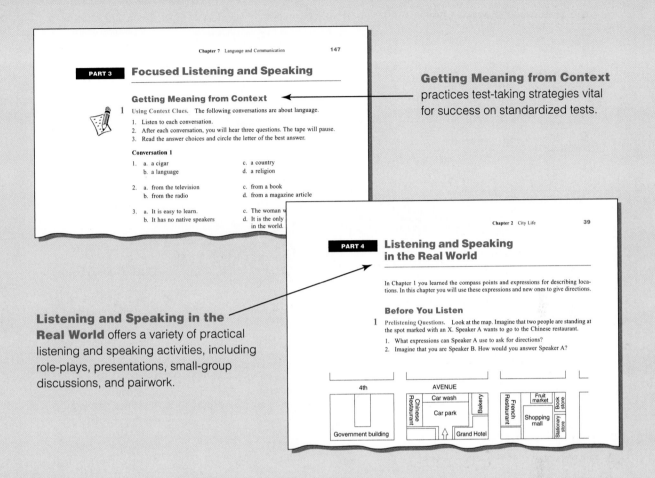

Getting Meaning from Context practices test-taking strategies vital for success on standardized tests.

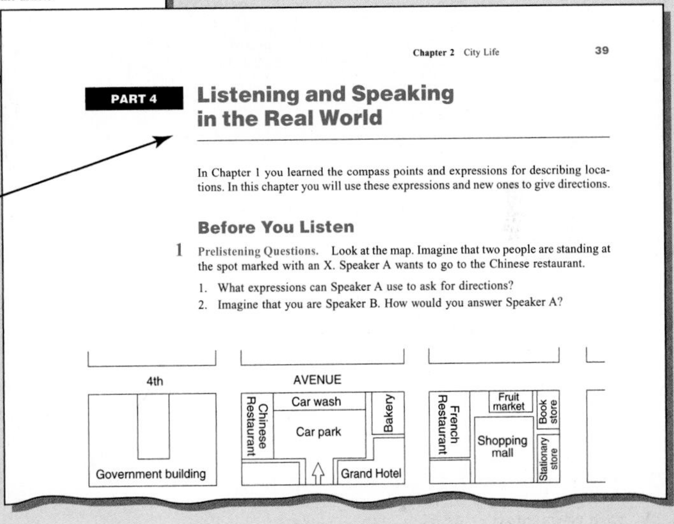

Chapter 2 City Life 39

PART 4 **Listening and Speaking in the Real World**

In Chapter 1 you learned the compass points and expressions for describing locations. In this chapter you will use these expressions and new ones to give directions.

Before You Listen

1 Prelistening Questions. Look at the map. Imagine that two people are standing at the spot marked with an X. Speaker A wants to go to the Chinese restaurant.

1. What expressions can Speaker A use to ask for directions?
2. Imagine that you are Speaker B. How would you answer Speaker A?

Listening and Speaking in the Real World offers a variety of practical listening and speaking activities, including role-plays, presentations, small-group discussions, and pairwork.

Don't forget to check out the new ***Interactions Mosaic*** Website at www.mhcontemporary.com/interactionsmosaic.

- Traditional practice and interactive activities
- Links to student and teacher resources
- Cultural activities
- Focus on Testing
- Activities from the Website are also provided on CD-ROM

Note-Taking Focus	Using Language	Speaking Activities	Video Topics
■ Using the introduction to predict lecture content ■ Indenting ■ Identifying key words ■ Abbreviating and using symbols	■ Showing interest ■ Accepting and refusing invitations ■ Asking for repetition	■ Problem solving: plagiarism situations ■ Role-playing invitations ■ Describing locations using maps	■ An Online English Class
■ Taking notes on statistics ■ Taking notes on transitions	■ Opening and closing conversations ■ Expressing frustration ■ Requesting and giving directions	■ Discussing crime ■ Role-playing phone conversations ■ Role-playing housing situations ■ Asking about places in the community	■ Garbage Car
■ Outlining	■ Requesting and giving advice ■ Accepting and rejecting advice	■ Talking about abilities ■ Using idioms about spending habits ■ Interviewing people about money ■ Problem solving: found money	■ A Teenage Stockbroker
■ Taking notes on causes and effects ■ Taking notes on statistics ■ Outlining	■ Apologizing and reconciling ■ Answering affirmative tag questions	■ Role-playing apologies ■ Discussing jobs ■ Problem solving: job interviews ■ Interviewing people about work	■ I Love My Job
■ Taking notes on examples ■ Summarizing	■ Asking for help or a favor ■ Expressing an opinion ■ Agreeing and disagreeing	■ Asking classmates for favors ■ Problem solving: division of housework ■ Comparing lifestyles ■ Talking about numbers, percentages, and statistics	■ Telecommuting
■ Taking notes on similarities and differences	■ Politely interrupting an action or a speaker ■ Generalizing	■ Discussing global electronic connections ■ Interviewing classmates about global experiences ■ Problem solving: dating dilemmas ■ Taking a trivia quiz	■ Teen Talk

(continued on next page)

Note-Taking Focus	Using Language	Speaking Activities	Video Topics
■ Classifying	■ Contradicting politely ■ Guessing	■ Discussing stereotypes ■ Problem solving: friendship ■ Guessing meanings of slang expressions ■ Doing a spelling scavenger hunt	■ Technology for the Disabled
■ Recognizing paraphrases	■ Talking about likes and dislikes ■ Expressing approval and disapproval	■ Giving an impromptu speech ■ Talking about fads ■ Problem solving: behaviors and fashion ■ Reading and writing personal ads	■ The Coffee Lover
■ Supporting a position with evidence	■ Introducing surprising information ■ Expressing interest or surprise	■ Telling true and false stories ■ Solving a science problem ■ Debating controversial topics ■ Talking about discoveries	■ Mapping the Human Genome
■ Digressing and returning to the topic	■ Expressing disbelief or skepticism ■ Answering negative tag questions ■ Talking about appearances and reality	■ Talking about superstitions ■ Discussing medical conditions ■ Discussing the Chinese zodiac ■ Problem solving: saving a life	■ A New Treatment for Back Pain
■ Taking notes on advantages and disadvantages	■ Arguing and conceding ■ Summarizing and concluding	■ Discussing controversial media topics ■ Problem solving: advertising ■ Summarizing a new story ■ Surveying people's television-viewing habits	■ Bye, Bye, Charlie Brown
■ Review of notetaking skills	■ Acknowledging a mistake	■ Problem solving: discrimination ■ Discussing the perfect world ■ Discussing social issues ■ Doing an oral report on a peacemaker	■ Justice and Racism

Chapter 1

Education and Student Life

IN THIS CHAPTER

Lecture:	College Courses in the United States
Note-Taking Focus:	Using the Introduction to Predict Lecture Content Indentation, Key Words, Abbreviations, and Symbols
Focused Listening:	Getting Meaning from Context Using Intonation to Understand a Speaker's Feelings
Using Language:	Showing Interest Accepting and Refusing Invitations Asking for Repetition

Did You Know?

- There are about 57 million teachers in the world. 46% are in Asia; of those, 20% are in China.[1]
- In 1996, women in the United States received 55% of all bachelor's degrees; 56% of all master's degrees; and 40% of all doctorates.[2]
- There are more than 800 million illiterate adults in the world today, and more than 100 million children are not in school.[3]
- Worldwide, women represent 94% of pre–primary school teachers, 58% of primary school teachers, and 48% of secondary school teachers.[4]

PART 1

Listening to Conversations

Before You Listen

In the following conversation, an international student meets an American teacher on a college campus and asks her for directions.

[1] *World Education Report,* 1998.

[2] *Digest of Education Statistics,* 1998.

[3] *World Education Report,* 2000, <http://www.unesco.org/education/information/wer/htmlENG/presentation.htm>.

[4] <http://unescostat.unesco.org/en/know/know0.htm>.

1 Prelistening Questions. Discuss these questions with your classmates.

1. What questions can you ask a person you are meeting for the first time? Are there questions or topics that are not polite?
2. When you are talking with people, how do you show that you are interested in what they are saying? For example, what do you say? What body language do you use?
3. Do you feel comfortable asking a stranger for directions?
4. What are some ways of asking for directions in English?

2 Vocabulary Preview. These sentences contain expressions from the conversation. Use the context to match the underlined words and expressions with their definitions.

Sentences	Definitions
1. I'm going to sign up for an exercise class at the gym.	a. ____ to succeed
2. She's planning to major in art at the University of Washington.	b. ____ to like or love (*slang*)*
3. I don't like classical music, but I am really into jazz.	c. ____ to study at a university (a subject or academic field)
4. You have to get a good education if you want to get ahead in life.	d. ____ to register
5. She has a successful career as a fashion designer.	e. ____ profession or job

Listen

3 Listening for Main Ideas.

1. Close your book as you listen to the conversation. Listen for the answers to these questions.
   1. Who are the speakers?
   2. Where are they?
   3. What do they talk about?
2. Compare answers with a partner.

Culture Note

In the United States, the words "college" and "university" both mean a school that gives academic degrees. However, a college can also be a two-year school where students take basic courses before transferring to a four-year institution to finish their degrees.

* "Slang" means very informal words and expressions that are used only in casual situations.

Stress

In spoken English, important words—words that carry information—are usually stressed. This means they are

- higher
- louder
- spoken more clearly

than other (unstressed) words. Stress is an important part of correct pronunciation. Listen to this example:

Good **lúck** on the **plácement** exam.

In this example, the words "luck" and "placement" are stressed.

4 Listening for Stressed Words.

1. Now listen to the conversation again. Some of the stressed words are missing. During each pause, repeat the phrase or sentence; then fill in the missing stressed words.

Anna: __________ me. Could you tell me where __________ Hall is?

Nancy: Oh, you mean __________ Hall?

Anna: Oh yeah, __________.

Nancy: Do you see that __________ building over there?

Anna: Uh, __________ the fountain?

Nancy: Yeah, that's it. Come on, __________ going there too. Are you here for the English __________ test?

Anna: Yes, I __________. How about __________?

Nancy: Actually, I'm one of the __________ teachers here.

Anna: Oh really? Maybe I'll be in your __________!

Nancy: It's __________. What's your __________?

Anna: Anna Maria Cassini, but __________ people call me Anna. And you?

Nancy: I'm Nancy Anderson. So, where are you __________?

Anna: From Italy.

Nancy: Aha. And, uh, how long have you __________ here?

Anna: Just __________ __________.

Nancy: Really? Your English sounds ______________!

Anna: Thanks. That's because my ______________ used to come here every summer when I was ____________. I can ___________ pretty well . . .

Nancy: Mmm-hmmm.

Anna: . . . but now I want to go to ______________ here, so I need to improve my skills, ______________ grammar and writing. That's why I signed up for this ______________ program.

Nancy: I see. Uh, what do you want to ______________ in?

Anna: International ______________. My father has an __________–export company, and he has a ______________ of business here. And I ______________ want to take ______________ classes, because I'm ______________ into art.

Nancy: Can't you study those things in Italy?

Anna: Of course, but you have to speak ______________ English these days to get ______________ in business. It's ______________ for my career if I go to college ______________.

Nancy: Well, here's Campbell Hall. Good ______________ on the ______________exam. It was nice ______________ you, Anna.

Anna: Thanks. You too.

Nancy: Bye now.

Anna: Bye bye.

2. Compare answers and read the conversation with a partner. Pay attention to the stressed words.

Reductions

FYI

Reduced forms are not acceptable in written English.

In spoken English, words that are not stressed are often shortened, or "reduced."

For example: "Could you tell me where Campbell Hall is?" changes to "Cudja tell me where Campbell Hall is?" Listen to the difference:

Long: could you
Short: cudja

Reduced forms are a natural part of spoken English. They are not slang.

5 Comparing Long and Reduced Forms. The sentences on the left side are from the conversation. They contain reduced forms. Listen and repeat them after the speaker. Note: You will hear the reduced forms only.

Reduced form	Long form
1. Cudja tell me where Kimbell Hall is?	Could you tell me where Kimbell Hall is?
2. Oh, y'mean Campbell Hall?	Oh, you mean Campbell Hall?
3. How boutchu?	How about you?
4. Whatcher name?	What's your name?
5. My family yoosta come here every summer.	My family used to come here every summer.
6. I wanna go ta college here.	I want to go to college here.
7. Whaddaya wanna major in?	What do you want to major in?
8. You hafta speak good English these days to get ahead in business.	You have to speak good English these days to get ahead in business.

6 Listening for Reductions.

1. Listen to the following conversation between an international student and a school office assistant. You'll hear the reduced forms of some words. Write the long forms in the blanks.

A: ___Could___ ___you___ help me, please? My name is Kenji Takamoto. I __________ __________ be a student in this school.

B: Oh yeah, I remember you. How are you?

A: Fine, thanks.

B: Can I help you with something?

A: Yes, I __________ __________ get an application for the TOEFL test.

B: __________ __________ the one in November? Let's see. They __________ __________ be here on this shelf. It looks like they're all gone. I'm sorry, you'll __________ __________ wait until they come in next week.

A: __________ __________ sending me one when they come in?

B: No problem. __________ __________ name and address?

2. Check your answers. Then read the dialogue with a partner for pronunciation practice.

After You Listen

7 **Vocabulary Review.** Discuss your answers to the following questions with a partner. Use the underlined vocabulary from Activity 2 in your answers.

1. If you are a student, what is your major, or what subject do you plan to major in at the university?
2. If you are working, what is your career, or what career would you like to have in the future?
3. Is it important for you to know English if you want to get ahead in your career?
4. Are you into art, like Anna Maria? If yes, what kind of art do you like?
5. Are you going to sign up for another English course after this one?

Using Language

Showing Interest

When people are talking, they want to show that they are listening and that they are interested in the conversation. English speakers do this by making eye contact, by nodding their heads,* and by using words and phrases that encourage the other speaker to continue.

Here are some expressions for showing interest:

Really?	Oh?
Yeah?	Oh yeah?
I see.	Mmmm—hmm
And?	Well?
Oh no!	

8 **Expressions for Showing Interest.** Read the completed script of the conversation in Activity 4. Circle all the phrases that Anna and Nancy use to show interest in what the other is saying.

9 **Showing Interest.** Work in pairs. Take turns telling each other a story about a very important event in your life. As one student speaks, the other should show interest by making eye contact, nodding, and using phrases of encouragement from the box.

Some sample topics (but feel free to choose your own!):

1. My favorite vacation
2. A serious accident
3. The best meal I have ever eaten
4. The day I met my (boyfriend / girlfriend / husband / wife)
5. My first day of high school / college / work

* "Nodding" means moving your head up and down to show agreement or to mean "yes."

PART 2

Listening to Lectures

Culture Note

There are three levels of degrees in most American and Canadian universities:

- *B.A. or B.S. (Bachelor of Arts / Science): after four years of study.*
- *M.A. or M.S. (Master of Arts / Science): after two additional years.*
- *Ph.D. (Doctor of Philosophy): after two or more additional years.*

Students who are studying for the B.A. are called undergraduates or "undergrads." Those studying for the M.A. or Ph.D. are called graduate (or "grad") students.

Before You Listen

Anna goes to an orientation meeting given by the academic advisor at her English language school. At the meeting, the advisor gives some information about typical undergraduate courses in the United States and Canada.

1 **Prelistening Quiz.** How much do you know about typical university courses in the United States and Canada? Take this short quiz and find out. Write T if a statement is true and F if it is false. Then discuss your responses with your classmates. When you listen to the lecture, you will learn the correct answers.

1. _____ Some undergraduate lecture classes may have 300 students in them.
2. _____ All courses at American and Canadian universities are taught by professors.
3. _____ The information in lectures is the same as the information in textbooks, so attending lectures is usually not necessary.
4. _____ All your homework will be read and corrected by your professor.
5. _____ A discussion section is a class where students meet informally to help each other with their coursework.
6. _____ The ability to write well is not very important for undergraduates.
7. _____ Only graduate students are required to do research.
8. _____ If you cheat and are caught, you might have to leave the university.

2 **Vocabulary Preview.** The following terms appear in the lecture. With your classmates, define the words you already know. Mark the words you do not know.

____ lecture	____ laboratory ("lab")	____ term paper
____ to take notes	____ experiment	____ plagiarism
____ to attend	____ requirement	____ cheating
____ discussion section	____ midterm exam	____ to fail a course
____ teaching assistant	____ quiz	____ to get kicked out

Listen

3 **Note-Taking Pretest.**

1. Listen to the lecture and take notes in any way you can. Don't worry about doing it the "right" way this first time; just do your best. Use your own paper.
2. Discuss the following questions with one or more classmates.
   1. Were you able to listen to the lecture and take notes at the same time? If not, why not?
   2. Did you try to organize your notes in any way? For example, did you separate the main ideas from the details?
   3. Did you write complete sentences?
   4. Compare notes with your classmates. How are they similar? Different?

Using the Introduction to Predict Lecture Content

Like a composition, a lecture usually has three parts: the introduction, the body, and the conclusion. You should listen very carefully to the introduction because it will usually contain two important pieces of information:

1. the topic of the lecture
2. a brief summary or list of the main ideas the speaker will talk about

Note: Lecturers often start their lectures with announcements, a review of the last lecture, or a story. You do **not** need to take notes on these things, so listen carefully to the lecturer's introduction before you start to take notes.

4 Taking Notes on the Introduction. Listen to the lecture introduction again and fill in the blanks.

Topic of the lecture:

____

____

____

Main ideas that the speaker will discuss:

____

____

____

Three Keys to Writing Effective Lecture Notes

Indentation. "Indent" means "move your text to the right." Indent to show the relationship between main ideas and specific details. Write main ideas next to the left margin. Indent about 1/2 inch (about 1.5 cm) as information becomes more specific. Most of the time your notes will have three or four "levels" of indentation.

Key words. When you take notes, do not write every word. Taking notes is not like writing a dictation. Write only the most important, or "key," words. Key words are usually nouns, verbs, adjectives, and adverbs.

Abbreviations and symbols. You can save time if you abbreviate (shorten) words and use symbols as much as possible. For example, write ↑ instead of "increase" or "go up." Look at the list of common abbreviations and symbols in the appendix on page 277. You can also create your own abbreviations and symbols as you take notes.

5 Identifying the Three Keys to Taking Effective Lecture Notes. Below are sample notes for the first part of the lecture. Look at the notes as you listen again. Notice how the writer used indentation, key words, abbreviations, and symbols.

Sept. 20, 2001

Topic: University System in U.S. & Canada

<u>3 Types of Univ. Courses (undergrad.)</u>

1. Lecture course: Prof. talks. Sts. take notes.
    - Important to take notes because
        - info in lec. ≠ info in books
        - exam q's based on lecs
    - Sts. listen to lecs. 4–6 hrs. / wk. per course
    - Lecs. given in large rooms cuz class size = 200+ students
2. Discussion section
    - smaller: 20–30 sts.
    - meets 2–3 hrs / wk
    - ask q's, go over HW
    - taught by TA (not prof)
3. Lab
    - for science majors
    - do experiments

6 **Indenting.** Below are notes for the second part of the lecture. However, the information is not indented correctly. Read the notes as you listen again. Then copy the notes on clean paper with three levels of indentation. Use the notes from Activity 5 as a model.

Course Requirements

tests or exams

midterm (in the middle of the course)

final (a big exam at the end of the course)

quizzes (small tests from time to time)

term paper = a large writing project

steps

choose a topic

do research in the library or on the Internet

use notes to write the paper in your own words

5–25 pgs. long

plagiarism

def.: copying

plag. = cheating

punishment

fail a course

get kicked out of univ.

After You Listen

7 **Defining New Vocabulary.** With a partner, look back at the words you marked as unknown in Activity 2 and discuss the meaning of each new term. Your teacher may ask you to write sentences with these new words.

8 Discussing the Lecture. Compare the American university system with systems in other countries or schools. Refer to your notes as necessary. Use the new vocabulary as you talk.

Topics to discuss:

- types of university courses
- who teaches university courses
- class sizes
- course requirements for different majors
- types of exams
- punishment for plagiarism

Example

"At universities in Italy, all the classes are lectures. We don't have discussion sections and we don't have TAs. If we need help we just ask friends. . . ."

On the Spot!*

Situation

Last year you took an American history course. There were 200 students in the class. One of the requirements of the course was a ten-page term paper. You worked hard on your paper and received an A.

This year a close friend of yours is enrolled in the same class. Your friend is a good student, but recently has had a sick mother, and he/she has been busy taking care of a younger brother and sister.

Your friend comes to you and asks to copy your research paper from last year. Your friend is sure that the professor will not remember the paper because there are so many students in the class.

Discussion Questions

Discuss the following questions in small groups.

1. Would you allow your friend to copy your paper in this situation? Why or why not?
2. Would your decision be different if your friend's mother were not sick?
3. Would your decision be different if you thought your friend might get caught?
4. Has a friend ever asked to copy from you? What did you do?

---

* You are "on the spot" when you have to make a difficult decision. This book contains On the Spot! activities, where you work with your classmates to solve difficult problems or discuss difficult situations.

5. Have you ever asked a friend if you could copy a paper? Why? How did you feel about it?
6. If a person cheats in school, do you think this person will also cheat in other areas of life? Why or why not?

Role-Play

Many universities in the United States and Canada have a "student affairs council." A council is a group of students who make decisions about how to punish students who break the university's rules. Suppose that in this situation, the student who copied the paper gets caught. The student affairs council meets to discuss the situation and decide on the student's punishment.

Roles

1. the student who cheated
2. the student who wrote the paper originally
3. the chairperson of the student affairs council
4. members of the student affairs council (all other classmates)

Procedure

The council should sit in a circle, if possible.

1. The chairperson begins the meeting and explains the case.
2. The council interviews the student who cheated.
3. The council interviews the student who wrote the paper originally.
4. After the students leave, the council decides what punishment, if any, the cheating students will receive.

Follow-Up

Write a letter from the student affairs council to the student who copied, informing the student of the council's decision.

PART 3 Focused Listening and Speaking

Getting Meaning from Context

When you listen to people talking in English, it is probably hard to understand all the words. However, you can usually get a general idea of what people are talking about. How? By using *clues* that help you to *guess*. These clues include words as well as nonverbal signals such as a speaker's voice, facial expressions, and gestures.

The ability to guess information is an important listening skill. Even if your vocabulary is small, it can help you understand what English speakers are saying. It can also help you do well on standardized listening tests such as the TOEFL.

1 **Using Context Clues.** The following conversations take place on a college campus.

1. Listen to each conversation.
2. After each conversation, you will hear a question. Stop the tape or CD.
3. Read the answer choices and circle the letter of the best answer.
4. Write the clues that helped you choose your answer. Discuss them with your teacher and classmates.
5. Start the recording again. You will hear a sentence with the correct answer.

Answers	Clues
1. a. in a bookstore b. in a library c. in a laboratory d. in an English class	
2. a. a chemist b. a secretary c. a roommate d. a TA	
3. a. chemistry b. history c. German d. business	

Focused Listening

Using Intonation to Understand a Speaker's Feelings

Intonation refers to the rising and falling direction of a speaker's voice. For example, when we ask yes/no questions in English, we use rising intonation: "Have you finished your homework yet?"

Tone of voice refers to the feeling in a speaker's voice. It tells us if the speaker is feeling excited, bored, angry, confused, disappointed, surprised, or many other feelings.

For example, listen to the sentence "I got 75% on the test" spoken in three different ways. What is the speaker's feeling in each case?

In the first case, the speaker's voice rises and falls a lot. It is energetic and happy. The speaker sounds excited. In the second case, the speaker is angry. Again the voice is energetic, but it sounds tense, unhappy. In the third case, we hear falling intonation and the voice lacks energy. The speaker sounds disappointed.

In short, meaning comes not only from words but also from the way we use our voices.

2 Listening for Intonation. In the items that follow, you will hear two conversations. Each of them is spoken in two ways. Use the differences in intonation and tone to decide what the speakers are feeling.

1A. a. excited
 b. uninterested
 c. angry

1B. a. happy
 b. uninterested
 c. angry

2A. a. excited
 b. worried
 c. bored

2B. a. happy
 b. worried
 c. bored

3 Using Intonation to Express Feelings. Work with a partner.

1. Each of you will read one sentence in different ways. Your partner should say which feeling you are trying to express each time.

 Student 1's sentence: You forgot the baby in the car.
 Student 2's sentence: You put my car keys in the refrigerator.

 Use intonation to express these feelings:

 a. angry b. surprised c. amused d. bored

2. Now write your own sentence. Say it to your partner in different ways. Your partner should guess which feeling you are trying to express.

Using Language

Accepting and Refusing Invitations

This is the script for Conversations 1A and 1B in Activity 2. Notice the expressions Ron uses to invite Kathy to the party and the expressions Kathy uses to accept or refuse.

Kathy: Hello?
Ron: Kathy? Uh, this is Ron, you know, from your history class?
Kathy: Oh, hi.
Ron: Listen, I was wondering . . . um, were you planning to go to Ali's party Saturday?
Kathy: Hmm. I haven't really thought about it yet.
Ron: Well, would you like to go?
Kathy: You mean, with you?
Ron: Yeah.
Kathy: Well, sure, Ron, I'd love to go. / Well thanks, Ron, but I just remembered that I'm busy that night.

4 **Expressions for Inviting, Accepting, and Refusing.** Complete this chart with expressions from the conversation. Add other expressions that you know.

Note: To **refuse** the invitation, Kathy does not say "No, thank you." Instead, she gives a reason for refusing. This kind of reason (which may or may not be true) is called an **excuse**, and refusing an invitation this way is called **making (or giving) an excuse**. Include in the chart some excuses that you have heard.

Inviting	Accepting	Refusing (with an excuse)

5 **Accepting and Refusing Invitations.** Work with a partner. Write a short (two minutes) conversation with these parts:

Part 1. Person A invites person B.

Part 2. Person B (a) accepts the invitation, or (b) refuses the invitation and offers an excuse.

Write about one of the following situations. Practice your conversation several times. Afterward, perform it for the class—without reading!

1. Person A invites person B to a foreign-language film. The film is very popular, but it is in a language that neither person understands.
2. Person A invites person B to a holiday party at Person A's parents' house. Person B has never met the parents.
3. Person A invites Person B to dinner at an expensive restaurant to celebrate Person B's birthday.

Now make a *real* invitation and see if your partner accepts or rejects it.

PART 4

Listening and Speaking in the Real World

In this section you will learn the compass points and expressions for describing locations. You will use this language again in Chapter 2, where you will learn how to give and follow directions.

Before You Listen

1 **Reviewing Compass Points.**

1. Study the picture of the compass. With your teacher, practice saying the names of the compass points: north, south, east, west, northeast, northwest, southeast, southwest.
2. With your teacher, determine where north is in your classroom. Stand up and face north. Select one student to call out directions. As the student calls a direction, everyone should turn and face that way.

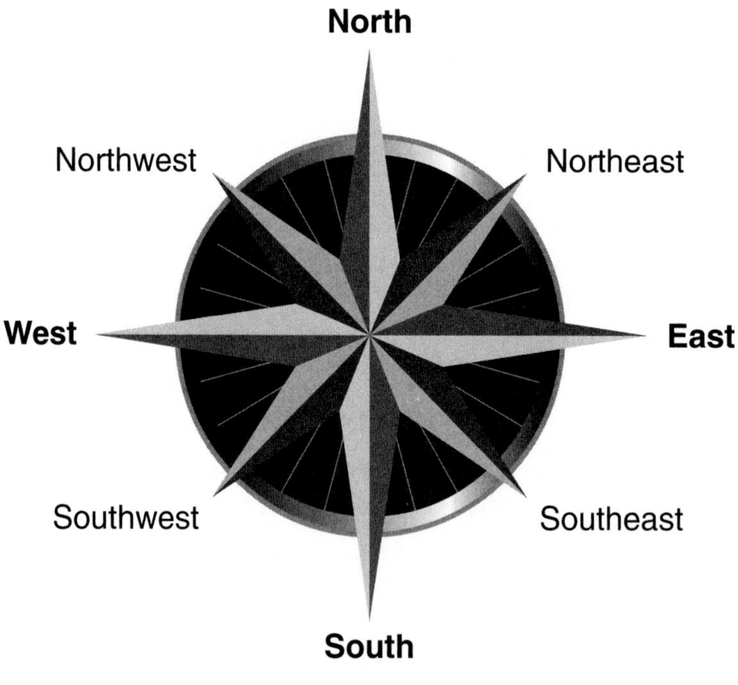

Listen

2 Pronouncing Expressions of Location.

1. Below are expressions for describing locations. Listen and repeat each expression after the speaker. Pay attention to stressed words.

   a. _____ on the (southeast) corner

   b. _____ at the intersection of

   c. _____ beside, next to the bank

   d. _____ across the street from (opposite)

   e. _____ on both sides of (the street)

   f. _____ in the middle of the block

   g. _____ around the corner from

   h. _____ down the street (from)

   i. _____ in the middle of the street

   j. _____ up the street (from)

   k. _____ between

2. Write the numbers from the map next to the matching expressions on this list.

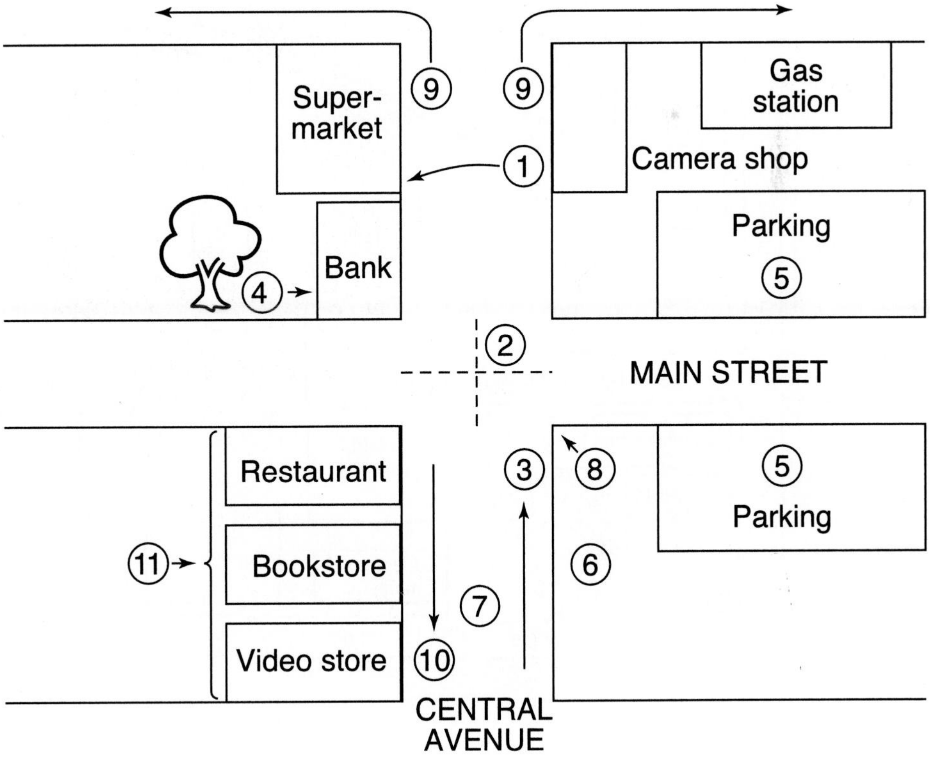

Language Tip

The prepositions *in, on, at* are confusing. Look at these examples:

	Hint
I live <u>on</u> Olympic Street	"on" + street
The school is <u>at</u> 3204 Glendon Avenue	"at" + address
Harvard University is <u>in</u> Boston (city). It is <u>in</u> Massachusetts (state). It is <u>in</u> the United States.	"in" + city, state, country

3 Understanding Expressions of Location in Context. Study this map of a college campus. Read the names of the buildings and streets. Then listen to statements about the map. Write T if a statement is true and F if it is false, based on the map. You will hear each statement twice.

1. _____
2. _____
3. _____
4. _____
5. _____
6. _____
7. _____
8. _____

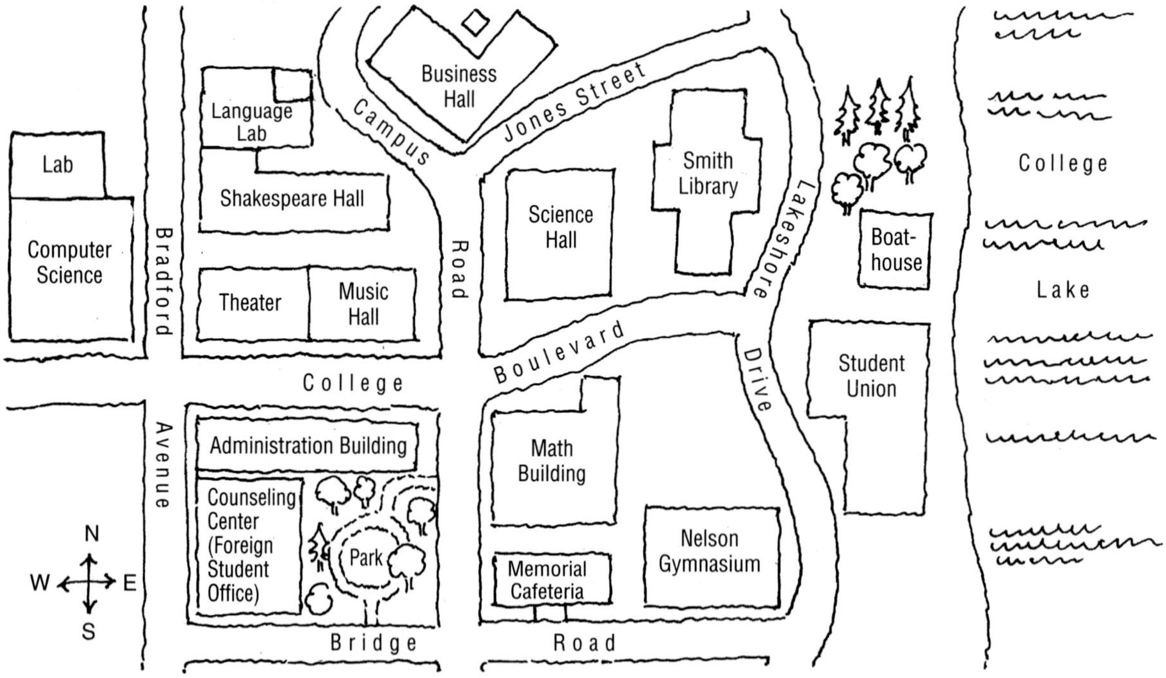

After You Listen

4 Using Expressions of Location. Write five true or false statements about the map. Use a different expression from Activity 2 in each statement. Then read your statements to one or more classmates, who will say if they are true or false.

____

____

____

____

____

Using Language

Asking for Repetition

Use the following expressions to ask a speaker for repetition:

I beg your pardon?	(formal)
Would you mind repeating that?	↓
Could you please repeat that?	
What did you say?	
Say it again, please.	
Pardon (me)?	
Excuse me?	
Sorry?	
What?	
Huh?	(informal)

5 Reading Maps for Locations. Work in pairs to ask and answer questions about locations. Student A should look at the map on page 254. Student B should look on page 264.

Video Activities: An Online English Class

Before You Watch. Discuss the following questions with your class or in small groups.

1. Do you ever use the Internet? What kinds of sites do you visit?
2. Do you ever do research for a paper online?
3. Have you ever taken an online course?
4. Do you know the expression "virtual reality"?

Watch. Check the following things students can do in Dr. Weshkey's virtual English class.

1. _____ get announcements
2. _____ listen to a lecture
3. _____ link to Websites for research
4. _____ construct a personal web page
5. _____ take tests
6. _____ talk to classmates
7. _____ send an e-mail to the teacher

Watch Again. Virtual courses have both advantages and disadvantages. Compete the chart below. Afterwards, share answers with your classmates.

	Advantage(s)	Disadvantage(s)
For students		
For parents		
For teachers		

After You Watch. Discuss the following questions.

1. Would <u>you</u> like to try a virtual course? In what subject(s)?
2. What kind of courses would work well online? What kind would not work well?
3. Do you think it would be possible to learn English online? Why or why not?

Chapter 2

City Life

IN THIS CHAPTER

Lecture:	Burglary Prevention
Note-Taking Focus:	Taking Notes on Statistics Listening for Transitions
Focused Listening:	Guessing Relationships between People
Using Language:	Opening and Closing Phone Conversations Expressing Frustration Requesting and Giving Directions

Did You Know?

- The world's cities with the largest populations are:
  1. Seoul, South Korea
  2. Sao Paolo, Brazil
  3. Bombay, India
  4. Jakarta, Indonesia
  5. Moscow, Russia
  6. Istanbul, Turkey
  7. Mexico City, Mexico
  8. Shanghai, China
  9. Tokyo, Japan
  10. New York City, U.S.A.
- In many U.S. cities it is illegal to cross in the middle of the street. Doing this is called "jaywalking." Visitors to the United States must remember to cross the street only at the corner; otherwise, a police officer can give them a ticket!
- The largest parking areas in the world are at the West Edmonton Mall, Alberta, Canada, and at the National Exhibition Centre, Birmingham, England. Each can hold 20,000 cars.

PART 1

Listening to Conversations

Before You Listen

The following telephone conversation is about an advertisement ("ad") for a roommate to share a house. The speakers are the owner of the house and a student looking for a place to live.

Roommate wanted to share 3 bdr. house near campus w/ 2 working people. Furnished room, semi-private bath, kitchen priv., backyard $700/month + util. Call Nancy or Jeff at 555-5949
STUDENT HOUSING

1 Prelistening Questions. Discuss these questions with your classmates.

1. Have you ever called someone about an advertisement? What kind of ad was it? How did you begin the conversation? What questions did you ask?
2. What will the student probably want to know about the room?
3. What will the owner probably want to know about the student?

2 Vocabulary Preview. These sentences contain expressions from the conversation. Use the context to match the underlined words and expressions with their definitions.

Sentences	Definitions
My roommate Sarah is a real (a) <u>slob</u>. She never (b) <u>lifts a finger</u> to clean up after herself. It really (c) <u>bugs</u> me that I have to do all the housework myself. I think it's time to find a new roommate!	1. ____ stop at someone's house for a short visit 2. ____ a dirty person (slang)
A: Are you going to Nadia's party tonight? *B:* No, I can't (d) <u>make it</u>. I have to study.	3. ____ can see easily 4. ____ irritates, annoys, bothers (slang)
A: Do you want to go out to dinner? *B:* Thanks, but I can't leave the house because my sister is going to (e) <u>come by</u> around 6 o'clock.	5. ____ helps with work 6. ____ come or go
A: Where is the language lab? *B:* Go upstairs. It's the first door on your right. You (f) <u>can't miss</u> it.	

Listen

3 Listening for Main Ideas.

1. Close your book as you listen to the conversation. Listen for the answers to these questions.
   1. Who are the speakers?
   2. What questions do they ask each other?
   3. What do they decide to do at the end?
2. Compare answers with a partner.

Stress

4 Listening for Stressed Words.

1. Now listen to the conversation again. Some of the stressed words are missing. During each pause, repeat the phrase or sentence; then fill in the missing stressed words.

Nancy: Hello?

Anna: May I speak to Nancy, please?

Nancy: ____________.

Anna: Uh hi, uh, my name is Anna, and I'm calling about the ____________ for rent. I saw your ____________ at the campus ____________ office.

Nancy: Oh, right. OK, uh, are you a ____________?

Anna: Well, right now I'm just studying ____________, but I'm planning to start college full-____________ in ____________.

Nancy: I see. ____________ are you living ____________?

Anna: I've been living in a ____________ with some other students, but I ____________ ____________ it there.

Nancy: Why? What's the ____________?

Anna: Well, ____________ of all, it's really ____________, and it's not very clean. The ____________ people in the house are real ____________. I mean they never lift a ____________ to clean up after themselves. It really ____________ me! I need a place that's cleaner and more ____________.

Nancy: Well, it's ____________ quiet here. We're not ____________ very much.

Anna: What do you ____________?

Nancy: I teach ____________ at the college.

Anna: ____________ a minute! Didn't we meet yesterday at the ____________ exam?

Nancy: Oh . . . ____________ the girl from Italy! ____________ was your name again?

Anna: Anna Maria.

Nancy: Right. What a ____________ ____________!

Anna: It really is. ____________ the ____________, who's Jeff? His name is also in the ____________.

Nancy: He's my ____________. He's a musician, but he's also taking classes in ____________ programming. How do you feel about having a ____________ roommate?

Anna: Well, okay, I guess, as long as he's ____________ and not too noisy.

Nancy: ____________ worry. He's really ____________ to live with.

Anna: OK. Um, is the ____________ safe?

Nancy: Oh sure. We haven't had ____________ problems, and you can ____________ to school from here.

Anna: Well, it sounds really nice. When can I come ____________ and ____________ it?

Nancy: Can you ____________ it this evening around ____________? Then you can meet ____________ too.

Anna: Yeah, 5 o'clock is ____________. What's the ____________?

Nancy: It's 3475 Hayworth Avenue. Do you ____________ where that is?

Anna: No, I don't.

Nancy: OK. From University Village you go seven blocks ____________ on Olympic Avenue. At the ____________ of Olympic and Alfred there's a stoplight. Turn ____________, and go up one and a half blocks. Our house is in the ____________ of the block on the ____________.

Anna: That sounds ____________.

Nancy: Yeah, you ____________ ____________ it. Listen, I've got to go. Someone's at the door. See you this ____________.

Anna: OK, see you ____________. Bye.

Nancy: Bye bye.

2. Compare answers and read the conversation with a partner. Pay attention to the stressed words.

Language Tip: Many students of English have difficulty with the phrase "by the way." Speakers use this phrase to introduce a new topic in a discussion or conversation. For example, in the conversation you heard:

Nancy: Oh . . . you're the girl from Italy! What was your name again?
Anna: Anna Maria.
Nancy: Right. What a small world!
Anna: It really is. By the way, who's Jeff? His name is also in the ad.

At first, Anna and Nancy are speaking about their meeting at the placement test the day before. Anna says "by the way" because she wants to interrupt this topic to ask a question about another matter.

Reductions

5 Comparing Long and Reduced Forms. The sentences on the left side are from the conversation. They contain reduced forms. Listen and repeat them after the speaker. Note: You will hear the reduced forms only.

Reduced form	Long form
1. Where're ya living now?	Where are you living now?
2. Whaddaya do?	What do you do?
3. How d'ya feel about having a male roommate?	How do you feel about having a male roommate?
4. Ya kin walk ta school from here.	You can walk to school from here.
5. When kin I come by 'n' see it?	When can I come by and see it?
6. Kinya make it this evening around five?	Can you make it this evening around five?
7. I've gotta go.	I've got to go.*

6 Listening for Reductions.

1. Listen to the following conversations. They contain reduced forms. Write the long forms in the blanks.

Conversation 1

Anna: Hey Jeff, ____________ ____________ ____________ going?

Jeff: I ____________ ____________ get a present for Nancy. It's her birthday, ____________ know.

Anna: Yeah, I know. ____________ ____________ ____________ think I should get her?

Jeff: Well, she likes music. ____________ ____________ a CD?

* "I've got to" means "I must."

Conversation 2

Nancy: ____________ ____________ ____________ like my new haircut, Anna?

Anna: It's great! Who's your hairstylist?

Nancy: His name's Jose.

Anna: ____________ ____________ give me his phone number?

Nancy: Sure, but he's always very busy. ____________ ____________ try calling him, but he might not be able ____________ see ____________ until next month.

Conversation 3

Jeff: ____________ ____________ ____________ ____________ ____________ do tonight, Nancy?

Nancy: Nothing special. I've ____________ ____________ stay home ____________ correct my students' compositions.

2. Check your answers. Then read the dialogue with a partner for pronunciation practice.

After You Listen

7 **Vocabulary Review.** With a partner, read the beginning of the phone conversation below. Then complete the conversation. Try to use all the idioms in the box. Perform your conversation in front of the class.

slob	lift a finger	bugs me	make it	come by	can't miss

Speaker 1: Hello?

Speaker 2: Hi __________ [name of partner]. This is __________ [your name].

Speaker 1: Oh hi! How are you?

Speaker 2: Well, I got a new roommate last week.

Speaker 1: Really? How is [he or she]?

Speaker 2: Terrible! . . .

Using Language

Opening a Phone Conversation

Read the beginning of the phone conversation between Anna and Nancy in Activity 4. Phone conversations between strangers often begin similarly. Typically, they contain these functions and expressions:

Function	Expressions
A caller asks to speak to a person	Can/ Could/ May I please speak to ___________? Is ___________ there? I'd like to speak to ___________.
The person identifies himself or herself.	Speaking. This is he / she. This is ___________.
The caller identifies himself or herself.	My name is ___________. [used by strangers talking for the first time.] This is ___________. [used when people know each other.]
The caller gives a reason for calling.	I'm calling about . . . I'm calling because . . . Let me tell you why I called.

Closing a Phone Conversation

Reread the end of the phone conversation between Anna and Nancy. It has these typical elements:

- The caller signals that the conversation is finished: "I've got to go."
- The other speaker uses a closing expression: "See you later. Bye."
- The caller uses a closing expression: "Bye."

Here are some other expressions that signal that you want to end the conversation:

- Well, thanks for the information.
- It was nice talking to you.
- I'll talk to you soon.
- Thanks for calling.
- I'll be in touch (with you).

8 **Role-Play.** Work in pairs to role-play the phone conversations. Be sure to use the expressions for opening and closing a phone conversation. Student A should look at page 255. Student B should look at page 265.

9 **Telephone Game.** For this activity your teacher will divide you into groups of five or six. Each person in the group will receive a number from 1 to 5 (or 6).

1. Exchange phone numbers with the people in your group.
2. Your teacher will give a "secret" message to the person in your group who got number 1.
3. This evening, person 1 will call person 2 in your group and give him or her the message. Person 2 will call person 3, and so on until everyone is called.
4. The next day, the last person will repeat the message in class. See if the message changed as it passed from person to person.

Remember: When you call your classmate,

ask for your classmate by name
identify yourself
say why you are calling
give the message
use correct expressions for ending the conversation

PART 2

Listening to Lectures

Before You Listen

GOOD NEIGHBORS PROTECT EACH OTHER.
THROUGH... NEIGHBORHOOD WATCH

In many American cities, neighbors have joined together to form a "Neighborhood Watch." This means that the neighbors agree to work together to prevent crimes in their area. Members of these groups watch out for unusual or suspicious activity in their neighborhood. If they see anything like that, they call the police. They do not try to stop crime by themselves.

At the first Neighborhood Watch meeting, a police officer usually comes to speak to the neighbors about crime prevention.

Last week there was a burglary in Nancy and Jeff's neighborhood. The people on their street decided to form a Neighborhood Watch. This is their first meeting. The police officer is speaking about ways to prevent crime.

NEIGHBORHOOD WATCH
PROGRAM IN FORCE
MEMBER NEIGHBORHOOD WATCH PROGRAM

1 Prelistening Discussion. Discuss these questions in small groups.

1. Explain the meaning of the following word pairs: neighbor / neighborhood; burglar / burglary; robber / robbery; crime (uncountable) / crimes (countable).
2. Is there much crime in the area where you live? What kind? Do you feel safe in your area?
3. Does your area have something like a Neighborhood Watch? Do you think it would be a good idea?
4. What are some things you can do to protect yourself and your home against crime?

2 Vocabulary Preview. The following terms appear in the lecture. With your classmates, define the words you already know. Mark the words you do not know.

_____ broke into (to break in)	_____ to have a hard time
_____ (car) theft	_____ to get into the habit
_____ the front / back (of)	_____ valuables
_____ a porch	_____ marks
_____ a backyard	_____ identify
_____ a timer	_____ a decal
_____ a deadbolt	_____ a right (noun)

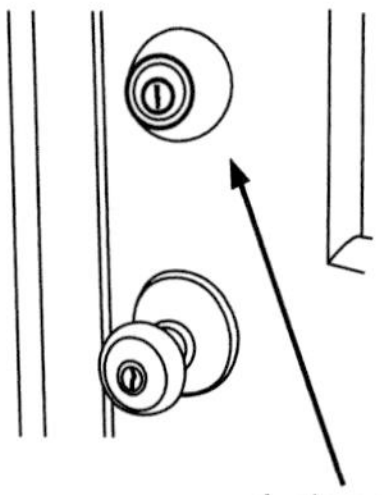

A deadbolt lock

Listen

Taking Notes on Statistics

"Statistics" are numbers that give facts about a situation. Often, statistics are expressed as a percentage or fraction; for example, "Thirty percent of the students in our class are men" or "I spend one-fourth of my salary on rent." Statistics are very common in lectures. The following terms appear frequently:

Nouns:

_______ percent
_______ number
_______ a half
_______ a third
_______ a quarter

Verbs:

_______ to increase, go up, rise
_______ to decrease, decline, go down
_______ to double

Other phrases:

_______ less than
_______ more than
_______ equal to or the same as

3 Abbreviating Statistics. Create abbreviations or symbols for the items in the statistics chart above and write them in the spaces.

4 **Taking Notes on Statistics.** Listen to sentences from the lecture. Use the abbreviations and symbols from the chart to take notes. You will hear each sentence twice.

1. ____________________
2. ____________________
3. ____________________

Exchange notes with a partner. Try to repeat the sentences from the tape by using your partner's notes.

Transitions (Connecting Words)

"Transitions" are words and phrases that connect the parts of a speech or composition. There are usually transitions *between* the major sections of a talk. In addition, we also use transitions to connect details *within* each main section.

For example:

"I came here tonight to give you some simple suggestions that will make it harder for burglars to break in to your homes. So let's get started. First of all, let's talk about lights outside your house . . ."

"Next, let's talk about lights inside the house . . ."

If you listen for transitions, you can tell when a new idea or topic is starting.

5 **Listening for Transitions.**

1. Below is a list of transitions from the lecture. Listen to the lecture. When you hear each transition, write the topic or suggestion that follows it.

First of all: outside lights

Next: ____________________

The next big topic I want to cover is: ____________________

    First of all: ____________________

    In addition: ____________________

My next suggestions are about: valuables

    First: ____________________

    Second: ____________________

My last piece of advice: ____________________

    The main thing is: ____________________

    Also: ____________________

    And one more thing: ____________________

2. Answer these questions with your classmates.
   1. How many main ideas did the speaker discuss? Which transitions introduced them?
   2. Why are some of the transitions indented in the chart above?
   3. When you take notes, should you write transitions in your notes? Why or why not?

6 Taking Notes Using Statistics and Transitions. Below are sample notes on the police officer's suggestions. Notice that they do not contain transitions; instead, the relationship among main ideas and details is shown by underlining, indenting, and listing.

Use your notes from Activities 4 and 5 to fill in the missing information. Remember to use abbreviations and symbols. If necessary, listen to the lecture again.

Date:

Ways to Prevent Crime

Intro: Crime ↑

Burglaries:

Last yr: ____________

This yr: ____________

Car theft: ____________

Ways to Prevent Burglaries:

1. Outside lights
   - need lights in front and ____________
   - turn on at ____________
2. ____________
   - use automatic ____________
   - in apt., have lights in ____________
3. ____________
   - ____________ are not safe
   - every door needs ____________
   - get special locks for ____________
4. ____________
   - put jewelry & cash in ____________
   - ____________ TV, stereo, etc.
5. ____________
   - When you go on vacation, ____________
   - If you see someth. unusual, ____________
   - Put ____________ in window

After You Listen

7 **Defining New Vocabulary.** With a partner, look back at the words you marked as unknown in Activity 2 and discuss the meaning of each new term. Your teacher may ask you to write sentences with these new words.

8 **Discussing the Lecture.** Discuss the following questions about the lecture and your own experience. Refer to your notes as necessary. Use the new vocabulary as you talk.

1. What advice did the police officer give about lights? Do you do these things in your house or apartment?
2. How does an automatic timer work? Do you use timers in your home?
3. What types of locks did the officer recommend? Do you use locks like that?
4. According to the officer, why should you mark your TV, stereo, and other valuables?
5. What is a decal? Where do people often put them? Do you have any?
6. How do people in a Neighborhood Watch help each other? Do you help your neighbors this way?
7. Has anyone ever broken into your home? If yes, what did the burglars steal?
8. What is the officer's opinion about keeping a gun in the house?

On the Spot!

Situation. You have come to the United States to study at an American university. You have rented a room in the home of a very nice American family. The neighborhood is quiet and pretty, and the house is near your school. You are comfortable and happy in your new home.

One day, while preparing food in the kitchen, you discover a gun inside a cabinet.

Discussion. Discuss the following questions in small groups.

1. Imagine that you have just discovered the gun. How do you feel?
2. What will you do next? Will you speak to the homeowners about the gun? What will you say?
3. Will you look for another place to live?
4. Imagine that the family with the gun lives next door to you. You have a young child, and this family also has a young child. The two children want to play together. Would you allow your child to play at this house?
5. If you lived in an area that had a high crime rate, would you feel safer if you had a gun in the house? Why or why not?
6. Do you believe that people have the right to own guns, or should gun ownership be forbidden by the government?
7. If a person has a gun illegally, what should the punishment be?

PART 3

Focused Listening and Speaking

Getting Meaning from Context

1 **Using Context Clues.** The following conversations take place in an apartment building.

1. Listen to each conversation.
2. After each conversation, you will hear a question. Stop the tape or CD.
3. Read the answer choices and circle the letter of the best answer.
4. Write the clues that helped you choose your answer. Discuss them with your teacher and classmates.
5. Start the recording again. You will hear a sentence with the correct answer.

Answers	Clues
Questions 1 through 3 are based on a conversation between a man and a woman.	
1. a. a neighbor b. the apartment manager c. Donna's father d. a repairman	
2. a. a repairman b. a painter c. an exterminator[1] d. a plumber[2]	
3. a. It's on the third floor. b. It's in bad condition. c. It's too expensive. d. It's cheap.	
Questions 4 and 5 are based on a conversation between two neighbors.	
4. a. He thinks it's very funny. b. He's surprised to see Donna. c. He's a little angry. d. He is happy to help Donna.	
5. a. He is happy to help Donna. b. He's surprised to see Donna. c. He's annoyed with Donna. d. He's very worried.	

[1] An exterminator is a professional who uses poison to kill insects.

[2] A plumber is a person who installs and repairs water pipes, sinks, toilets, etc.

Focused Listening

Guessing Relationships between People

The way people address each other in the United States and Canada can give clues about their relationship. Here are some examples:

- In formal situations, it is polite to use the titles "Sir" or "Ma'am" when you are talking to your boss, an older person, or someone important. In such cases it is also correct to use a title with the person's last name, for example, "Ms. Adams" or "Dr. Snow."
- On the other hand, two people who are equal in age or position usually use each other's first names.
- In casual situations, many people like to use "pet" names to speak to people they know well. For example:
  - Married people, people in love, or relatives speaking to children: honey, dear, sweetheart, darling
  - Children to parents: Mom, Mommy, Mama, Dad, Daddy, Papa
  - Children to grandparents: Grandma, Granny, Grammy, Grandpa
  - Friends: pal, buddy, brother, sister

2 **Listening for Relationships between People.** Role-play the dialogue below with a partner. Listen for the titles or pet names that your partner adds to show the relationships between the speakers.

Speakers

1. two friends
2. a boss and an assistant
3. a grandmother and grandson
4. a boyfriend and girlfriend
5. a waiter and a customer

Dialogue

A: Can I get you anything to drink?

B: Just water, thanks.

Using Language

Expressing Frustration

"Frustration" is the way people feel when they cannot get what they want, even after many attempts. For example, suppose your neighbor's dog wakes you up every night. You complain to your neighbor many times, but the situation does not improve.

In this situation you will feel *frustrated.*

The underlined idioms in the following sentences mean that a speaker is frustrated. Notice the grammar in each sentence.

- My roommate is a total slob! She never cleans up after herself! I am fed up with her mess!
- Mother (to fighting children): I've had it with your fighting! Go outside right now. I want some quiet in here!
- Student: I've been working on this physics problem for three hours. I'm sick of it!

3 **Role-Play.** Work in pairs to role-play situations in an apartment building. Student A should look at page 255. Student B should look at page 265.

4 **Follow-up Discussion.** Discuss the following questions with your classmates.

1. Do you live in an apartment? If yes, does your building have a manager? What responsibilities does he or she have?
2. In Activity 1, you learned that a person who kills insects is called an exterminator. Below is a list of other professionals who work in homes. Use a dictionary to find out what each person does. Then tell your group if you have ever called this person to fix a problem in your home. Describe the problem.

plumber	carpenter	roofer	plasterer
bricklayer	electrician	architect	

3. Tell your classmates about any other problems you have had in your home or with your neighbors. Also, explain what you did to solve the problem(s).

PART 4

Listening and Speaking in the Real World

In Chapter 1 you learned the compass points and expressions for describing locations. In this chapter you will use these expressions and new ones to give directions.

Before You Listen

1 **Prelistening Questions.** Look at the map. Imagine that two people are standing at the spot marked with an X. Speaker A wants to go to the Chinese restaurant.

1. What expressions can Speaker A use to ask for directions?
2. Imagine that you are Speaker B. How would you answer Speaker A?

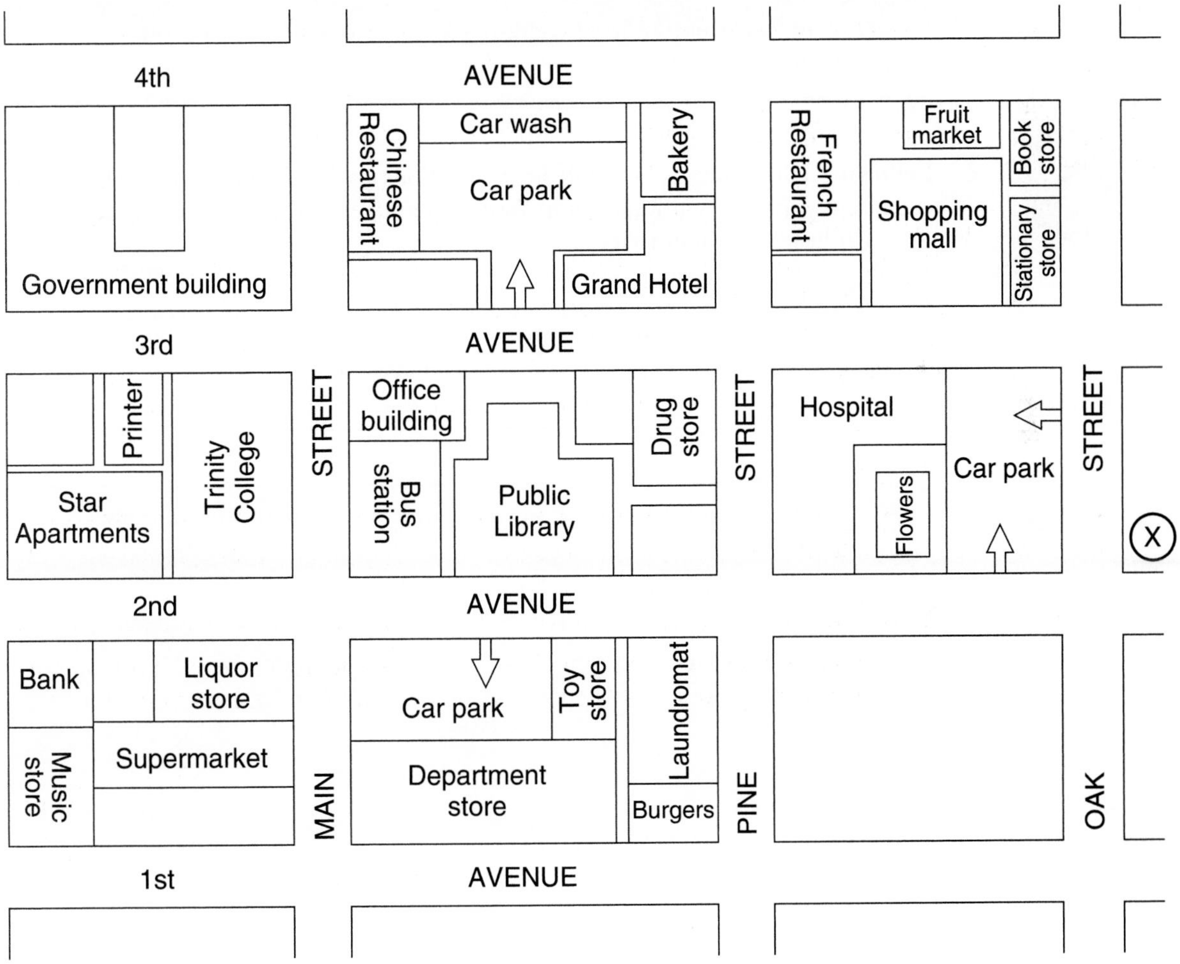

Listen

Requesting and Giving Directions

You can use the following expressions to *request* directions.

Excuse me, where is _________?
Can / could you tell me where _________ is?
How do I get to _________?
Do you know where _________ is?

When giving directions, use the imperative. Say "Go three blocks" Do not say "*You* go three blocks." You can use the following expressions to *give* directions.

Verbs: go, walk, drive, turn

Directions: up/down the street; north, south, east, west; right, left; straight

Distance: half a block, one mile, two kilometers

Prepositions: on the left / right; on _________ Street; (Also see Chapter 1, page 19.)

2 **Following Directions.** You will hear directions based on the map. At the end of each item you will hear a question. Write the answer to the question in the spaces. You will hear each item twice.

1. ________________________________
2. ________________________________
3. ________________________________
4. ________________________________

After You Listen

Saying You Don't Understand

If you don't understand your partner's directions, use one of these expressions. Then ask your partner to repeat, using the expressions you learned in Chapter 1, page 21.

I don't understand.

I'm confused

I don't get it.

I'm lost.

I'm in the dark.

I didn't catch that.

I'm not following you.

3 **Requesting and Giving Directions.** Work in pairs to request and give directions using maps. Student A should look at page 256. Student B should look at page 266.

Video Activities: Garbage Car

Before You Watch. Discuss the following questions with your class or in small groups.

1. Where do you usually put the garbage from your home?
2. When trash is collected in your city, where does it go?
3. Why is it important to collect and dispose of trash properly?
4. Did you ever have a trash collection problem in the city where you live?

Watch. Watch the video and discuss the following questions with your classmates.

1. What was left in front of Ann Porter's home?
2. What is her problem?
3. Has the city where she lives tried to help her?
4. How does she feel?
5. Why is the situation dangerous?

Watch Again. Read the following statements. Write (T) if they are true and (F) if they are false.

1. _____ The car belongs to one of Ann Porter's neighbors.
2. _____ The car smells bad.
3. _____ The car has been in front of her house for a week.
4. _____ The police have come out to see the car.
5. _____ The car is a fire hazard.
6. _____ The city is going to take the car away tomorrow.

After You Watch. Work in small groups. Imagine that you are Ann Porter and some of her neighbors. You are meeting to discuss the garbage problem in your neighborhood. First, discuss the problem. Second, make a list of ideas for solving the problem. Share your list with your class.

Chapter 3

Business and Money

IN THIS CHAPTER

Lecture: Entrepreneurs
Note-Taking Focus: Outlining
Pronunciation: Can versus Can't
Focused Listening: Teens versus Tens
Using Language: Requesting and Giving Advice

Did You Know?

- The new European currency, the euro, was introduced electronically on January 1, 1999. The coins and notes will be introduced on January 1, 2002, and will replace the local money in 11 European nations.
- In 1998 online retail ("e-tail") sales were $7.2 billion, double the amount in 1997.[1]
- Books are the most popular online product order, with over half of Web shoppers ordering books (one online bookseller, Amazon.com, which started in 1995, had revenues of $610 million in 1998), followed by software, audio CDs, and personal computers.[2]

PART 1

Listening to Conversations

Before You Listen

In the following conversation, Jeff talks with his father about borrowing money.

1 **Prelistening Questions.** Discuss these questions with your classmates.

1. Who is paying your expenses while you are in school?
2. Is it easy or difficult for you to manage your money?
3. What would you do if you needed more money right now?
4. Do you know anyone who works and goes to school at the same time?

---

[1] <http://www.infoplease.com/ce6/bus/A0816716.html>.

[2] <http://www.infoplease.com/ce6/bus/A0816716.html>.

2 Vocabulary Preview. These sentences contain expressions from the conversation. Use the context to match the underlined words and expressions with their definitions.

Sentences	Definitions
1. It's hard to live alone in the United States because everything costs <u>an arm and a leg</u>.	a. _____ a person who does not like to spend money
2. It's hard for me <u>to make ends meet</u> because I don't earn enough money.	b. _____ a lot of money
3. It's no use asking my father for money because he's such a <u>tightwad</u>.	c. _____ a limited amount of money that a person can spend each month, based on income
4. I can't go away on vacation because I'm <u>broke.</u>	d. _____ without any money
5. I can't buy everything I want, because I am living on <u>a budget</u>.	e. _____ to pay all one's bills

Listen

3 Listening for Main Ideas.

1. Close your book as you listen to the conversation. Listen for the answers to these questions.
   1. What is Jeff's problem?
   2. What is his father's response?
   3. How does Jeff feel at the end of the conversation?
2. Compare answers with a partner.

Stress

4 Listening for Stressed Words.

1. Now listen to the conversation again. Some of the stressed words are missing. During each pause, repeat the phrase or sentence; then fill in the missing stressed words.

Dad: Hello?

Jeff: Hi, Dad.

Dad: Hello, Jeff. How _____________ you?

Jeff: I'm fine Dad. How's Mom? Did she get over her _____________?

Dad: Yes, she's _____________ now. She went back to _____________ yesterday.

Jeff: That's good . . . um, Dad, I need to _____________ you something.

Dad: Sure, son, what ____________ it?

Jeff: Well, uh, the truth is, I'm ____________ again. Could you ____________ me $200 until the end of the month?

Dad: Broke again? Jeff, when you moved ____________ with Nancy, you said you could ____________ ends ____________. But this is the ____________ time you've asked me for help!

Jeff: I know, I know, I'm sorry. But my old guitar broke, and I had to buy a ____________ one. I ____________ ____________ on a broken guitar, right?

Dad: Look Jeff, if you want to play in a ____________, that's OK with me, but you ____________ keep asking ____________ to pay for it!

Jeff: OK, OK, you're right. But what do you think I ought to ____________? Everything costs an ____________ and a ____________.

Dad: Well, first of all, I think you had better go on a ____________. Make a list of all your ____________ and all your expenses. And then it's simple. Don't ____________ more than you ____________.

Jeff: But that's ____________ the problem! My expenses are ____________ larger than my income. That's why I need to borrow money from ____________.

Dad: Then maybe you should work more hours at the ____________ store.

Jeff: Dad! I ____________ work 15 hours a week! How can I ____________ and ____________ and find time to play with my band?

Dad: Come ____________, Jeff, when ____________ was your age . . .

Jeff: I know, I know. When ____________ were my age you were already ____________ and working and going to school . . .

Dad: That's right. And if I could do it, why can't ______________?

Jeff: Because ______________ not ______________, Dad, that's why!

Dad: All right, Jeff, calm down. I don't ______________ you to be like me. But I ______________ ______________ you any more money. Your mother and I are on a budget ______________, you know.

Jeff: Maybe I should just drop ______________ of school, ______________ full-time, and play in the band in the evenings. I can go back to school ______________.

Dad: I wouldn't do that if I were you . . .

Jeff: Yeah, but you're ______________ me, remember? It's my life!

Dad: All right, Jeff. Let's not ______________. Why don't you ______________ about this very carefully and call me ______________ in a few days. And in the meantime, you'd ______________ find a way to ______________ for that new guitar.

Jeff: Yes, Dad.

Dad: Good-bye, son.

Jeff: Bye.

Jeff: Tightwad . . .

2. Compare answers and read the conversation with a partner. Pay attention to the stressed words.

Language Tip: The words "borrow" and "lend" are confusing. Look at this example:

Jeff wants to *borrow* money from his father, but his father doesn't want to *lend* money to him.

An easy way to remember the difference is like this:

borrow = take

lend = give

Also notice the grammar:

to borrow (something) from (someone)

to lend (something) to (someone)

Reductions

5 Comparing Long and Reduced Forms. The sentences on the left side are from the conversation. They contain reduced forms. Listen and repeat them after the speaker. Note: You will hear the reduced forms only.

Reduced form	Long form
1. I need ta ask you something.	I need to ask you something.
2. This is the third time you've ast me for help.	This is the third time you've asked me for help.
3. My old guitar broke, 'n' I hadta buy a new one.	My old guitar broke, and I had to buy a new one.
4. Whaddaya think I oughta do?	What do you think I ought to do?
5. If I could do it, why cantchu?	If I could do it, why can't you?
6. Why donchu think about this very carefully 'n' call me back in a few days?	Why don't you think about this very carefully and call me back in a few days?

6 Listening for Reductions.

1. Listen to the following conversation between a bank teller and a customer. You'll hear reduced forms from Chapters 1, 2, and 3. Write the long forms in the blanks.

Customer: Hi, my name is Chang Lee.

Teller: How ____________ I help you?

Customer: I ____________ ____________ check my balance.

Teller: OK. ____________ I have your account number, please?

Customer: 381335.

Teller: Your balance is $201.

Customer: OK. ____________ I ____________ my father ____________ wire me some money. I'd like __________ know if it's arrived.

Teller: I'm sorry, your account doesn't show any deposits.

Customer: Oh, no. I need ____________ pay my rent tomorrow. ____________ ____________ ____________ think I ____________ ____________ do?

Teller: Well, the computer's a little slow today. __________ __________ __________ come in again tomorrow? Or you __________ call us. Here's the number.

Customer: OK, thanks.

Teller: You're welcome.

2. Check your answers. Then read the dialogue with a partner for pronunciation practice.

After You Listen

7 **Vocabulary Review.** Write a question using each of these words. Then use your questions to interview a classmate.

1. borrow ______________________________
2. lend ______________________________
3. earn ______________________________
4. income ______________________________
5. spend ______________________________

8 **Review of Idioms.** Work in pairs to practice the idioms from this section. Student A should look at page 257. Student B should look at page 267.

Pronunciation

Can versus Can't

To hear the difference between "can" and "can't," you must listen to the differences in vowel quality and in sentence stress.

Examples

1. You **can búy** a cheap house these days. (Pronounce: kin buy)
2. You **cán't búy** a cheap house these days. (Pronounce: kant buy)

9 **Pronouncing *Can* and *Can't*.** Listen and repeat the following pairs of sentences. Place an accent mark over the stressed words. The first one is done for you.

Affirmative	Negative
1. Jeff **can pláy** on a broken guitar.	1. Jeff **cán't pláy** on a broken guitar.
2. Jeff's father can pay for his new guitar.	2. Jeff's father can't pay for his new guitar.
3. Jeff can work more hours at the computer store.	3. Jeff can't work more hours at the computer store.
4. I can lend you more money.	4. I can't lend you more money.
5. Jeff can go back to school later.	5. Jeff can't go back to school later.

10 **Distinguishing between *Can* and *Can't*.** Listen to the sentences. Decide if they are affirmative or negative. Circle *can* or *can't*.

1. can can't
2. can can't
3. can can't
4. can can't
5. can can't
6. can can't
7. can can't
8. can can't
9. can can't
10. can can't

11 **Talking about Abilities.**

1. Look at the following list of activities. With a partner, take turns making sentences with *can* and *can't*. After you make a sentence, your partner will say if your statement was affirmative or negative. This will tell you if your pronunciation was clear.

   Example

   A: I can drive a stick-shift car.

   B: Affirmative.

   A: Correct.

   a. sew
   b. cook
   c. stand on my head
   d. do a handstand
   e. waterski
   f. snow ski
   g. sing
   h. dance
   i. drive a stick-shift car
   j. pilot a plane
   k. understand my teacher
   l. understand the English news on TV
   m. run a mile (1.6 kilometers)
   n. run a marathon
   o. speak Latin
   p. speak your native language

2. Ask your partner about additional skills or abilities that are not on the list.
3. Tell the class three things your partner can and can't do.

Using Language

Asking for advice	Giving advice	Accepting advice	Rejecting advice
Can you give me any advice? What should I do? What do you suggest/ recommend/advise?	You ought to . . . I advise you to + verb I suggest that you + verb	Thanks for the advice. That sounds like a good idea. Thanks. I'll do that.	Thanks, but I don't think that's a good idea. Thanks. I'll think about it. Thanks, but I'm not so sure.

12 **Recognizing Expressions of Advice.** Reread the conversation in Activity 4. Find one place where Jeff asks his father for advice. Find four places where his father gives him advice. Fill in the chart with the language they use.

Asking for advice	Giving advice
1.	1. 2. 3. 4.

13 **Role-Play.** With a partner, role-play one of the following situations. Use expressions from the chart. Your teacher may ask you to perform your role-play in front of the class.

Situation 1

Person A is spending more money each month then he or she is earning. Person B gives suggestions for helping Person A to manage money. (Example: Don't use credit cards.)

Situation 2

Person A bought a radio and paid cash for it. Unfortunately, he or she didn't keep the receipt. Two days later the radio broke. Person A asks Person B for advice on how to get his or her money back.

Situation 3

Person A doesn't trust banks and keeps all his/her extra money in a box under the bed. Person B explains why this is a bad idea and gives Person A advice about safer places to keep money.

Situation 4

Person A, an American student, is planning a vacation to Person B's home city. Person A asks Person B for advice on ways to have a good time without spending a lot of money. (Example: Person A asks about inexpensive places to stay and eat.)

PART 2

Listening to Lectures

Before You Listen

The following lecture is about people who start new businesses or industries—they are called *entrepreneurs*—and about the process they follow in creating their businesses.

Time magazine's 1999 Person of the Year, Jeff Bezos, founder of Amazon.com

1 Prelistening Discussion. Discuss these questions in small groups.

1. Have you ever seen or heard the word "entrepreneur"? Tell what you know about this word.
2. What personality characteristics do you think successful businesspeople need to have? Make a list on the board. Write both the noun and adjective forms of the words.

   Example

   creativity / creative

3. Give examples of people you know who have started their own businesses. Which of these characteristics did they have?
4. Which of these characteristics do *you* have? Do you think you would be a good businessperson?

2 **Vocabulary Preview.** The following terms appear in the lecture. With your classmates, define the words you already know. Mark the words you do not know.

____ to have something in common	____ to take risks	____ to solve
____ to surf the Internet	____ to found	____ to hire
____ a brilliant idea	____ a refugee	____ a team
____ a quality	____ to identify	____ to raise capital
____ vision	____ a solution	

Listen

3 **Taking Draft Notes.** Listen to the lecture and take notes in the best way you can. Use your own paper.

Outlining

In Chapters 1 and 2 you learned how to indent to show the relationship between main ideas and specific details. You can also show this relationship by using an outline. An outline looks like this:

I. Major topic
   A. Division of major topic
      1. Detail concerning division A
      2. Second detail
   B. Second division of major topic
II. Second major topic
Etc.

You can see that outlines use indentation together with letters and numbers to organize information. Outlining is a very common way of taking notes in English.

Fred Smith

Debbi Fields

Andrew Grove

4 Outlining the Lecture. Here is a sample outline of the first part of the lecture. Use your notes from Activity 3 to fill in as much information as you can. Remember to use abbreviations and symbols and write key words only. Listen again if necessary.

Date:

Topic: Entrepreneurs

I. Intro
   A. Example: ______________________
   B. Def. of entrep.: ______________________

II. Characteristics
   A. ______________________
      1. Ex.: ______________________
   B. ______________________
      1. Ex.: ______________________

III. Diffs. in background
   A. ______________________
      1. Ex.: ______________________
   B. some rich, some poor
   C. many ent. are ______________________.
      1. Ex.: ______________________
   D. ______________________
   E. ______________________
      1. Ex.: ______________________

5 Taking Notes on a Process. Here is an outline of the second part of the lecture. Listen again and fill in the steps in the entrepreneurial process.

IV. Entrepreneurial process

A. Identify a problem

B. ______________________

C. ______________________

D. ______________________

E. ______________________

F. ______________________

After You Listen

6 Defining New Vocabulary. With a partner, look back at the words you marked as unknown in Activity 2 and discuss the meaning of each new term. Your teacher may ask you to write sentences with these new words.

7 Discussing the Lecture. Discuss the following questions about the lecture and your own experience. Refer to your notes as necessary. Use the new vocabulary as you talk.

1. Match each person with the company he or she founded. Have you ever used any of these companies' products?

a. Jeff Bezos	____ Microsoft Corporation
b. Bill Gates	____ Federal Express
c. Andrew Grove	____ Mrs. Fields Cookie Company
d. Debbi Fields	____ Intel
e. Fred Smith	____ Amazon.com

2. What qualities do all entrepreneurs have in common? Do you have these qualities? Would you like to be an entrepreneur?
3. Do you enjoy surfing the Internet? What sites do you like to visit?
4. In what ways are entrepreneurs different from each other?
5. What are the six steps in the entrepreneurial process?
6. Why are entrepreneurs cultural heroes in the United States?

Talk It Over

Become an Entrepreneur! In small groups, pretend that you are an entrepreneurial team. Design a product or service together. Don't worry if your idea seems impossible. Use your imagination! Use the following questions to guide you. When you are finished, make a presentation to your classmates. Use pictures, diagrams, or charts to make your presentation more interesting.

1. Think of a problem, need, or opportunity that you would like to address.
2. Invent a solution to the problem. It can be a product or a service.
3. Design a business plan. Make decisions about the following items:
   a. Will you need any special equipment?
   b. Where will your business be located?
   c. What special people will you need to hire in order to produce your product or service?
   d. Where or how will you get the money to create and market your product or service?
   e. Where, when, and how will you test-market it?
   f. How will you obtain capital to make and sell your product?

PART 3

Focused Listening and Speaking

Getting Meaning from Context

1 **Prelistening Questions.** Discuss these questions with your classmates.

1. Most American banks offer many different services. Look at the list in Activity 2. Define the unfamiliar items.
2. Which of these services are offered by your bank? Which ones have you used?
3. Have you ever tried banking by phone, by mail, or online?

2 **Using Context Clues.** You are going to hear some advertisements about banking services.

1. Listen to each advertisement.
2. After each advertisement, you will hear a question. Stop the tape or CD.
3. Read the answer choices and write the letter of the best answer in the blank next to the question.
4. Start the recording again. You will hear a sentence with the correct answer.

1. The speaker is talking about ____	a. a safety deposit box
2. The speaker is talking about ____	b. a savings account
3. The speaker is talking about ____	c. a home improvement loan
4. What can't the woman find? ____	d. an automated banking machine
5. The speaker is talking about ____	e. a credit card
	f. travelers' checks
	g. a car loan

Focused Listening

Teens versus Tens

In American English it is hard to hear the difference between the "teens"—numbers 13 to 19—and the "tens"—numbers 30 to 90. To tell them apart, pay attention to the following phonetic differences:

1. In the teen numbers, the "t" is pronounced like the */t/* in *ten.*
   For example: seventeen
2. In the ten numbers, the "t" is pronounced like the */d/* in *dog.*
   For example: seventy
3. Many speakers stress the ten numbers on the first syllable and the teen numbers on the last. For example:
   thírty   thirtéen

Some speakers stress both sets of words on the first syllable. In that case it may be almost impossible to hear the difference. You may have to ask a speaker to repeat the number.

3 Pronouncing Teens and Tens. Listen to the tape and repeat the pairs of numbers after the speaker.

1. thirteen	thirty
2. fourteen	forty
3. fifteen	fifty
4. sixteen	sixty
5. seventeen	seventy
6. eighteen	eighty
7. nineteen	ninety

4 Distinguishing between Teens and Tens. Listen to the tape and circle the numbers you hear.

1. $40.10	$14.10
2. $16.99	$60.99
3. 18%	80%
4. 90	19
5. 630	613
6. 216	260
7. 40.5	14.5
8. $2,250	$2,215
9. 7064	1764
10. 8090	1890

5 Pair Practice with Teens and Tens. Work in pairs to practice teens and tens. Student A should look at page 257. Student B should look at page 267.

On the Spot!

Situations. Read the following situations and decide what you would probably do in each case. Circle the letter of your answer, or write your own answer in the space provided.

1. While walking down the street, you find a wallet. It contains $100 (or the equivalent), and an identification card with the owner's name, address, and phone number. What would you do?
   a. Call the owner and arrange to return the wallet with the money.
   b. Keep the money and mail the empty wallet to the owner.
   c. Keep the money and throw away the wallet.
   d. Take the wallet with the money to a police station.
   e. Other: ______________________________

2. Same situation as No. 1, but the wallet contains only five or six dollars. What would you do?

3. You went to the bank to take money out of your account. By mistake, the bank teller gave you more money than you requested. What would you do?
   a. Return the extra money immediately. The amount doesn't matter.
   b. Keep the extra money.
   c. It depends on the amount.
   d. Other: ______________________________

4. You went to your favorite department store and bought four items. When you got home, you noticed that the clerk only charged you for three items. What would you do?
   a. Keep the item and use it myself.
   b. Keep the item but give it to a friend or to charity.
   c. Return the item to the store.
   d. Other: ______________________________

Discussion Questions. Discuss the following questions in small groups.

1. What answers did you select for the situations? Explain your choices.
2. Have any of these situations ever happened to you? What did you do with the money?
3. Do you think you are an honest person?

PART 4

Listening and Speaking in the Real World

Most adults in the United States have a checking account. Once a month they receive a *statement* from the bank, which lists all their *deposits* and *withdrawals* for the month. At that time they must *balance their checkbook*. This means they fill in missing information and check to make sure the bank did not make a mistake.

Before You Listen

1 **Prelistening Questions.**

1. Do you have a checking account at a bank?
2. How often do you write checks?
3. How often do you balance your checkbook?
4. In Activity 3 you can see a sample page from a couple's checkbook record. It has six columns. What kind of information is in each column?

2 **Vocabulary Preview.** The words and expressions in the left column are used in the listening exercise. Match them with their definitions.

Expressions	Definitions
1. balance (noun)	a. ____ a monthly percentage that is paid on money that is borrowed or owed
2. to balance a checkbook (verb)	b. ____ to write on a check or in a checkbook record
3. to pay off (a credit card)	c. ____ the amount of money in an account
4. interest (noun)	d. ____ to pay all of a large bill at the same time
5. to enter (an amount)	e. ____ to record all the transactions in a checking account; most people do this once a month

Listen

3 **Balancing a Checkbook.** George and Martha Spendthrift have a joint checking account; that is, they share one checking account and both of them can write checks from it. Here is one page from their checkbook record. Listen as they try to balance their checkbook. Fill in the missing information.

CHECKBOOK RECORD

NAME: George & Martha Spendthrift

ACCOUNT: 132-98804

NO.	DATE	DESCRIPTION	PAYMENT	DEPOSIT	BALANCE
200	10/25		30.21		490.31
201	10/27	Electric Company	57.82		
202	10/27	Time Magazine			
203	10/30		70.00		327.49
204	11/1	Compu-Tech	125.00		202.49
205		Dr. Painless	40.00		162.49
	11/1	Deposit		1234.69	
206	11/2				985.18
207	11/4	Visa Payment	155.00		830.18
208	11/8		305.00		525.18
209	11/10	traffic ticket			

After You Listen

4 **Discussion.** Discuss the following questions in small groups.

1. Look at the checkbook record. What could the couple do to spend less money?
2. Do you think a joint checking account is a good idea? Why or why not?
3. Who manages the money in your family? What system does he or she use?

Language Tip: Question Openers

Before asking someone a question, especially a personal question, it is polite to use one of the following "openers":

- Excuse me, can / could / may I ask you a question?
- Can / could / may I ask you something?
- Do you mind if I ask you a (personal) question?

5 **"Find Someone Who . . ."** Walk around the room and find one person who fits each description below. Write that person's name in the blank space. Then move on and talk to a different person. Collect as many names as possible in the time you have.

Example

You read: "Find someone who . . . has a black wallet."

You ask a classmate: "Excuse me, can I ask you something? Do you have a black wallet?"

Find someone who . . .

Item	Name
is not carrying any money today	
works or has worked in a bank	
has a checking account	
sews his or her own clothes	
has her or his own business	
has borrowed money to buy a car	
has a credit card	
has used an ATM machine this week	
knows how to read the stock market numbers in the newspaper	
owns a house or apartment	
bought something and returned it to the store the next day	
takes the bus to school or work	
ate dinner in a restaurant last night	

Talk It Over

Interview. Attitudes about money vary from culture to culture, family to family, and person to person. Use the following questions to interview someone outside your class about his or her attitudes. Take notes in the spaces provided. When you return to class, share in small groups what you've learned.

Name of the person interviewed: ______________________________

Questions	Answers
1. Would you normally ask a friend how much money he or she makes?	
2. Would you feel comfortable borrowing money from your relatives? When? How much?	
3. If you borrowed a dollar from a classmate, how soon would you return the money?	
4. Ask a man: How would you feel if your wife earned more money than you? Ask a woman: How would you feel if you earned more money than your husband?	
5. If you want to buy an expensive item like a car, do you pay the listed price or do you bargain for a lower price?	
6. When you buy something expensive, do you pay for the whole thing at one time or do you make payments (pay a little each month)?	
7. Do you use credit cards? Where?	
8. Do you think children should receive money (an "allowance") from their parents to spend as they like? At what age should they begin receiving it?	

Video Activities: A Teenage Stockbroker

Before You Watch. Discuss the meanings of the following words and expressions with your classmates. Check the meanings in a dictionary if necessary. Then complete the definitions below.

1. Stocks and shares — Stocks and shares are kinds of ______________________
2. Stock exchange — A stock exchange is ______________________
3. Investor — An investor is a person who ______________________
4. Risk — For an investor, a risk means ______________________

Watch. Discuss the following questions with your classmates.

1. Talk about Dan. How old is he? What is unusual about him?
2. Where is Dan standing at the beginning of the video?

Watch Again. Read the following statements. Write (T) if they are true and (F) if they are false.

1. _____ Dan has been trading stocks for six years.
2. _____ Dan has never lost money on the stock market.
3. _____ Dan dropped out of high school and now spends all his time trading stocks.
4. _____ Dan publishes all his wins and losses on his Website.
5. _____ Dan plans to buy a house in Malibu (California) when he is 19.

After You Watch. Imagine that you are Dan, a 17-year-old millionaire. In small groups, answer the questions below.

1. Will you finish high school?
2. Will you go to a university? If yes, what will you major in?
3. What will you do with your money: spend it, save it, reinvest it, or a combination?
4. Will you give any money to your family, friends, or charity?
5. In what ways will this money change your life and your relationships with people?

Chapter 4

Jobs and Professions

IN THIS CHAPTER

Lecture:	The Changing Job Market
Note-Taking Focus:	Taking Notes on Causes and Effects Review: Taking Notes on Statistics Review: Outlining
Focused Listening:	Understanding the Intonation of Tag Questions
Using Language:	Apologizing and Reconciling Answering Affirmative Tag Questions

Did You Know?

- Experts forecast that American workers starting out now will switch careers (careers, not jobs!) an average of more than three times during their lives.[1]
- The ten most stressful and least stressful jobs in the United States:[2]

Most stressful

1. president of the United States
2. firefighter
3. senior corporate executive
4. professional race car driver
5. taxi driver
6. surgeon
7. astronaut
8. police officer
9. professional football player
10. air traffic controller

Least stressful

1. medical records technician
2. janitor
3. forklift operator
4. musical instrument repairer
5. florist
6. actuary
7. appliance repairer
8. medical secretary
9. librarian
10. bookkeeper

- Americans rank their jobs eighth in importance below children's education, family life, health, and other items. Europeans rank work fourth, and Japanese rank work second (after health).

PART 1

Listening to Conversations

Before You Listen

In the following conversation, Jeff, Anna, and Nancy talk about jobs.

[1] *Money* magazine, June 1, 1990.

[2] *The Wall Street Journal,* 1999, cited at <http://go.grolier.com/ea-online/wsja/text/ch04/tables/bi111.htm>.

1 Prelistening Questions. Discuss these questions with your classmates.

1. Nancy is a teacher; Jeff plays guitar in a rock band; Anna is an international student. What job problems might each of them have?
2. Look at the picture. What are classified ads? Why is Jeff reading them?
3. How do people in different countries find jobs?
4. Have you ever had a job? What was your first job?

2 Vocabulary Preview. These sentences contain expressions from the conversation. Use the context to match the underlined words and expressions with their definitions.

Sentences	Definitions
1. I'm <u>not in the mood</u> to go to a movie tonight.	a. ____ an expression of surprise
2. He has two jobs because he is <u>supporting</u> his mother.	b. ____ terrible (slang)
3. <u>What</u> <u>on earth</u> happened to you?	c. ____ paying (someone's) expenses
4. He <u>spends</u> a lot of <u>time</u> playing his guitar.	d. ____ don't want
5. A: How was your day today? B: It was <u>the worst</u>.	e. ____ uses, passes time

Listen

3 Listening for Main Ideas.

1. Close your book as you listen to the conversation. Listen for the answers to these questions.
   1. Why is Jeff reading the classified ads?
   2. What jobs has Jeff had?
   3. What job problems do the three speakers have?
2. Compare answers with a partner.

Stress

4 Listening for Stressed Words.

1. Now listen to the conversation again. Some of the stressed words are missing. During each pause, repeat the phrase or sentence; then fill in the missing stressed words.

Anna: Hey, Jeff, what's going ______________?

Jeff: Oh, I'm looking at the ______________ ads. It looks like I have to get a ______________.

Anna: I thought you ______________ a job, at a computer store or something.

Jeff: Yeah, but that's ______________-time. I need something ______________-time.

Anna: Really? But what about ______________? What about your ______________? How can you work full-time?

Jeff: Well, to tell you the ______________, I'm probably going to drop ______________ of school for a while. I'm just not in the ______________ for ______________ these days. I'd rather spend my time ______________with my band. But my father won't ______________ me if I'm not in school.

Anna: I see . . . Well, what kind of job do you want to ______________?

Jeff: I don't really ______________. I've done ______________ of different things. I've been a ______________, a taxi driver, a house painter. And I'll never forget my ______________ job; it was in a potato chip factory.

Anna: A potato chip factory? What on earth did you do ______________?

Jeff: Believe it or not, I was a potato chip ______________. My job was to take out the ______________ ones before they went into the ______________.

Anna: That sounds like a pretty ______________ job!

Jeff: It was the ______________. And I haven't eaten a ______________ potato chip since I ______________ that job.

Nancy: Hi, what's so ___________?

Jeff: Do you remember my job at the ___________ chip factory?

Nancy: Oh yeah. That was pretty ___________. But actually, it doesn't sound so bad to me right now.

Anna: Why, Nancy? What's ___________?

Nancy: Oh, I don't know. Sometimes I think I've been ___________ too long. Lately I haven't been as ___________ about my job as I ___________ to be.

Anna: How long have you been ___________?

Nancy: Twelve years. Maybe it's time to try something ___________.

Anna: Like ___________?

Nancy: Well, I've always wanted to be a ___________. I could . . .

Jeff: Oh, ___________ listen to her, Anna. She ___________ talks this way when she's had a bad day at school. At least you ___________ a ___________, Nancy. Look at me: I'm ___________, and Dad won't ___________ me any more money . . .

Nancy: Oh, stop ___________. If you're so poor, why don't you go ___________ to the potato chip factory?

Anna: Listen you two, stop ___________. Look at me! I ___________ work at ___________ because I'm an international student.

Jeff: Okay, okay. I'm ___________, Nancy. Tell you what. Let's go out to ___________. ___________ pay.

Nancy: But you're ___________!

Jeff: All right, ___________ pay!

2. Compare answers and read the conversation with a partner. Pay attention to the stressed words.

Reductions

5 Comparing Long and Reduced Forms. The sentences on the left side are from the conversation. They contain reduced forms. Listen and repeat them after the speaker. Note: You will hear the reduced forms only.

Reduced form	Long form
1. What's goin' on?	What's going on?
2. I'm probably gonna drop outa school for a while.	I'm probably going to drop out of school for a while.
3. A potato chip factory? What on earth didja do there?	A potato chip factory? What on earth did you do there?
4. What kinda job dya wanna get?	What kind of job do you want to get?
5. I've done lotsa different things.	I've done lots of different things.
6. *Anna:* Why, Nancy? What's wrong? *Nancy:* Oh, I dunno.	*Anna:* Why, Nancy? What's wrong? *Nancy:* Oh, I don't know.
7. If you're so poor, why doncha go back to the potato chip factory?	If you're so poor, why don't you go back to the potato chip factory?

6 Listening for Reductions.

1. Listen to the following conversation. It contains reduced forms. Write the long forms in the blanks.

Manager: I'm ____________ ____________ ask you some questions, okay? What ____________ ____________ jobs have you had?

Applicant: I've had ____________ ____________ different jobs. I ____________ ____________ work in a plastics factory.

Manager: ____________ ____________ ____________ do there?

Applicant: I ____________ ____________cut sheets of plastic.

Manager: ____________ ____________ ____________ ____________ ____________ do here?

Applicant: I ____________ ____________, . . . I'll do anything . . . I'm broke, I ____________ ____________ make some money right away.

Manager: Well, it looks like we're ____________ ____________ have an opening next week. I'll call you.

Applicant: Thanks.

2. Check your answers. Then read the dialogue with a partner for pronunciation practice.

After You Listen

7 **Vocabulary Review.** Work in pairs to practice the new vocabulary. Student A should look at page 258. Student B should look at page 268.

Using Language

Culture Note

To reconcile with someone after a disagreement, Americans have the following customs:

- *They can do something nice for the person. ("I'll wash the dishes tonight.")*
- *They can buy the person a gift.*
- *They can say that they will change their behavior in some way. ("Next time I'll be more polite to your brother.")*

Apologizing and Reconciling

At the end of the conversation Jeff and Nancy have a short argument. It ends like this:

Anna: Listen you two, stop arguing. Look at me! I can't work at all because I'm an international student.

Jeff: Okay, okay. I'm sorry, Nancy. Tell you what. Let's go out to dinner. I'll pay.

Nancy: But you're broke!

Jeff: All right, *you* pay!

Notice that Jeff does two things. First he *apologizes* to Nancy. He says "I'm sorry." Then he *reconciles* with her. This means that he offers to do something nice for her—to take her out to dinner—so that she will not be angry anymore. Here are some expressions you can use to apologize:

- I'm sorry
- I apologize
- (Please) Forgive me
- I beg your pardon (formal)

8 **Role-Play.** Prepare short dialogues with a partner for the following situations. Take turns apologizing and reconciling. Then role-play one of the situations for the class.

1. You forgot your boyfriend's / girlfriend's birthday.
2. You came to work late. As you came in, your boss was standing by the door waiting for you. Your boss is angry.
3. You had a loud party in your apartment, and your neighbors are very upset with you.
4. While arguing with your roommate, you called him or her "stupid" and slammed the door on your way out of the room.
5. On a crowded bus, you stepped on a person's foot three times. Now the person is annoyed with you.

Talk It Over

Discussion. Work in groups of three to four students and discuss the following questions.

1. In the conversation, Anna complains that she can't work because she is an international student. This is the law in the United States. However, some international students find low-paying jobs illegally in places like restaurants and gas stations.
   a. Do you think this law is fair?
   b. What might be the reasons for this law?
   c. If you were a student in the United States and needed money, would you try to find a job?
2. After twelve years of teaching, Nancy is thinking about changing careers. This is a common practice in the United States and Canada, especially among people in high-stress careers like teaching.
   a. Is it easy for people to change careers in other countries?
   b. Why do you think it is more common in the United States than in other places?
   c. If, after working for several years, you discovered that you hated your career, what would you do?
3. In the United States and Canada, it is very common for people to go to college and have jobs at the same time.
   a. Do you think this is common in other countries?
   b. Do you or any of your friends have jobs right now? What kind?

PART 2

Listening to Lectures

Before You Listen

In the following lecture, a job counselor is speaking to a group of students about changes in the U.S. job market and future job possibilities.

1 Prelistening Discussion. Study the graph and answer the questions that follow.

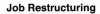

Job Restructuring

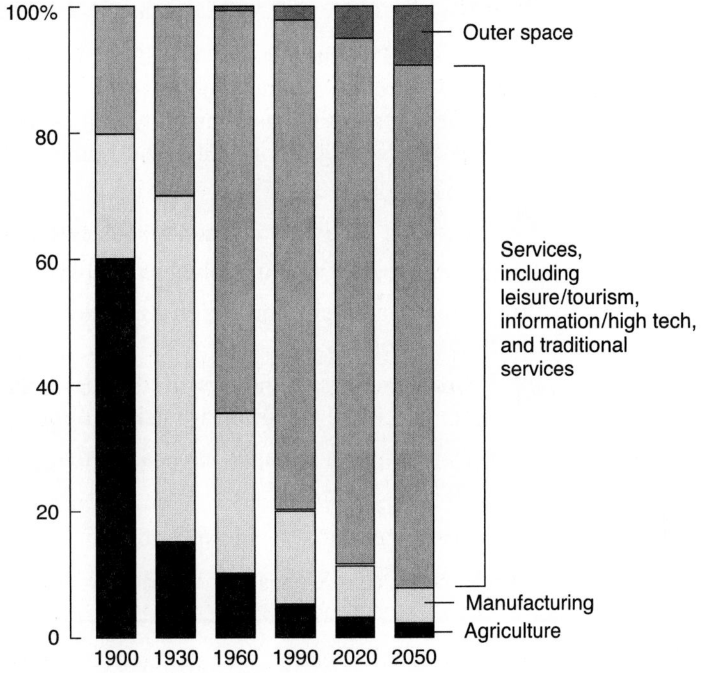

Source: Bureau of Labor Statistics

1. What is the meaning of "job restructuring"?
2. What information is given in this graph?
3. What years are covered?
4. Define the terms "agriculture," "manufacturing," and "services." What has happened to each of these categories? What will happen in the future?
5. If you are a student, what kind of work do you want to do after you graduate? What are your chances of finding a good job in the field of your choice?

2 Vocabulary Preview. The following terms appear in the lecture. With your classmates, define the words you already know. Mark the words you do not know.

____ job market	____ automation	____ to earn a salary
____ shift (noun and verb)	____ competition	____ training
____ manufacturing	____ labor costs	____ benefits
____ service (or services)	____ health care	____ pension
____ nine out of ten	____ hourly	____ bottom line

Listen

Taking Notes on Causes and Effects

To understand the main points in the lecture, you need to recognize the relationship between *causes* (reasons) and *effects* (results) in the changing job market. Study the examples below. Identify the cause and effect in each sentence. (Note: Some sentences begin with the cause, some with the effect. In which sentences can you switch the order?)

1. The (first, second, etc.) **cause** of unemployment is automation.
2. The number of factory jobs has decreased **because of [due to]** robots.
3. Factories are using more robots **because [since]** they are cheaper than human workers.
4. Human workers cannot work 24 hours a day; **as a result, [therefore,]** more and more factories are using robots.
5. Labor costs are cheaper in Asia, **so** many American factories are moving there.

Many people use arrows in notes to indicate cause and effect. For example,

X → Y means that X causes Y. In other words, X is the cause and Y is the effect.

3 **Taking Notes on Cause-and-Effect Statements.** Take notes on the five sentences from the explanation box. Remember to abbreviate, use symbols, and write key words only.

1. 1st cause of unemp. = automation
2. ______________________
3. ______________________
4. ______________________
5. ______________________

Now compare notes with a classmate. There are several correct ways of taking notes on these sentences.

4 **Creating Abbreviations.** Following are key words from the lecture. Create abbreviations for them before you listen.

Words	Abbreviations
number	
service	
manufacturing	
population	
percentage	

5 **Listening and Taking Notes on Causes and Effects.** Listen to cause-and-effect statements from the lecture and take notes. You will hear each statement twice.

Example

You hear: "In many cases, automation causes unemployment."

You write: *automation → unemp.*

1. ______
2. ______
3. ______
4. ______
5. ______

6 **Taking Notes on Statistics.** The lecture contains many statistics about jobs. Go back to Chapter 2, page 32 and review the section titled Taking Notes on Statistics. Then listen to sentences from the lecture and take notes. You will hear each sentence twice.

1. ______
2. ______
3. ______
4. ______
5. ______

Exchange notes with a partner. Try to repeat the sentences from the tape by using your partner's notes.

7 **Taking Draft Notes.** Listen to the lecture and take notes in the best way you can. Use your own paper. Listen specifically for the following information:

How has the U.S. job market changed?

Why?

What are some problems connected with today's job market?

25 Occupations with Fast Growth, High Pay, and Low Unemployment, 1996–2000

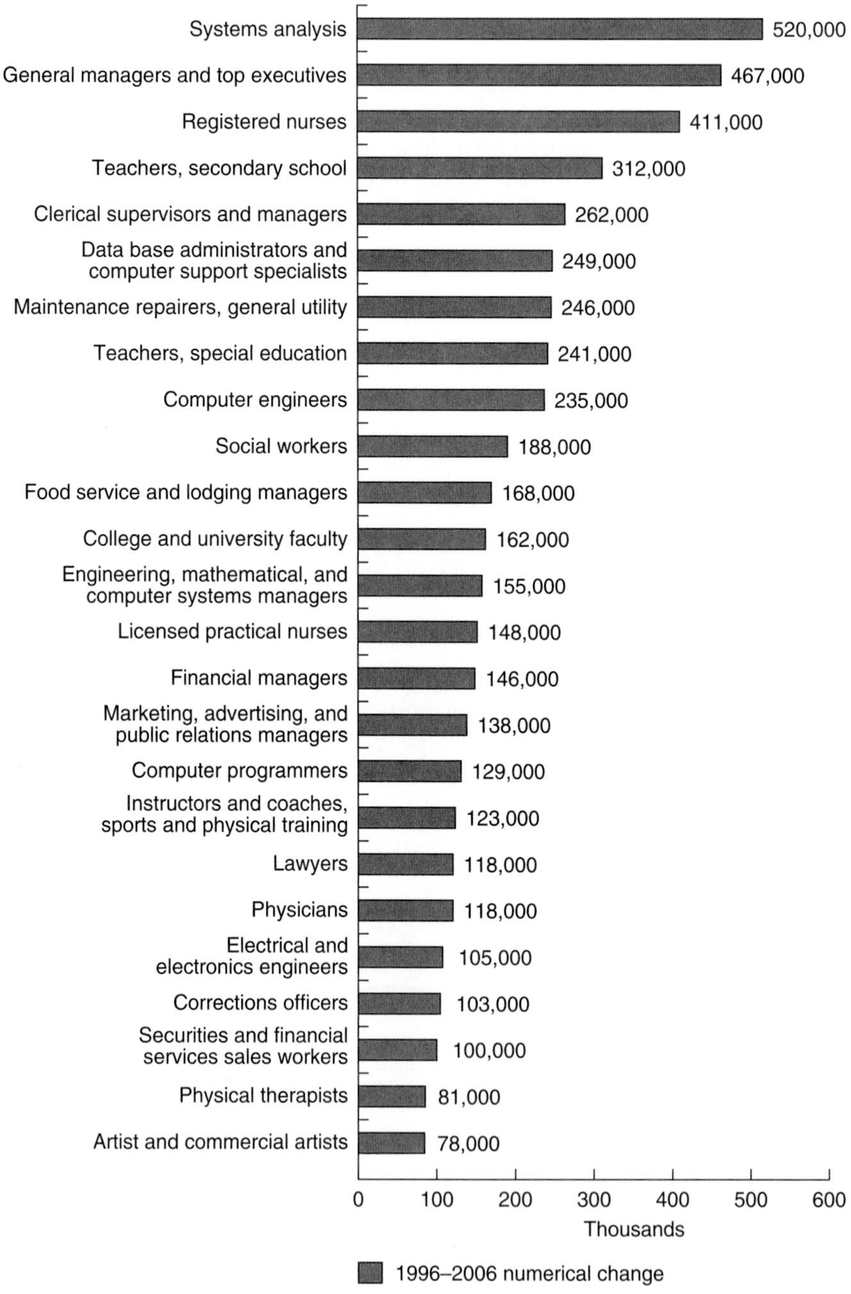

Source: Bureau of Labor Statistics

After You Listen

8 **Outlining the Lecture.** Complete the outline with the information from Activities 3 through 7. Listen again if necessary.

The Changing U.S. Job Market

I. Change in U.S. workforce: from ____________ to ____________

A. Definitions

1. ______________________________

e.g.: ______________________________

2. ______________________________

e.g.: ______________________________

B. Stats:

1. 100 yrs. ago: ______________________________

2. ______________ : ______________

3. By 2020: ______________________________

II. ______________________________

A. Manufac. ↓

1. ______________________________

2. ______________________________

a. ex: 3/98 to 11/99, ______________________________

B. ______________________________

1. ______________________________

2. ______________________________

a. ex.: ______________________________

b. ex.: ______________________________

III. Problems w/ serv. econ.

A. ______________________________

1. 30% of Am. wkrs. ______________________________

B. ______________________________

IV. Conc.

A. 18/25 best jobs ______________________________

B. ______________________________

9 **Vocabulary Review.** Use vocabulary from the box to complete the summary of the lecture.

salaries	automation	benefits
shift	manufacturing	nine out of ten
competition	training	labor
service	bottom line	

One hundred years ago, the United States had a ______________ (1) economy. This meant that most people made things by hand or machine. In contrast, today the United States has a ______________ (2) economy, in which ______________ (3) workers, or 90 percent, provide services instead of making products. There are several reasons for this important ______________ (4) in the U.S. economy. The first is ______________ (5). It is cheaper to use robots than human workers in factories. Another reason is ______________ (6) from foreign countries where ______________ (7) costs are lower than in the United States. Therefore, many products that used to be manufactured in the United States are now made overseas.

There are many different kinds of service jobs. Some jobs pay very well, especially in the computer industry. However, at least one-third of all service jobs pay very low ______________ (8) because they don't require much ______________ (9). Another problem is that many service jobs don't offer ______________ (10) such as health insurance. The ______________ (11) for people who want to get a secure job with good pay is this: Get a good education.

10 **Discussing the Lecture.** Use your notes and experience to discuss the following questions. Use the new vocabulary as you talk.

1. Define the terms "service economy" and "manufacturing economy." Give examples of jobs that fall in each category.
2. How has the American workforce changed?
3. What are the reasons for these changes?
4. Has a similar change occurred in other countries? Why?
5. What problems do service jobs have in the United States? Is it the same in other countries?
6. Look at the chart of "25 occupations with fast growth, high pay, and low unemployment, 1996–2006." Which of these jobs would you like to have? What would you need to do to prepare yourself for this job?

On the Spot!

Situation. A new supermarket is opening in your neighborhood. The company needs to hire four people immediately. They are a manager, a checker,[1] a stock clerk,[2] and a butcher.[3] You are going to role-play job interviews for these people.

Instructions

1. Choose four people to be interviewers. Each interviewer will interview the applicants for one of the jobs available.
2. All other students will play the role of job applicants. The teacher will tell you which position you are applying for.
3. You will receive a paper with the information you need for your role. Try to learn it by heart so that you don't have to read it. When you are interviewed, add information to your role as you like. Note: The applicants' information is located on page 274.
4. The class should divide into groups. Each group consists of an interviewer and all the interviewees for that job. The interviewer will interview each interviewee for five minutes. The four groups should have their interviews at the same time.
5. After all the interviews are finished, the interviewers will report to the class. They will tell which applicant they picked for the job and why they chose that person.

---

[1] A checker is the same thing as a cashier or checkout clerk.

[2] Stock clerks put new merchandise on the shelves of a supermarket. They often work at night.

[3] A butcher cuts and prepares meat.

PART 3

Focused Listening and Speaking

Getting Meaning from Context

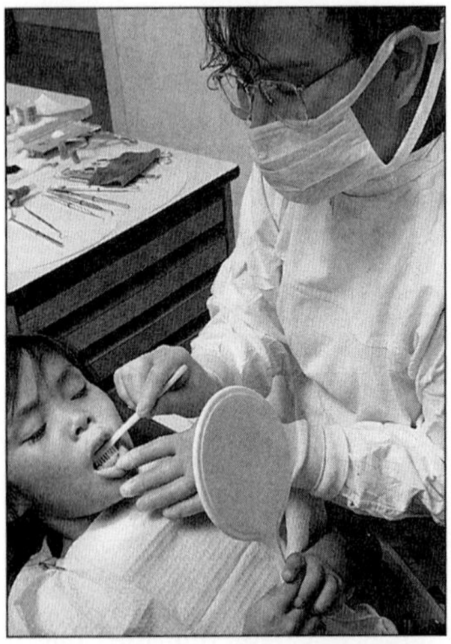

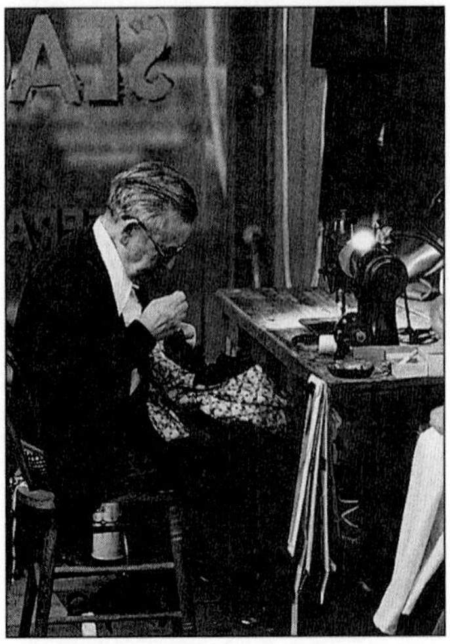

1 **Prelistening Questions.** Look at the photos on page 80 and the list of jobs in Activity 2. For each job, discuss:

1. What does this person do?
2. What education or training is needed for this job?
3. Would you enjoy doing this job?

2 **Using Context Clues.** The following conversations take place at work.

1. Listen to each conversation.
2. After each conversation, stop the tape or CD. Write the letter of each speaker's job in the blank.
3. Then listen to the next part of the conversation to hear the correct answer.

	a. architect
1. What's the woman's job? _____	b. computer programmer
	c. accountant
2. What's the woman's job? _____	d. restaurant host
	e. dentist
3. What's the man's job? _____	f. police officer
	g. construction worker
4. What's the woman's job? _____	h. medical receptionist
	i. tailor
5. What's the man's job? _____	j. plumber

Talk It Over

Game: Twenty Questions. In this game, one person thinks of a job but does not tell the class what it is. The class tries to guess by asking a maximum of 20 Yes or No questions.

Examples

"Can you do this job outdoors?"

"Is a college education necessary for this job?"

"Is this job normally done by women?"

The student who correctly guesses the occupation wins. If no one guesses after 20 questions, the same person leads another round.

Focused Listening

Understanding the Intonation of Tag Questions

Normally when we ask a question, we do not know the answer. Then we form a question in the usual way, for example, "Are you from China?"
If English speakers *think* they know the answer to a question, but they *aren't sure*, they often form tag questions with *rising intonation*:

You're from China, aren't you? You speak Chinese, don't you?

The rising intonation means that the person is asking for information.
In contrast, it is also possible to form tag questions with *falling intonation*, like this:

It's nice weather, today, isn't it That test was hard, wasn't it?

Tag questions with falling intonation are not real questions. Rather, they are a way of making conversation or small talk. Often, people do not answer tag "questions" that have falling intonation.

3 **Recognizing the Intonation of Tag Questions.** Listen to these ten tag questions. Decide if they are "real" questions (if the speaker is really asking for information) or if the speaker is just "making conversation." Put an X in the correct column.

Question	Real question	Making conversation
1.		
2.		
3.		
4.		
5.		
6.		
7.		
8.		
9.		
10.		

Using Language

Answering Affirmative Tag Questions

In Activity 3, the main verb in each sentence was affirmative, and the verb in the tag was negative.* Here is the proper way to *answer* such questions:

Tag with rising intonation:	**Meaning of answer:**
A: You're from China, aren't you? *B:* Yes, I am.	Speaker A is correct. Speaker B is from China.
A: We have homework tonight, don't we? *B:* No, we don't.	Speaker A is mistaken, so Speaker B corrects him.
Tag with falling intonation:	**Meaning of answer:**
A: It's really cold today, isn't it? *B:* Yes, and I don't have a jacket.	Speaker B agrees with Speaker A.

4 **Asking and Answering Affirmative Tag Questions.** Work in pairs to ask and answer tag questions. Student A should look at page 258. Student B should look at page 268.

PART 4

Listening and Speaking in the Real World

Before You Listen

1 **Prelistening Discussion.**

1. Do you think managing a house and children is a real job? Why or why not?
2. It is estimated that homemakers work as many as 60 hours a week. Is (or was) your mother or father a full-time homemaker? How many hours does/did she or he work each week?
3. Make a list of skills that a homemaker needs to have, for example, cooking, financial planning.

* You will practice tag questions with negative main verbs ("You're not American, are you?") in Chapter 10.

2 Vocabulary Preview. The idioms in the box are related to work in the home. Discuss their meanings. Write the meaning of each item on the line. Note which expressions use "do" and which use "make."

to fix (breakfast, lunch, dinner)	____________________
to do the dishes	____________________
to make the beds	____________________
to balance the family budget	____________________
to do the laundry	____________________
to water the lawn (garden)	____________________
to shop for groceries	____________________

3 Predicting. The pictures in Activity 4 show a typical day in the life of an American homemaker. The pictures are not in the correct order. With a partner, look at each picture and describe what is happening using the vocabulary from Activity 2. Then try to predict the order of the pictures.

Listen

4 **Sequencing Events.** Listen to the woman describe her day. Write numbers under the pictures to show the order in which each activity occurred. If two things happened at the same time, give them the same number. Pay attention to time words ("before," "after," "during," etc.) and verb tenses. (Note: Only *some* of her activities are shown in the pictures.) Then compare answers with a partner.

_____

_____

_____

_____

_____

_____

_____

_____

_____

_____

After You Listen

5 Discussion. Discuss the following questions in small groups.

1. Compare the woman's day with a typical day in your life or a typical day in your mother's or father's life. Discuss the similarities and differences.
2. Which tasks does the woman's husband do? How does this compare to your family?
3. If you have children, who takes care of them?
4. Would you like to have this woman's life? Why or why not?

6 Talking about "Men's" and "Women's" Jobs.

1. Below is a list of jobs. What is your *first* idea about them: Are they "men's" jobs, "women's" jobs, or both? Put a check in the column that describes your thinking.

Job	Men	Women	Both
computer programmer			
nurse			
architect			
college professor			
bus driver			
film director			
police officer			
computer software salesperson			
mail carrier			
lawyer			
pilot			
administrative assistant			
manager of a company			
telephone repairperson			
firefighter			
diplomat			
farmer			

2. With two or three classmates, compare your charts. Why did you make the choices you did?
3. While traveling or living in new countries, have you been surprised to see women doing what were traditionally men's jobs or vice versa? Where? What kinds of jobs?

Talk It Over

Interview. Interview someone outside of class about his or her work experience.

1. Make a list of questions to ask the person.

    1. What do you do?
    2. How long have you been working at your present job?
    3. How many jobs have you had in your life?
    4. What was the worst or strangest job you ever had?
    5. ______________________________
    6. ______________________________
    7. ______________________________
    8. ______________________________
    9. ______________________________

2. Prepare a short oral report about your interview. Tell about the person you interviewed and the most interesting things you learned about him or her.

    You may begin your report like this:

    > "I interviewed Mr. Richard Baldwin. He works as the student advisor at the English Language Center. He has worked in this job for eight years. Mr. Baldwin had many other jobs before this one. The worst job was in college, when he worked as a dishwasher in the dormitory . . ."

Video Activities: I Love My Job

Before You Watch. Discuss these questions in small groups.

1. Have you ever had a job? If you have, did you like it? If you have had many jobs, which one was your favorite? Why?
2. Describe your ideal job. Why does this kind of job appeal to you?
3. Do you know anyone who is retired? What are the advantages and disadvantages of being retired?

Watch. Watch the video one time. Then discuss the following questions with your classmates.

1. Describe Lu. What does she look like? How old is she, probably?
2. Why do customers love Lu?
3. How does Lu feel about her job?
4. What kind of restaurant is Nicolosi's, probably?

Watch Again. Write answers to the following questions.

1. What skills does Luella have that make her good at her job?
2. What does it mean to "kill people with kindness"?
3. Have you ever known a wonderful waiter or waitress like Lu?
4. Why do you think Luella is still working?

After You Watch. What is important to you in a job? Read the choices below. Put a check in the column that describes your thinking. Then sit in small groups and compare your answers with those of your classmates.

	Very important	Important	Not very important
Having a job that I love			
Making a lot of money			
Working alone			
Working with a team of people			
Doing different things every day			
Having the power to make independent decisions			
Helping people			
Working outdoors			

Chapter 5

Lifestyles Around the World

IN THIS CHAPTER

Lecture: The Changing Family
Note-Taking Focus: Taking Notes on Examples
Focused Listening: Linking
Using Language: Asking for Help or a Favor
Expressing an Opinion
Agreeing and Disagreeing
Talking about Numbers, Percentages, and Statistics

Did You Know?

- The average age for marriage in the United States was 27 for men and 25 for women in 1998.
- In 1998, the average family size in the United States was 3.18 children per woman. The world average was 3.4.
- In 1980 there were 651,000 interracial couples in the United States. In 1996, that number had almost doubled, to 1,260,000.
- Americans own 112 million pet cats and dogs, and most consider the animals to be members of the family.
- All of Africa has approximately the same number of telephones as does the city of Tokyo, Japan.*

PART 1

Listening to Conversations

Before You Listen

Jeff and Nancy have a neighbor named Margie. In the following conversation, she comes over to ask Jeff for a favor.

1 **Prelistening Questions.** Discuss these questions with your classmates.

1. What is a single mother or a single father?
2. Why do you think that the number of single mothers and fathers is growing?
3. Do you think it is difficult to be a single parent? Why or why not?
4. What does it mean to "ask someone for a favor"? Give an example.

* <http://www.unesco.org/education/educprog/wer/wer.htm>.

2 Vocabulary Preview. These sentences contain expressions from the conversation. Use the context to match the underlined words and expressions with their definitions.

Sentences	Definitions
1. I will <u>look into</u> your problem as soon as I have time.	a. ____ to see if someone is OK
2. If I don't <u>take off</u> right this minute, I'm going to miss my bus.	b. ____ not modern
3. My mother is very <u>old-fashioned</u>. That's why I fight with her all the time.	c. ____ check; find information about something.
4. Time is <u>running out</u> for me to finish this paper. It's due tomorrow!	d. ____ ending
5. My mother is sick. I want to <u>check up on</u> her on my way home from work.	e. ____ leave

Listen

3 Listening for Main Ideas.

1. Close your book as you listen to the conversation. Listen for the answers to these questions.
   1. What does Margie want from Jeff? Why?
   2. What is Nancy thinking about?
   3. Why is Anna surprised?
2. Compare answers with a partner.

Stress

Many verbs in English consist of two or three words. The first word is a verb and the second or third word is usually a preposition. In most of these verbs, the *second* word receives the stress. Listen to these examples:

The plane **took óff** at seven o'clock.

John **takes cáre** of his mother.

Please **drop** me **óff** at the corner.

4 Listening for Stressed Words.

1. Listen to the following sentences from the conversation. They contain two- and three-word verbs. During each pause, repeat the sentence; then fill in the missing stressed words.

    1. Come on ________________.
    2. They're having a problem with the computer and they want me to look ________________ it right away.
    3. If he wakes ________________, here's his bottle and some toys.
    4. Listen, I've got to take ________________.
    5. Thanks so much, Jeff, for helping me ________________.
    6. I take ________________ of him from time to time when Margie's busy.
    7. I sometimes feel like time is running ________________.
    8. I could never bring ________________ a baby by myself.
    9. I'd better check ________________ on Joey.

2. Compare answers and discuss the meaning of the idioms with a partner. Then take turns reading the sentences using the correct stress.
3. Now listen to part of the conversation again. Some of the stressed words are missing. During each pause, repeat the phrase or sentence; then fill in the missing stressed words.

Anna: Hey, Jeff, I didn't know you liked ______________.

Jeff: Well, Joey is ______________. I take care of him from time to time when Margie's ______________. And then ______________ does favors for ______________ in return. Like last week she lent me her ______________, and sometimes she bakes ______________ for me.

Anna: What does her ______________ do?

Jeff: She's not ______________. I don't think she ______________ was, actually.

Anna: Never?

Jeff: ______________, ______________. I think she's ______________ being a ______________ mother.

Anna: Is that very ______________ in the United States?

Jeff: Well, it's becoming ______ and ______ common. Even ______________ been talking about it.

Nancy: Hi, you two. Uh, ______________ have I been talking about?

Jeff: Having a______________.

Nancy: Oh yeah, I ______________ about it. I sometimes feel like ______________ is running out. What if I ______________ get married?

Anna: Maybe I'm ____________-____________, but I could ______________ bring up a baby by ______________. I think it would be so difficult . . .

Nancy: Yeah, but ______________ forget, I wouldn't have to do it by myself. I have "Uncle Jeff" here to help with ______________. Right, Jeff?

Jeff: We'll see. Speaking of babysitting, I'd ______________ check up on Joey.

4. Compare answers and read the conversation with a partner. Pay attention to the stressed words.

Reductions

Sometimes the letter "h" is not pronounced at the beginning of English words. In a few words, like "honest" and "hour," it is never pronounced. In other cases, the "h" is pronounced except in the following situations:

- when a pronoun or auxiliary word beginning with */h/* is unstressed, <u>and</u>
- when it does not come at the beginning of a phrase

When these two conditions exist, the */h/* sound is dropped, and the word with the "h" is connected to the previous word. Listen and repeat the following examples:

1. Long: Is he asleep?
   Short: /izzi/ asleep?
2. Long: Where have you been?
   Short: /where uv/ you been?
3. Long: He's so little.
   The */h/* is not dropped because it is at the beginning of the phrase.

5 **Listening for Reductions.** Listen to the following sentences from the conversation. Repeat them after the speaker. Draw a slash (/) through any reduced /*h*/ sounds that are dropped.

Example

Is h̸e asleep?

1. If he wakes up, here's his bottle and some toys.
2. Thanks so much, Jeff, for helping me out.
3. I take care of him from time to time when Margie's busy.
4. What does her husband do?
5. Hi, you two. Uh, what have I been talking about?
6. Having a baby.
7. Don't forget, I wouldn't have to do it by myself. I have Uncle Jeff here to help with babysitting.

After You Listen

6 **Vocabulary Review.**

1. Work in pairs to practice the new vocabulary. Student A should look at page 259. Student B should look at page 269.
2. Discuss your answers to the following questions with a partner.
    1. Do you sometimes argue with your parents because you think their ideas are old-fashioned? Give examples.
    2. Do you feel that time is running out for you to learn English?
    3. Would you look into raising a baby by yourself?

Using Language

Asking for Help or a Favor

In the conversation, Margie asks Jeff for a favor, and Jeff agrees. They say:

Margie: Can you do me a big favor? I just got a call from the office. . . . Would you mind watching Joey until I get back?

Jeff: Sure, no problem.

Sometimes it is necessary to say "no" when someone asks us for help or a favor. In that case, we usually apologize and give a reason why we cannot help. For example, Jeff might have said, "I'm really sorry, Margie, but I have to go to work now."

The following expressions are used for talking about favors.

Asking for a favor	**Responding**	
	Yes	**No**
Can / could you do me a (big) favor?	Sure / Yes / Okay / Yeah / Of course.	I'm sorry, but . . . I'd like to, but . . . I wish I could, but . . .
Can / could I ask you for a favor?	No problem. I'd be glad to. What do you need?	I really can't.
Will / can / could you (please) + verb?		Let me think about it.
Could you give / lend me a hand (with something)?		
Can / could you help me with (something)?		
Would you mind verb + *-ing*?	No, not at all.*	

7 **Asking for a Favor.** Work in pairs to practice asking for help and responding. Student A should look at page 259. Student B should look at page 269.

* The answer "No, not at all" means that the speaker *doesn't mind doing* something. In other words, the speaker agrees to do it.

8 Role-Play.

1. In pairs, take turns asking for help or favors and responding in each of the following situations. Then role-play one of the situations for the class.
    1. You ask a classmate if you can copy his or her lecture notes because you were absent.
    2. You want to ask out a cute girl or guy from your biology class. You ask his or her best friend if he or she can introduce you.
    3. You ask your teacher if you can take your final exam one day early because you bought a cheap plane ticket that leaves for Hawaii on the day of the exam.
    4. You ask a colleague if you can borrow $5 until you have a chance to get some cash.
    5. You ask your brother if you can live with him and his wife for the next three months so that you can save some money to go on vacation with your friends.
    6. You ask a friend if you can borrow his or her favorite sweater to wear on a very special date.
    7. In a crowded movie theater, you ask the person sitting next to you if he or she will change seats with you because the person sitting in front of you is very tall.
2. In groups, discuss whether you would feel comfortable asking for favors in these situations.

PART 2 Listening to Lectures

Before You Listen

This lecture is about changes in the American family and how some businesses are responding to those changes.

1 Prelistening Discussion. Discuss these questions in small groups.

1. Look at the photo of a "typical" American family from a 1950s television show. How would you describe the family members? What do you know about their lifestyle?
2. How has the "typical" American family changed since the 1950s?
3. How are families changing in your community? Why?

2 Vocabulary Preview. The following terms appear in the lecture. With your classmates, define the words you already know. Mark the words you do not know.

____ cost of living	____ flexible, flexibility	____ to transfer
____ opportunity	____ a policy	____ to commute
____ a homemaker	____ a benefit	____ a daycare center
____ to volunteer	____ maternity leave (noun)	____ can / can't afford

Listen

Taking Notes on Examples

In English there are many expressions to signal examples. Here are a few:

For example
For instance
As an example
Such as
To give (one) example

In notes, people often use the abbreviation *e.g.* (from Latin *exempli gratia)* to indicate an example.

3 Taking Notes on Examples. You will hear statements supported by examples. The statements are written here in note form. Listen and take notes on the missing examples. Be sure to indent the examples and use abbreviations, symbols, and key words. You will hear each item twice.

1. Today women are wking. in profs. not open 30–40 yrs. ago

2. Now most Am. homes don't have full-time homemaker → new probs.

3. Some comps. give new parents pd. vacation.

Exchange notes with a classmate. Use your partner's notes to try to restate the items you heard.

Language Tip: Summaries

A summary is a short review of the main points of a lecture (or composition). Summaries often appear in the conclusion, but they are also found in the body of a lecture, where they function as a transition between main ideas. These expressions signal that the speaker is summarizing. You do not need to take notes on summaries unless you missed the information the first time.

To summarize
In summary
To review (what I've been talking about)
Let's review the main points up to now
So far, I have talked about

4 Taking Draft Notes. Listen to the lecture and take notes in the best way you can. Use your own paper. Listen specifically for this information:

1. How has the American family changed?
2. What are businesses doing to meet the needs of modern families?

After You Listen

5 **Outlining the Lecture.** Here is a sample outline of the lecture. Use your notes from Activities 3 and 4 to fill in the missing information. Remember to use abbreviations and symbols. Listen to the lecture again if necessary.

Topic: Changes in the American Family

I. "Typical" Am. fam

A. 1950s: ______________________________

____

____

B. Stats:

1. 1965: 35% of Am women worked

2. ______________________________

____

____

3. ______________________________

____

____

II. ______________________________

____

____

A. ______________________________

____

____

B. Women have > opp. than 40 yrs. ago.

e.g. ______________________________

____

____

III. Most fams. don't have ______________ anymore → new probs.

e.g. ______________________________

____

____

IV. ______________________________

Examples:

A. ______________________________

B. If co. transfers worker, they try to find job for husb. / wife

C. ______________________________

D. ______________________________

E. ______________________________

V. Very few cos. can afford these progs. Gov. should ______________________________

6 **Defining New Vocabulary.** With a partner, look back at the words you marked as unknown in Activity 2 and discuss the meaning of each new term. Your teacher may ask you to write sentences with these new words.

7 **Discussing the Lecture.** Discuss the following questions about the lecture and your own experience. Refer to your notes as necessary. Use the new vocabulary as you talk.

1. Why are more and more American women working these days? (Give two reasons.) How does this compare with other countries?
2. With both mothers and fathers working, what new problems do American families have?
3. Review the five ways in which American businesses are responding to the needs of working parents. For each one, talk about the advantages and disadvantages (a) to workers, (b) to employers.
4. Why don't <u>all</u> American companies offer these programs to their employees?
5. Of the five policies, which one would be the most useful for you and your family?

On the Spot!

The following story appeared in the *Los Angeles Times* on August 2, 1997. Read it with your classmates and discuss the questions that follow.

Husband Sues Wife over Housework*

Tokyo—A 33-year-old Japanese woman divorced her husband after he demanded that every day she cook him breakfast, iron his pants and clean the house. The woman worked full time, but the husband said it was the wife's job to do all the housework.

The husband, a 35-year-old public servant, filed a lawsuit demanding that the wife pay him about $38,000 because she did not live up to her end of the marriage arrangement.[1]

---

1. If you were the judge in this case, what would you decide? Do you agree with the wife or the husband? Why? (To find out what really happened, turn to page 275.)

[1] She did not do the things that her husband expected her to do.

The newspaper article continues:

> Increasingly, young [Japanese] women delay marriage or even refuse to get married because of the long-established expectations that women alone should raise the children and take care of the housework. Surveys show the average age at which Japanese women marry has risen to 27, with an increasing number now deciding not to tie the knot[2] at all.

2. Compare the situation of Japanese women and women in other countries. Are women in other countries getting married later? Do some women refuse to get married? Why?

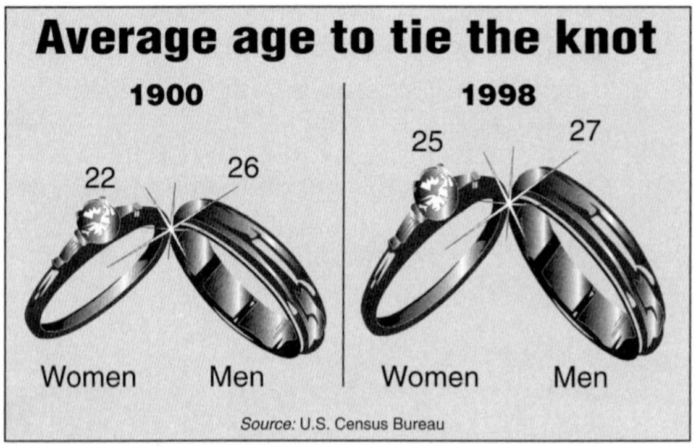

3. In your opinion, whose job is it to take care of children and do housework? Why?

PART 3

Focused Listening and Speaking

[2] to get married

Focused Listening

Linking

In writing, words are separated by spaces. For example: "Please put it in a box." In speech, words are separated by pauses. However, some words don't have pauses between them. They are *linked,* or *connected.*

For example: Please **púdidinabóx**.

Words are linked according to the following rules:

1. In a phrase, when a word ends in a consonant and the next word starts with a vowel, the two words are linked. For example:

   an‿eye where‿are run‿out‿of put‿it‿in‿a box

2. If a word ends in the vowel sounds */iy/, /ey/, /ay/,* or */oy/,* and the next word starts with a vowel, the words are linked with the sound */y/.* For example:

   the‿end of say‿it my‿aunt enjoy‿it

3. If a word ends in the vowel sounds */uw/, /ow/,* or */aw/,* and the next word starts with a vowel, the words are linked with the sound */w/.* For example:

   you‿are late show‿us how‿are you

Note*:* Don't try to memorize these rules. If you practice listening to English a lot, you will learn the rules naturally.

1 Pronouncing Linked Phrases. Listen and repeat the linked phrases.

Rule 1: Consonant + vowel

1. fifty dollars‿a month
2. the check‿is late
3. to care‿about
4. in an‿apartment
5. get‿a job

Rule 2: Vowel + vowel

6. the_end of (the month)
7. people my_own age
8. come see_us
9. no way_out
10. the toy_is broken

Rule 3: Vowel + vowel

11. grow_up
12. go_on
13. who_is it
14. now_it's ready
15. new_art

2 Pronouncing Sentences.

1. Listen and repeat these sentences. Notice the stress, intonation, linking, reductions, and pauses.
    1. She's always broke by the end of the month.
    2. No one cares about poor people in this country.
    3. It'll be interesting to see if Sara gets an A in the course.
    4. There's an old apple on the table in the living room.
    5. Please drop off the October rent check in the afternoon.
    6. I usually wake up at seven, but today my alarm clock didn't go off.
    7. The birthday party is going to be at Ellen's apartment.
    8. He walked out of the house with a big bag full of old clothes.
2. With a partner, take turns reading the sentences again. Pay attention to stress, intonation, linking, reductions, and pauses.

Getting Meaning from Context

3 **Using Context Clues.** You're going to hear several people talking about their lifestyles.

1. Listen to each conversation.
2. After each conversation, you will hear a question. Stop the tape or CD.
3. Read the answer choices and circle the letter of the best answer.
4. Then listen to the next part of the conversation to hear the correct answer.

1. a. factory worker
   b. retired person
   c. landlord
   d. a fashion model

2. a. police
   b. teachers
   c. friends
   d. parents

3. a. is a day-care worker
   b. has never been married
   c. is divorced
   d. is married now

4. a. with his parents
   b. in a college dormitory
   c. alone
   d. with roommates

5. a. a retirement home
   b. a house with friends
   c. an apartment
   d. a hospital

Using Language

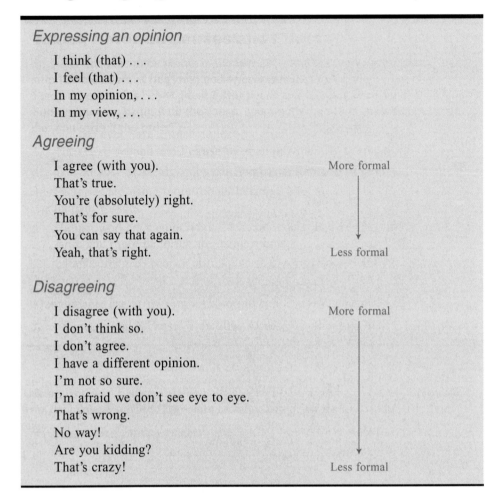

Expressing an opinion

I think (that) . . .
I feel (that) . . .
In my opinion, . . .
In my view, . . .

Agreeing

I agree (with you).	More formal
That's true.	↓
You're (absolutely) right.	
That's for sure.	
You can say that again.	
Yeah, that's right.	Less formal

Disagreeing

I disagree (with you).	More formal
I don't think so.	↓
I don't agree.	
I have a different opinion.	
I'm not so sure.	
I'm afraid we don't see eye to eye.	
That's wrong.	
No way!	
Are you kidding?	
That's crazy!	Less formal

4 Discussing Lifestyles. In this section you heard the following five speakers:

1. a retired man living on Social Security (money that retired people receive each month from the U.S. government)
2. a teenage girl who feels that her parents treat her like a baby
3. a single father whose children live with him
4. a young man who lost his job and moved back into his parents' house
5. an elderly woman living in a retirement home

Discuss the following questions with your classmates. Use expressions for saying your opinion, agreeing, and disagreeing.

1. Do (did) you know any people like the ones on the tape? If yes, tell about their lifestyles. What problems or difficulties do (did) these people have?
2. As a teenager, how is / was your relationship with your parents? Do / Did you ever feel that your parents treat you like a baby?
3. In your opinion, is it the government's responsibility to give money to people when they retire? If not, whose responsibility is it?

PART 4

Listening and Speaking in the Real World

In this section you are going to compare lifestyles in different countries. In Chapter 2, page 32, you practiced taking notes on statistics. Review the vocabulary from that page. In this section you will continue to learn how to talk about numbers and percentages.

Before You Listen

Numbers and Percentages

The following examples show how to talk about numbers and percentages. Pay close attention to prepositions.

In 1999, 55 percent of the students at the English Language Center were from Asia.

In 1999, the percentage of Italian students rose (fell, etc.) by 12 percent.

The percentage of Algerian students fell (increased, etc.) from 15 percent to 9 percent.

The number of Algerian students decreased (rose) from 15 to 9.

The divorce rate in 1995 was 4.4 per 1,000 people.

The number of children declined to 1.6 per family.

1 **Prelistening Discussion.** The following questions are about your community.

1. As far as you know, is the number of working women increasing, decreasing, or staying the same?
2. What is happening to the divorce rate?
3. With whom do older people usually live? Are more older people choosing to live alone than in the past?

Listen

2 Completing Graphs.

1. Here are three incomplete graphs. The numbers at the bottom represent years. In Graphs 1 and 3, the numbers on the left represent percentages. In Graph 2 they represent numbers. Listen to the information and complete the graphs. The first item is done for you.
2. Compare your graphs with those of another student. Do they look the same?

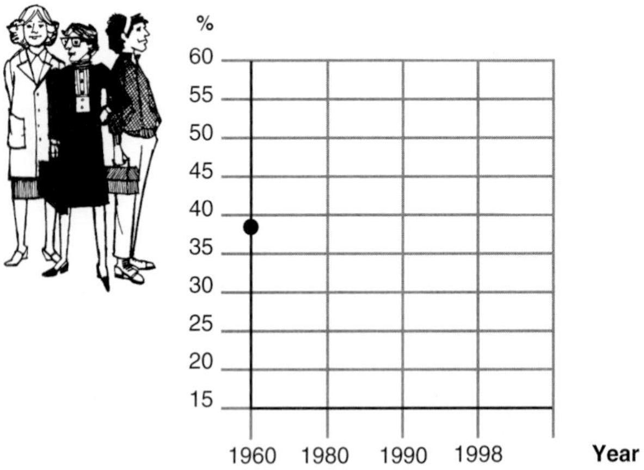

1. Women in the U.S. Working Population, 1960–1998

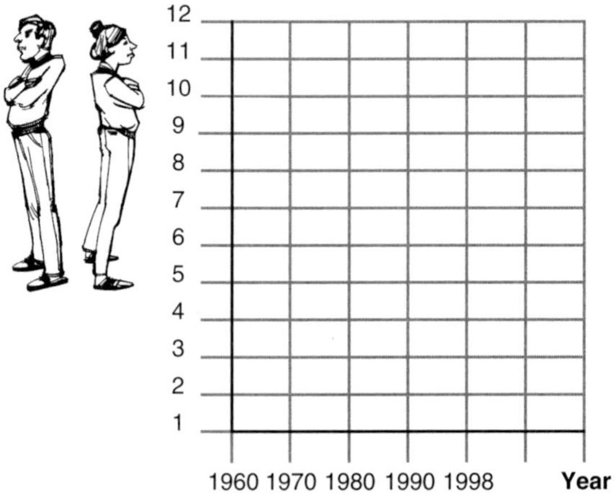

2. U.S. Divorce Rate, 1960–1998 (per 1,000 people)

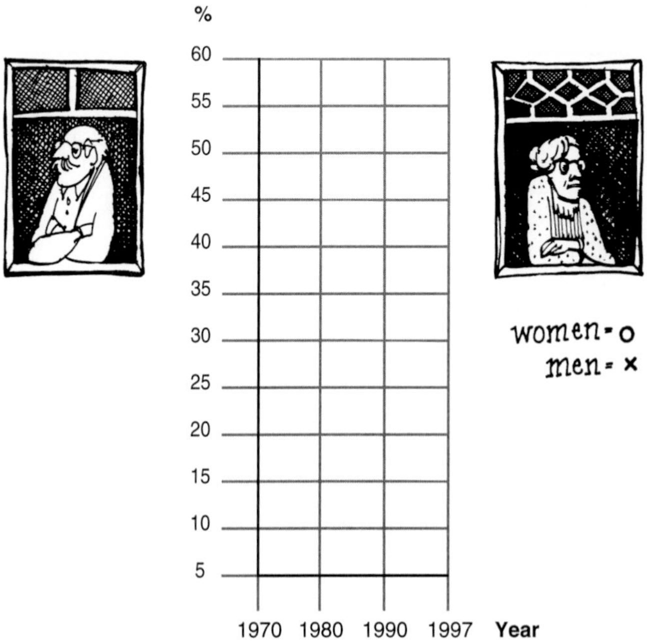

3. People in the U.S. over Age 65 Living Alone, 1970–1997

After You Listen

3 Talking about Statistics.

1. Write five True or False statements based on the information in the graphs. Then take turns saying your statements to one or more partners. If a statement is false, your classmate(s) should correct it.

   Example

   A: In 1990, 10.8% of elderly men lived alone.

   B: That's false. In 1990, 21.5% of elderly men lived alone.

2. Discuss your answers to the following questions with a partner.
   1. Are you surprised by the information you learned in Activities 1 and 2?
   2. In what way(s) is the situation in the United States different from other countries?

Talk It Over

Comparing Lifestyles in Different Countries. The following charts are from the 1999 World Factbook.[1] They contain information about lifestyles in different countries. However, the charts are not complete. Work in groups of three. Take turns asking and answering questions about the information in your chart. Fill in the missing information.

Examples

Q: What was the average life expectancy in France?

A: The life expectancy in France was 78.63 years. (Note: It is OK to say "almost 79 years.")

Q: What was the per capita income in Russia?

A: The per capita income in Russia was $4,000.

Q: How many children did the average woman have in Mexico?

A: The average woman had 2.85 children. (Note: You may say "between 2 and 3 children.")

[1] *The World Factbook,* 1999, <http://www.odci.gov/cia/publications/factbook/index.html>.

Chart A

Country	# children per woman	Life expectancy	TV sets per person	per capita GDP[2]
Korea	1.79	74.3	.2	$12,600
United States	2.07	76.23		31,500
Argentina	2.66	74.76	.2	10,300
France	1.61	78.63	.5	22,600
Senegal		57.83	.006	1,600
Thailand	1.82	69.21	.05	6,100
Mexico	2.85	72	.13	8,300
Italy	1.22	78.51	.3	20,800
Saudi Arabia	6.34	70.55	.2	9,000
China (PRC)	1.8	69.92	.24	3,600
Egypt	3.33	62.39	.07	2,850
Iran	2.45	69.76	.1	5,000
Russia		65.12	.37	4,000
Japan	1.48		.8	23,100
Turkey	2.41	73.29	.16	

Chart B

Country	# children per woman	Life expectancy	TV sets per person	per capita GDP
Korea	1.79	74.3	.2	
United States	2.07		1.27	31,500
Argentina	2.66	74.76	.2	10,300
France	1.61	78.63	.5	22,600
Senegal	6.11		.006	1,600
Thailand	1.82	69.21	.05	6,100
Mexico	2.85	72	.13	8,300
Italy	1.22	78.51	.3	20,800
Saudi Arabia	6.34	70.55	.2	9,000
China (PRC)		69.92	.24	3,600
Egypt	3.33	62.39	.07	2,850
Iran	2.45	69.76		5,000
Russia	1.34	65.12	.37	4,000
Japan	1.48	80.11	.8	23,100
Turkey	2.41	73.29	.16	6,600

[2] GDP means "gross domestic product." This number refers to the amount of money spent on each person in a country per year.

Chart C

Country	# children per woman	Life expectancy	TV sets per person	per capita GDP
Korea	1.79	74.3	.2	$12,600
United States	2.07	76.23	1.27	31,500
Argentina	2.66	74.76	.2	
France	1.61	78.63	.5	22,600
Senegal	6.11	57.83	.006	1,600
Thailand	1.82		.05	6,100
Mexico	2.85	72	.13	8,300
Italy	1.22	78.51	.3	
Saudi Arabia	6.34	70.55	.2	9,000
China (PRC)	1.8	69.92	.24	3,600
Egypt		62.39	.07	2,850
Iran	2.45	69.76	.1	5,000
Russia	1.34	65.12		4,000
Japan	1.48	80.11	.8	23,100
Turkey	2.41	73.29	.16	6,600

Discussion.

1. Based on the information in the charts, which five countries are the richest?
2. Which five countries are the poorest?
3. Compare the number of the children per woman, the life expectancy, and the TV sets per person for the richest and poorest countries. What general statements can you make, based on this information? Make complete sentences.

   Example

   The poorest countries usually have the largest number of children per woman, and the richest countries have the smallest number. For example, in Japan, the average woman has 1.48 children, but in Senegal, the average woman has more than 6 children.

Video Activities: Telecommuting

Before You Watch. Discuss the following questions with your class or in small groups.

1. Is traffic a problem in your area?
2. What can people in your area do to avoid sitting in traffic on the way to work?
3. Are businesses in your area doing anything to help workers who have to travel a long time to get to work?

Watch. Discuss the following questions with your classmates.

1. How does David Carroll reduce his commuting time?
2. Where does Marty Barrazo work?

Watch Again. Read the statements below. Say if they are true (T) or false (F). Then watch the video again and check your answers.

1. _____ David Carroll spends an hour commuting to work.
2. _____ David's company allows flexible work hours.
3. _____ Marty Barrazo works for an Internet company.
4. _____ He commutes three hours a day to the community computer center.
5. _____ Many people don't know that the community computer center exists.
6. _____ The computer center has very modern computers.
7. _____ Marty Barrazo is always grumpy when he gets home.

After You Watch. Discuss the following questions in small groups.

1. What method of transportation do you use to come to school?
2. How much time do you spend commuting to and from school each day?
3. If you didn't have to commute, what would you do with your extra time?
4. Is telecommuting possible in your career or future career?

Chapter 6

Global Connections

IN THIS CHAPTER

Lecture:	Cultural Differences
Note-Taking Focus:	Taking Notes on Similarities and Differences
Focused Listening:	Blending Consonants
Using Language:	Politely Interrupting an Action or a Speaker Generalizing

Did You Know?

- The world's population officially reached 6 billion on July 19, 1999.
- The smallest nations in the world are:

Vatican City	17 square miles
Monaco	75 square miles
Nauru	8.2 square miles

- Number of online users worldwide: 257.5 million[1]
- The World Wide Web now contains some 1.2 billion pages and doubles in size each year.[2]
- Language use online:[1]

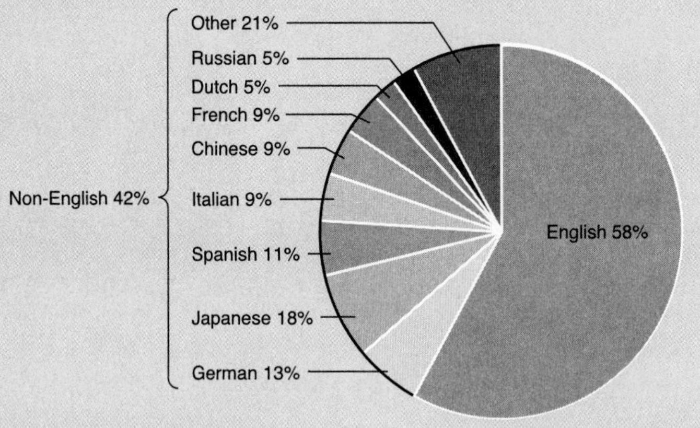

PART 1

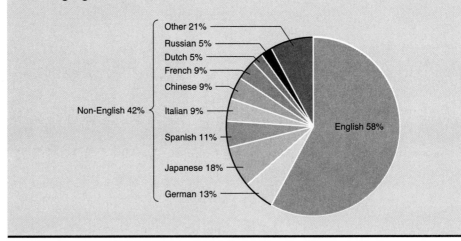

Listening to Conversations

Before You Listen

In the following conversation, Jeff helps Anna make a decision about buying a computer.

BIZARRO By DAN PIRARO

[1] *Los Angeles Times,* January 25, 2000.

[2] *Newsweek,* August 9, 1999, p. 51

1 Prelistening Questions. Discuss these questions with your classmates.

1. Do you own a computer, or do you use one frequently? What do you use it for?
2. Which is easier for you: writing by hand or on the computer?
3. How can computers help people all over the world keep in touch with each other?

2 Vocabulary Preview.

1. The following computer terms are used in the conversation. Define them with your classmates. If you are not sure about a term, look it up in a dictionary.

Computer Terms

chat	(to) post a message
discussion group	(to) search (the World Wide Web); to do a search
e-mail	(to) surf the Net
the Internet	(Web) site
online	word processing

2. These sentences contain expressions from the conversation. Use the context to match the underlined words and expressions with their definitions.

Sentences	Definitions
1. Hi Anna. <u>What's up?</u>	a. ____ have a desire to do something
2. I need to lose weight. <u>From now on</u> I'm not going to eat any desserts.	b. ____ communicate with someone on a regular basis, usually by phone or e-mail
3. Let's stay home tonight. I don't <u>feel like</u> going out.	c. ____ a greeting, similar in meaning to "How are you" or "What's happening?"
4. Do you use e-mail to <u>keep in touch with</u> your family?	d. ____ beginning at this time
5. John spends hours every night <u>surfing the Net</u>.	e. ____ exploring the Internet

Listen

3 Listening for Main Ideas.

1. Close your book as you listen to the conversation. Listen for the answers to these questions.
    1. Why is Anna thinking about getting a computer?
    2. What does she learn from Jeff?
    3. What does she finally decide?
2. Compare answers with a partner.

Stress

4 Listening for Stressed Words.

1. Now listen to part of the conversation again. Some of the stressed words are missing. During each pause, repeat the phrase or sentence; then fill in the missing stressed words.

Jeff: But ______________, Anna, there are lots of ______________ things you can do with a computer besides word processing and e-mail.

Anna: Yeah? Like ______________?

Jeff: Well first of all, there's the ______________, of course.

Anna: Yeah, I know, you seem to be ______________ all the time. What do you do, ______________ the ______________?

Jeff: Sometimes. But ______________ I use the Internet to get information about things that I'm ______________ in and to talk with people all over the world about ______________.

Anna: How do you do ______________?

Jeff: Do you know what a ______________ group is?

Anna: No.

Jeff: Well, it's a kind of ______________, except that it meets ______________, and uh, ______________ who's interested can ______________ the group. If you're a ______________, you can go online ______________you want and read ______________ sent in by other members, and of course you can also ______________ to any message you want. Um, here, look.

Jeff: Here. I belong to a discussion group about ______________ ______________. Remember my friend Hiroshi, the ______________ from Japan? Here's a message he posted talking about . . . hip hop in ______________.

Anna: Jeff, this is very ______________. Are there discussion groups for people learning ______________?

Jeff: I don't know . . . let's do a quick ______________ . . . OK, look here.

Anna: Wow! So many ______________!

Jeff: Look, this one has 25 different discussion groups and live ______________. You can communicate with people from all over the world in ______________ time.

Anna: That sounds like ______________! And if I ______________ a computer, I could do ______________ at home . . . I ______________ have to do all my work in the computer lab at ______________.

Jeff: So what do you ______________, Anna? Is it ______________ getting a computer?

Anna: Yeah, I guess it is. Would you ______________ helping me pick one ______________?

Jeff: ______________ at ______________. Do you have ______________ to go shopping this ______________?

Anna: Let's go!

2. Compare answers and read the conversation with a partner. Pay attention to the stressed words.

Intonation

Intonation in Questions and Requests

Information questions have a rising-falling intonation pattern:

- Where do you live?

Yes or No questions and requests have a rising intonation pattern:

- Are you ready to go?
- Could you please repeat that?

5 **Practicing Intonation of Questions.** Listen to the following items from the conversation and repeat them after the speaker.

Yes or No questions

1. Am I interrupting?
2. Do you know what a discussion group is?
3. Are there discussion groups for people learning English?

Request for help

4. Would you mind helping me pick one out?

Information questions

5. What's up?
6. What's the problem?
7. How do you do that?

6 **Identifying Intonation Patterns.** Listen to the following sentences. Repeat each sentence after the speaker; then circle the rising arrow for rising intonation, and the falling arrow for rising-falling intonation.

1. ↗ ↘
2. ↗ ↘
3. ↗ ↘
4. ↗ ↘
5. ↗ ↘
6. ↗ ↘

After You Listen

7 **Vocabulary Review.** Discuss the following questions with a partner. Use the underlined vocabulary in your answers.

1. To whom would you say "<u>What's up</u>"? Why?

   a. a friend b. a professor c. a child d. your boss

2. This morning you were the last person to leave your house. When you went out, you forgot to lock the doors and windows. When you returned home in the afternoon, you discovered that burglars had entered your house and stolen many valuable items. What can you do <u>from now on</u> to protect your home against burglary?
3. It is a cold but beautiful Saturday morning. Last night it snowed, but today the weather is calm. What do you <u>feel like</u> doing today?
4. What methods of communication do you use to <u>keep in touch with</u> your family and friends?
5. How much time do you spend each week <u>surfing the Net</u>? What kinds of sites do you like to explore?
6. In the city where you live, is it <u>worth</u> owning a car, or is it better to use public transportation?

Using Language

At the beginning of the conversation, Anna knocks on the door and asks Jeff, "Am I interrupting?" In many cultures it is impolite to interrupt a person who is speaking or working. However, most Americans are accustomed to interruptions and don't mind them. Here are some expressions that English speakers use to interrupt politely.

Politely interrupting an action

Excuse me (for interrupting), but . . . (I have a message for you.)
I'm sorry to interrupt, but . . .
I hate to interrupt, but . . .
Pardon me, but . . .

Am I interrupting?
Can / May I interrupt?
Do you mind if I interrupt?

Politely interrupting a speaker

Can / Could / May I say something here?
I'd like to say something.
Wait (a minute). (I have a question.)

8 **Role-Play.** Work in groups of three students. In each of the situations, two people are talking and a third person interrupts. Take turns playing the role of the interrupter.

1. Two businesspeople are having a meeting. They are talking about a computer problem. An assistant knocks on the door, enters, interrupts politely, and tells one of the businesspeople that the boss is on the phone and wants to talk to him or her right away. The businessperson thanks the assistant.
2. After class, a teacher is talking to a student about a grammar problem. Another student interrupts, says she or he forgot her or his homework, and asks for permission to bring it the next day. The teacher says OK.
3. Two students are doing a vocabulary exercise together. The teacher interrupts and tells one of them that she needs to speak to him or her during the break. The student agrees.
4. Two friends are having coffee together. They are talking about the party last weekend. A third friend interrupts and asks if he or she can join them. They invite the third student to sit down.

9 **The Interrupting Game.** Work in groups of four to five students. Your teacher will give each student in the group a topic to discuss.

1. When it is your turn, start speaking about your topic.
2. Your classmates will interrupt you often, using the expressions in the explanation box.
3. When you are interrupted, answer the person who interrupted you, but then return to your topic. Follow the example.

Example

Speaker: Last night I went to a baseball game . . .

Student 1: Excuse me for interrupting, but which one?

Speaker: The Red Sox and the Yankees. Anyway, I went to the game and got to my seat . . .

Student 2: Sorry, but where was your seat?

And so on.

4. The game ends when the speaker finishes the story.

Talk It Over

Interview. Work with a partner. Take turns interviewing each other about your experiences as "global citizens." Use the following questions; feel free to add others that interest you. Concentrate on using correct stress and intonation patterns.

1. Do you enjoy traveling?
2. How many different countries have you visited?
3. How many languages do you speak?
4. What is the strangest food that you have ever eaten?

5. Do you use e-mail? Are you connected to the Internet?
6. Would you like to live or work in another country for several years? Which country?
7. Would you marry a person from another country? If so, what languages would you want your children to learn?
8. In your current or future work, how important is contact with the international community?
9. Right now you are studying English. Which other languages do you think you will need to learn in the future?

PART 2

Listening to Lectures

Before You Listen

The lecture in this chapter is about misunderstandings that can occur if people from different countries do not know about each other's customs.

1 **Prelistening Discussion.** Discuss these questions in small groups.

1. Have you ever had guests from other countries come to your home? If so, did they behave in any way that was different from what you expected? How did you react to their behavior?
2. Have you ever traveled to or lived in other countries? If so, have you ever insulted someone or embarrassed yourself because you didn't know the local customs?
3. Do you try to learn about other countries' customs and traditions? Where do you get your information?

2 **Vocabulary Preview.** The following terms appear in the lecture. With your classmates, define the words you already know. Mark the words you do not know.

____ insulted	____ title (of a person)	____ universal
____ misunderstanding (noun)	____ vary	____ variation
____ to illustrate	____ utensils	____ embarrassment
____ a hug	____ chopsticks	____ to interact with
____ a bow	____ generous	

Listen

Taking Notes on Similarities and Differences

Taking notes on differences

The following sentence is from the lecture:

> "In the United States, greetings involve some sort of touching. . . . On the other hand, Asian people aren't as comfortable touching in public."

Here are sample notes for this sentence. The contrasting items are written on different lines. Notice the use of indenting, key words, and abbreviations:

Greetings
    U.S.: involve touching
    Asia: not comf. touching

Taking notes on similarities

Similar items may be written on the same line. For example: "The Japanese, like many other Asian people, give gifts quite frequently."

Jap. + other Asians give gifts freq.

Expressions signaling similarity and difference

The following expressions are used in the lecture.

Differences:	*Similarities:*
on the other hand	is similar to
in contrast	also
however	like
while	

3 **Taking Notes on Similarities and Differences.** Listen to sentences with similarities and differences. Complete the notes. You will hear each sentence twice.

1. Ams = quick to use 1st names.

   ____

   ____

2. Egypt: leave food on plate.

   ____

   ____

3. Bolivia: eat everyth. on plate.

   ____

   ____

4. Many Jap. bow when they greet

   ____

   ____

5. U.S., CA, + West. countries:

   ____

   ____

Now, exchange notes with a classmate. Use your partner's notes to try to restate the items you heard.

4 **Taking Draft Notes.** Listen to the lecture and take notes in the best way you can. Use your own paper. Listen for examples of similarities and differences among people from different cultures.

After You Listen

5 Outlining the Lecture. Here is a sample outline of the lecture. Use your notes from Activities 3 and 4 to fill in the missing information. Remember to use abbreviations and symbols. Listen to the lecture again if necessary.

____

____

Intro: ______________________________

____

I. Greetings

  A. No. America + West. countries: ______________________________

  B. Asia: ______________________________

    1. ______________________________

    2. ______________________________

II. ______________________________

  A. Americans: ______________________________

  B. ______________________________

  C. ______________________________

III. ______________________________

  A. Utensils

    1. ______________________________

    2. ______________________________

    3. ______________________________

  B. ______________________________

    1. Egypt, China: ______________________________

    2. ______________________________

IV. ______________________________

  A. ______________________________

    1. for dinner: bring flowers, wine, small gift

    2. business: ______________________________

  B. Jap. + other Asians: ______________________________

  ____

  C. ______________________________

    e.g.: ______________________________

V. ______________________________

____

6 **Defining New Vocabulary.** With a partner, look back at the words you marked as unknown in Activity 2 and discuss the meaning of each new term. Your teacher may ask you to write sentences with these new words.

7 **Discussing the Lecture.** Discuss the following questions about the lecture and your own experience. Refer to your notes as necessary. Use the new vocabulary as you talk.

1. Explain the "rules" for greeting people in your community. What body language do you use? Do you bow, shake hands, hug, or kiss? Does it depend on your relationship to the person?
2. Is it customary to kiss a person you have just met? Would you feel embarrassed if this happened to you?
3. Discuss the use of names. For example, how do you address the following people: your teacher, your grandparents, your parents, your boss, your boyfriend or girlfriend, your husband or wife, your children? What titles do you use when speaking to these people?
4. Discuss the customs connected with giving gifts. What is your custom on the following occasions: birthdays; holidays; special events, such as graduations, the birth of a baby, or a wedding. Which gifts are polite? Which gifts are considered rude?
5. Why is it important for people everywhere to know about other people's customs and traditions?

On the Spot!

Situation. One day you meet a young man or woman. You begin talking and discover that the two of you have many opinions and ideas in common. You enjoy each other's company so much that you agree to meet for coffee the following day.

In the following weeks you meet many more times. As you get to know each other better, you begin to fall in love and talk about the future. However, there is a serious problem. Your parents have told you that they expect you to date people from the same background (race, religion, education, or social class) as

you. However, your new boyfriend / girlfriend comes from a very different background. You know that your parents will be angry if you decide to keep seeing this person.

You must make a decision. Will you continue seeing this person, knowing that your parents will disapprove, or will you end the relationship now, before it becomes more serious?

Discussion. Discuss the following questions in small groups.

1. Have you ever had a friend, boyfriend, or girlfriend who came from a different background than you? What was the difference? What did your parents say about this relationship?
2. Could you fall in love with/or marry a person from a different background than you? What would your parents say if you wanted to do this?
3. In your opinion, is it important for two people in a romantic relationship to be similar in race, nationality, religion, economic status, or educational level? Why or why not?
4. If two people come from different backgrounds, what problems might they have in their relationship?
5. What are the advantages of two people from different backgrounds getting married?

PART 3 Focused Listening and Speaking

Focused Listening

Blending Consonants

When one word ends in a consonant and the next word begins with the same consonant, the two consonants are *blended*, or pronounced as one sound. There is no pause between the two words.

For example:

black + cat = */blákát/*

big + girl = */bígírl/*

famous + singer= */fámousínger/*

1 Pronouncing Names with Blended Consonants. Here are some typical English names. Listen to the tape and repeat them after the speaker. Blend the consonants so that each name sounds like one word.

1. Alan Norton
2. Pat Thompson
3. Philip Pearson
4. Dick Cantor
5. Brad Davis
6. Meg Gray
7. Tom Madison
8. Peter Ramsey
9. Val Lewis
10. Trish Sherman
11. Cass Saxon
12. Seth Thayer

2 Saying Phrases with Blended Consonants. Circle the blended sounds in the following phrases. Then practice saying the phrases. Finally, listen to the tape to check your pronunciation.

Example

a fat tiger

1. a bad day
2. June ninth
3. a car radio
4. a tall ladder
5. hot tea
6. a dangerous street
7. eight times

3 Pronouncing Sentences. Practice saying these sentences with correct linking, blending, stress, reductions, and intonation. Then listen to the tape to check your pronunciation.

Example

The air was full of fall leaves.

1. We need to cancel our dinner reservations.
2. I live with three roommates.
3. Have a good day.
4. I don't know her phone number.
5. This song is so sad.
6. We're ready to take a walk.
7. Did he put his black coat away?
8. She bought an expensive vase.

Getting Meaning from Context

4 **Using Context Clues.** You are going to hear short passages about customs in different countries.

1. Listen to each passage.
2. After each passage, you will hear a question or statement. Stop the tape or CD.
3. Read the answer choices and circle the letter of the best answer.

1. a. It is rude to arrive late for dinner.
   b. If you arrive for dinner exactly on time, the hosts probably will not be ready for you.
   c. You should never be late for a business appointment.
   d. University students have difficulty organizing their time.

2. a. comfortable
   b. bored
   c. nervous
   d. grateful

3. a. Japanese people are friendlier than Americans.
   b. Americans smile more than people from other cultures.
   c. A smile can have different meanings in different cultures.
   d. A smile has the same meaning in the United States and Puerto Rico.

4. a. an old tradition
   b. a way to make trees healthier
   c. how to use old shoes
   d. couples who have many children

5. a. disapprove of you
   b. give you special treatment
   c. help your business
   d. arrest you

Using Language

Generalizing

To speak about your daily routine or typical activities, use the present tense with any of these adverbs.

generally	typically	most of the time	as a rule
in general	normally	usually	ordinarily

Examples

Most of the time I wear shoes from Italy.

I usually drink French or Colombian coffee for breakfast.

Typically I leave for work in my Japanese car at 7:30 A.M.

5 **Reading.** In the following passage, a writer from Los Angeles, California, describes his typical day in that international city.

> This is the typical day of a relatively typical soul in today's diversified world. I wake up to the sound of my Japanese clock radio, put on a T-shirt sent me by an uncle in Nigeria, and walk out into the street, past German cars, to my office. Around me are English-language students from Korea, Switzerland, and Argentina all on this Spanish-named road in this Mediterranean-style town. On TV, I find, the news is in Mandarin; today's baseball game is being broadcast in Korean. For lunch I can walk to a sushi bar, a tandoori palace, a Thai cafe, or the newest burrito joint (run by an old Japanese lady). Who am I, I sometimes wonder . . . And where am I?
>
> *—Pico Iyer*

1. Discuss the following questions about the passage.
    1. How many imported products does the writer use, and where do they come from?

       (Example: Japanese clock radio)
    2. What does the writer see around him on the street?
    3. What languages does the writer hear on television?
    4. Which foods does the writer mention, and where do they come from?

2. Prepare a short presentation about *your* typical day as an international citizen. Use expressions for generalizing in your presentation.
    1. Use the questions in No. 1 to guide you. For example: Which imported products do you use every day?
    2. Make a list of other activities and products that are part of your daily routine.
    3. Organize your presentation in chronological order, i.e., from the time you get up in the morning and until you go to bed at night. Do not include every detail of your day; include only those activities and products that have an international aspect.
    4. Remember to use expressions for generalizing from the explanation box.
    5. Speak for two to three minutes. If possible, use one or more visual aids in your presentation.

PART 4

Listening and Speaking in the Real World

FYI

trivia [noun, plural] *matters or things that are very unimportant; unimportant or useless details; little-known facts*

A popular party game in the United States is called Trivial Pursuit. This game tests people's knowledge of detailed facts ("trivia") in a wide variety of categories, such as world geography, movies, computers, and many more. Many Americans enjoy playing trivia games or taking trivia quizzes in magazines and newspapers.

Before You Listen

1 **Sharing Experiences.**

1. Have you ever played a trivia game? With whom did you play? Did you enjoy the game? Did you win?
2. Do you know anyone who is a "trivia expert"? Describe this person.
3. Is there any topic or area in which you are an expert? How did you acquire your knowledge or skill?

Listen

2 Taking a Trivia Quiz.

1. In the following conversation, Georgie reads a trivia quiz to her friend Kevin. As she asks the questions, circle *your* answers in the chart. Then listen to the next part of the conversation, and you will hear the correct answer.

1.	a. The United States	5.	a. 8
	b. Canada		b. 6.5
	c. Russia		c. 5
	d. China		d. 3.5
2.	a. France	6.	a. Mexico
	b. The United States		b. Russia
	c. Italy		c. England
	d. China		d. Greece
3.	a. Finland	7.	a. German
	b. Japan		b. Spanish
	c. Canada		c. Japanese
	d. Mexico		d. Chinese
4.	a. Finland	8.	a. Moscow
	b. Japan		b. New York
	c. the United States		c. Tokyo
	d. Brazil		d. London

2. What score did *you* get on the quiz? Compare with your classmates.

After You Listen

3 Design a Trivia Game. Write five trivia questions about your country and submit them to your teacher. Your teacher will select questions to be used in a class trivia competition.

You may write questions about:

geography
history
customs
products
cities
people
natural resources
tourist attractions

Talk It Over

Choosing Your Dream Vacation. Work in small groups. Look at the photos and answer the questions that follow.

FYI

Students are often confused about the correct use of the words "trip" and "travel." Study these examples:

I took a trip to Boston. (noun)

I don't like to travel on boats. (verb)

Traveling is her favorite hobby. (noun)

1. Can you guess where each photo was taken? What do you know about this place? For example,
   - the weather
   - the attractions
   - places to stay
   - dangers
2. Have you ever visited any of these places or similar ones? If so, tell your group about your trip.
3. If you could choose *one* of these places to take an all-expenses-paid vacation, which one would you choose? Why?

Video Activities: Teen Talk

Before You Watch. Discuss these questions in small groups.

1. What are the most common problems that teenagers have?
2. How do teenagers get help when they have a problem?
3. If you have a problem, do you think it's easier to talk to a stranger or to someone you know?

Watch. Discuss the following questions in a group.

1. What is "Teen Talk"?
   a. a magazine
   b. a Website
   c. a school group
2. On Teen Talk, teenagers can . . . (Choose 2 answers)
   a. talk to other teens about their problems
   b. see advertisements for products they might like
   c. get help with homework
   d. learn about resources to help them with their problems

Watch Again. Fill in the answers.

1. List three examples of problems that the users of Teen Talk discuss.

a. ____

b. ____

c. ____

2. The teen girl believes that just ____________________ about something can help teens to solve problems.
3. The "number 1 goal" of Teen Talk was to give teens a place to go to find ____________________.

After You Watch. Discuss these questions in small groups.

1. Do you think a Website like Teen Talk could be a useful way for you and your friends to get help with problems?
2. What resources exist in your community to help teens who are depressed or in trouble?
3. If you were in some kind of crisis, where would you go for help?

Chapter 7

Language and Communication

IN THIS CHAPTER

Lecture: Differences between American and British English
Note-Taking Focus: Classifying
Focused Listening: Interjections
Using Language: Contradicting Politely
Guessing

Did You Know?

- The total number of languages spoken in the world today: 6,528.
- Language Distribution*

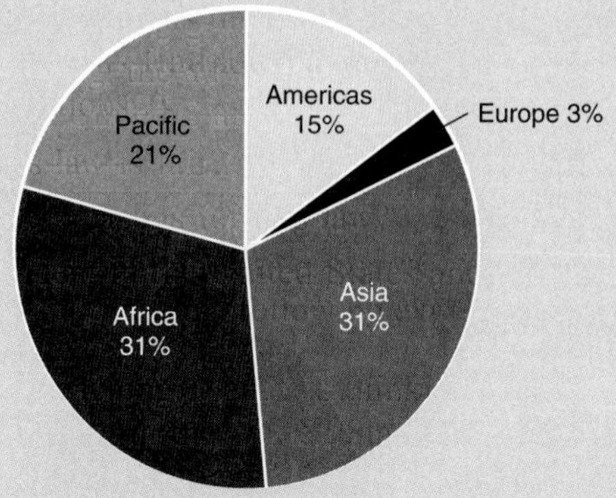

- Number of people who speak English as a first language: 427 million
  Number of people who speak English as a second language: 350 million
- The world's top ten languages, based on number of native speakers:

1. Mandarin Chinese
2. English
3. Spanish
4. Hindi
5. Arabic
6. Portuguese
7. Bengali
8. Russian
9. Japanese
10. German

PART 1

Listening to Conversations

Before You Listen

In the following conversation, Nancy and Anna talk about friendliness and friendship in the United States.

---

* *Los Angeles Times,* January 25, 2000, p. A14.

1 Prelistening Questions.

Discuss these questions with your classmates.

1. What is the difference between "friendliness" and "friendship"?
2. Have you ever had a friend from another culture? How did you meet? Was it difficult for you to communicate with this person at first?
3. Do you have a best friend? How long have you known this person?

2 Vocabulary Preview.

These sentences contain words and expressions from the conversation. Use the context to match the underlined items with their definitions.

Sentences	Definitions
1. (At a restaurant) *Host:* Your table is not ready yet. Would you like to have a seat in the lobby for a few moments?	a. _____ a close, trusting relationship
2. (Two students are talking) *A:* I don't like Mary. She's so two-faced! *B:* Yeah, she's nice when she's with you, but she says nasty things about you behind your back.	b. _____ to sit down
3. The student from Brazil was popular because of her warmth and friendliness.	c. _____ confused or without information
4. If a good friend lied to me, I would end my friendship with her.	d. _____ to understand
5. It's hard to make friends with people if you don't speak their language well.	e. _____ very tired and nervous
6. After the teacher explained the math problem five times, the students finally began to catch on.	f. _____ a warm and open way of behaving and talking
7. I don't know what our teacher wants us to do. I am completely in the dark.	g. _____ to establish a close relationship with someone
8. I've been working very hard and I am totally stressed out. I need a vacation!	h. _____ hypocritical; dishonest

Listen

3 Listening for Main Ideas.

1. Close your book as you listen to the conversation. Listen for the answers to these questions.
    1. What is the relationship between Karen and Anna?
    2. Why is Anna upset?
    3. What does Nancy say about friendship and friendliness in the United States?
2. Compare answers with a partner.

Stress

4 Listening for Stressed Words.

1. Now listen to part of the conversation again. Some of the stressed words are missing. During each pause, repeat the phrase or sentence; then fill in the missing stressed words.

Anna: I don't understand Americans.

Nancy: Huh?

Anna: Did you ___________ what she said? "I'll call you, we'll go to a ___________." But every time I try to pick a ___________ day or time, she says she's _____, she has to check her ___________. And then she ___________ calls me.

Nancy: Um hmm . . .

Anna: Why do Americans say things they don't ___________? They ___________ so nice, like they ___________ say, "How are you," but then they keep on ___________ and don't even wait for your __________. They're so . . . how do you say it . . . ___________ -faced?

Nancy: I know it ___________ that way sometimes, Anna. But it's ___________ ___________. It's just that for Americans, friendliness and friendship ___________ always the same thing.

Anna: What do you ___________?

Nancy: Well, as you know, Americans can be very ___________ and friendly. For example, they ___________ you to sit down, they ___________ you questions, they ___________ you all about their families. So naturally you think they're trying to make ___________ with you. But in reality, friendship, ___________ friendship, takes ___________ to build. It doesn't happen ___________.

Anna: So, when people say "How are you," they're just being ___________? They don't really ___________?

Nancy: Not exactly. The thing you have to ___________ is that "How are you" isn't a ___________ question. It's more of a ___________, a way of saying hello.

Anna: Aha, I ___________ it! And "Have a nice day" is just a ___________ way to say good-bye?

Nancy: Exactly. ___________ you're catching on.

Anna: But I'm ___________ in the dark about Karen. Does she ___________ to be my friend or ___________?

Nancy: It's _____ to say. It sounds like she's pretty stressed _____ right now. Maybe she'll have more time after the ___________. I guess you'll just have to be ___________.

Anna: OK. Thanks for the ___________, Nancy.

2. Compare answers and read the conversation with a partner. Pay attention to the stressed words.

Intonation

Statements with Rising Intonation

You heard the following exchange in the conversation:

Anna: So, when people say "How are you," they're just being polite? They don't really care?

Nancy: Not exactly.

Note that Anna's questions are actually statements—"They're just being polite? They don't really care?"—with rising intonation. This way of talking is often used in rapid, informal English, especially when the speaker is surprised or expects an affirmative answer.

5 **Understanding Statements with Rising Intonation.** Listen to the following "statement questions" and rewrite them as "true" questions in the spaces.

Example

You hear: "You're going to work?"

You write: "Are you going to work?"

1. ______________________________
2. ______________________________
3. ______________________________
4. ______________________________
5. ______________________________

After You Listen

6 **Vocabulary Review.** Work in pairs to practice the new vocabulary. Student A should look at page 260. Student B should look at page 270.

Using Language

Contradicting Politely

"To contradict" means to say the opposite of what someone else has just said. We contradict people if we disagree with them or if they have made a mistake. For example, in the conversation, Anna has some incorrect ideas about American friendliness. She says,

> Why do Americans say things they don't mean? They act so nice, like they always say "How are you," but then they keep on walking and don't even wait for your answer. They're so . . . how do you say it . . . two-faced?

In her answer, Nancy contradicts Anna and corrects her wrong idea; notice the language she uses:

> I know <u>it seems</u> that way sometimes, Anna. <u>But it's not true</u>. It's just that for Americans, friendliness and friendship aren't always the same thing.

There are polite and impolite ways to contradict people. Here are some common expressions that are used for this purpose:

Polite	Well, you might think . . . but actually . . . Well, actually . . . It's true that . . . but . . . Well, as a matter of fact, . . . No, that's wrong. That's not true.
Rude	You're wrong. What are you talking about? That's ridiculous.

FYI

stereotype (noun) *an idea or impression about types or groups of people that is too simple, too general, and often negative.*

Example
One stereotype about Americans is that they are rich and care only about money. This description is a stereotype because it is too general.

7 Contradicting Stereotypes. Discuss stereotypes with your classmates and practice contradicting each other politely.

1. Working alone

   Complete the following sentence with adjectives or nouns.

   Americans are ____.

2. Whole-class activity
   1. Compare your answers in No. 1 with those of your classmates. One student should write the answers on the board.
   2. With your class and teacher, discuss the following questions:
      a. Which statements are stereotypes? Remember, a stereotype is a statement that is too simple, too general, and often negative.
      b. How can you modify the statements so that they are not stereotypes? In other words, if someone said one of these statements, how would you correct the speaker?
      c. Do we generally have stereotypes about people who are similar to us or different from us? Why?
      d. Are stereotypes ever funny?

3. Pairwork

Take turns stating stereotypes about these groups and then politely correcting those stereotypes.

Americans	movie stars	athletes	artists

Example

Student 2: Americans are only interested in money.

Student 1: I know it seems that way, especially if you don't know many American people personally. But actually, Americans can be very generous. They donate a lot of food and money to charities.

On the Spot!

What Is Friendship? Look at the following list of situations. Discuss the following questions in small groups.

Situations

- take care of you when you are sick
- lend you money
- take you or pick you up from the airport during school or work hours
- give you a gift on your birthday
- help you with your homework
- disagree with you
- tell you secrets
- help you move to a new house or apartment
- always tell you the truth
- take care of your pets or your children if you go away on vacation
- invite your relatives to his or her home
- other ____________________

Questions

1. Would you expect a friend to do these things for you?
2. Would you do these things for a friend?

PART 2 Listening to Lectures

Before You Listen

This lecture is about some differences between British and American English.

"Do you have an elevator?"

"Have you got a lift?"

1 **Prelistening Discussion.** Discuss these questions in small groups.

1. Which English-speaking countries have you visited (if any)?
2. Did you notice anything special about the way people there speak English?
3. Which accent of English is easiest for you to understand: American, British, Australian, or something else?

2 **Vocabulary Preview.** The following terms appear in the lecture. With your classmates, define the words you already know. Mark the words you do not know.

____ a sample	____ a dialect	____ noticeable
____ a standard	____ a category	____ identical
____ a majority	____ unique	____ while, whereas (for contrast)
	____ uniqueness	

Listen

Classifying

Lectures are often organized by classification. That is, the lecture topic is classified, or divided, into several smaller subtopics, or categories. A well-organized lecturer will announce these categories in the introduction to the lecture. You should listen for this information because it helps you to plan how you will organize and write your notes.

3 **Classifying Lecture Organization.** Listen to the introductions from three lectures. Identify the subtopics and write them in the spaces.

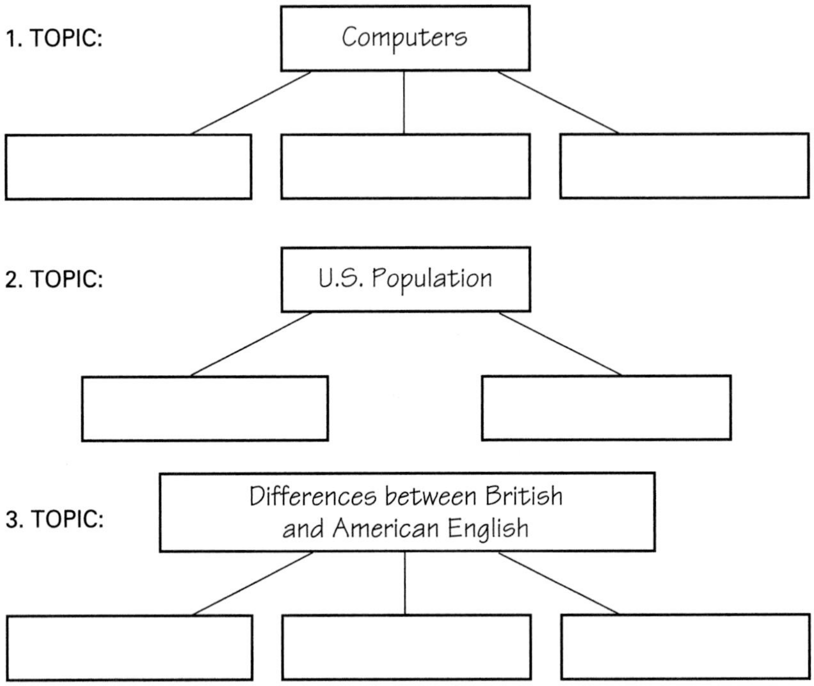

4 **Taking Draft Notes.** Listen to the lecture and take notes in the best way you can. Use your own paper.

Language Tip

Some Vocabulary Differences between American and British English

American English	**British English**
apartment	flat
bathroom	toilet
garbage can	dustbin
soccer	football
raincoat	mackintosh
quotation marks (punctuation)	inverted commas
lawyer	solicitor
pharmacist	chemist
truck	lorry
elevator	lift
cookie	biscuit
dessert	sweet

After You Listen

5 Outlining the Lecture. Here is a sample outline of the lecture. Use your notes from Activity 4 to fill in the missing information. Remember to use abbreviations and symbols. Listen to the lecture again if necessary.

Differences between American and British English

I. ____

____

	Sound	Am E	RP
1.	"a"	/ae/	/a/
2.	__________	__________	"New Yok"
3.	__________	"liddle," "twenny-one"	__________

II. ____

____

- Eng. has over ____________________ words
- # of vocab diffs between Am E and RP is quite ____________________
  ____________________.
- most diffs are words from daily ____________________.
- Examples:

Am E	RP
__________	__________
__________	__________
__________	__________
__________	__________

III. ____

____

- Am E and RP nearly identical
- A few diffs.:

	Grammar feature	Am E	RP
1.	Verbs	__________	__________
2.	__________	government is	government are
3.	__________	__________	__________

IV. ____

____

6 **Defining New Vocabulary.** With a partner, look back at the words you marked as unknown in Activity 2 and discuss the meaning of each new term. Your teacher may ask you to write sentences with these new words.

7 **Discussing the Lecture.** Discuss the following questions about the lecture and your own experience. Refer to your notes as necessary. Use the new vocabulary as you talk.

1. What is meant by *standard* English? How is the standard different in the United States or Canada and Great Britain?

2. Why are most speakers of American and British English able to understand one another with little difficulty?

3. In what *category* can you find the biggest difference between American and British English: pronunciation, vocabulary, or grammar? Where do you find the smallest variation? Give a few examples of differences between them. Use the words "*while*" and "*whereas*" to state the contrast.

   Example

   In standard American English, people use the verb "have," whereas speakers of British English do not. British English speakers use the verb "have got."

4. What language or languages are spoken by the *majority* of people in your community?

5. Are there *dialects* in your community's language? Are there any *unique characteristics*? Give a few examples of differences between the standard language and the dialect. Use the words "*while*" and "*whereas*" to state the contrast. See No. 3 for an example.

6. If you ever have children, do you want them to be bilingual or bidialectal? Why is this important or advantageous?

PART 3

Focused Listening and Speaking

Getting Meaning from Context

1 **Using Context Clues.** The following conversations are about language.

1. Listen to each conversation.
2. After each conversation, you will hear three questions. The tape or CD will pause.
3. Read the answer choices and circle the letter of the best answer.

Conversation 1

1. a. a cigar
   b. a language
   c. a country
   d. a religion

2. a. from the television
   b. from the radio
   c. from a book
   d. from a magazine article

3. a. It is easy to learn.
   b. It has no native speakers
   c. The woman wants to learn it.
   d. It is the only artificial language in the world.

Conversation 2

4. a. to buy more bees
   b. to kill the bees
   c. to repair the roof
   d. to learn more about bees

5. a. direction
   b. distance
   c. quantity
   d. taste

6. a. the study of language
   b. the study of insects
   c. the study of dancing
   d. the study of communication

Conversation 3

7. a. grandmother
   b. pet
   c. car
   d. friend

8. a. She sold it.
   b. It was stolen.
   c. It stopped working.
   d. It was in an accident.

9. a. Often they have no meaning.
   b. They always come from Italian.
   c. They usually start with the letter "c."
   d. They are often named after fast animals.

Focused Listening

Interjections

Interjections are sound combinations that have specific meanings in spoken English. However, they are not "real" words, so they are not written.

Interjections	Meanings
uh-huh	1. Yes
uh-uh	2. No
oh-oh	3. I made a mistake. Something is wrong.
huh?	4. What?
oops	5. I dropped something. I made a mistake.
ouch!	6. That hurts!

2 Understanding Interjections. Listen to the short conversations. Choose the number of the *second* speaker's meaning from the chart, and write the number in the blanks.

Conversation 1: ______________________________

Conversation 2: ______________________________

Conversation 3: ______________________________

Conversation 4: ______________________________

Conversation 5: ______________________________

Conversation 6: ______________________________

3 Using Interjections. Work in pairs to practice using interjections. Student A should look at page 260. Student B should look at page 270.

Using Language

Guessing

The functions in this section are used for guessing or speculating about the identity or meaning of something. They indicate that a speaker is hesitant or unsure. For example:

A: What language is this? I don't recognize it.

B: Hmm. I suppose it's something Scandinavian. It looks like Swedish, but it might be Danish.

Here are some expressions you can use for guessing:

I guess	I suppose	It might be	It looks like
I think	I'd say	It could be	

4 **Guessing Meanings of Slang Expressions.** These items contain American slang expressions. Read the sentences with your classmates and use expressions from the box to guess what the underlined expressions mean. Then turn to page 275 to check your answers.

Example

"That movie was a real bomb."

Student 1: I think it means the movie was terrible.

Student 2: Yeah, but it could also mean that the movie was great.

Student 3: I guess it means that the movie was long and boring.

Slang expressions	Possible meanings
1. Jenna freaked out when she saw her boyfriend kissing another girl.	
2. On Saturday afternoon I like to shoot some hoops with my brothers.	
3. The furniture in this store is really cheesy.	
4. Teenage boys always act goofy when they're around girls.	
5. If I don't take a vacation soon, I'm going to lose it.	
6. Whenever I'm unhappy I pig out on ice cream.	
7. Don't tell Bob any secrets. He's a real blabbermouth.	
8. Kyle was bummed out when he got a C on his chemistry test.	
9. We were wiped out after playing two hours of basketball.	
10. I was going to ask my boss for a raise, but at the last minute I chickened out.	

PART 4

Listening and Speaking in the Real World

One common contest in American schools is called a spelling bee. In a spelling bee competitors are given words to spell out loud. They remain in the game as long as they spell correctly, but if they make a mistake they must leave the game.

Before You Listen

1 **Prelistening Questions.**

1. Are you a good speller in your native language?
2. Do you spell well in English?
3. Give examples of words that are hard to spell in English.
4. How can a person become a better speller?

Listen

2 **Identifying Spellings.** Listen to a spelling bee in an American high school class. The words are taken from a list of commonly misspelled words.* As you listen, circle the letter of the spelling you hear **even if it is wrong**! During the pause, check whether you think the spelling is right or wrong. Continue listening, and you will hear the correct spelling.

Spelling	Right	Wrong	Spelling	Right	Wrong
1. a. tryes b. tires (c.) tries	✔		6. a. ninty b. ninety c. ninnty		
2. a. chose b. choose c. choise			7. a. analyze b. analize c. analise		
3. a. effect b. affect c. effete			8. a. posibility b. possibilety c. possibility		
4. a. quizes b. kwizzes c. quizzes			9. a. misterious b. mysterious c. mesterious		
5. a. suceed b. succede c. succeed			10. a. lightening b. litening c. lightning		

* The list was published in the *Los Angeles Times* on April 16, 2000. The original list of the 25 most commonly misspelled words was taken from the *Student's Book of College English,* 1992.

After You Listen

3 **Class Spelling Bee.** Have a spelling bee in your English class. Use words that you have learned in Chapters 1 through 6 of this textbook.

Talk It Over

A Scavenger Hunt. In a scavenger hunt, individuals or teams search for a list of items. The team that finishes first, or the team that collects the largest number of items, is the winner.

Do a scavenger hunt for misspelled words. Divide into pairs or small teams. Your teacher will tell you where to search and how much time you have. Your task is to collect examples of misspelled words on signs, billboards, and shop fronts in your community. You can also look in magazine or newspaper advertisements.

Video Activities: Technology for the Disabled

Before You Watch. Discuss the following in small groups.

1. What are *disabilities*? Do you have a friend or a relative who is *disabled*?
2. Define these terms: paraplegic, quadriplegic
3. What are some of the difficulties that disabled people have in an "abled" world?

Watch. Discuss the following questions in small groups.

1. Guido Corona is blind. How does technology help him to see?
2. The man in the wheelchair cannot use his hands. How can he use a computer?
3. What percentage of Americans have a disability?

Watch Again. Read the questions below. Fill in the blanks. Then watch the video again to check your answers.

1. The IBM Home Page Reader allows ________________ people to access everything on the Web. It was created by a person with a ________________.

2. The man in the wheelchair is able to use a computer with the help of a device called Track 2000. With this program, the man can move the computer cursor by moving his ________________, and he can "right click" and "left click" a mouse by twitching his ________________.

After You Watch. Below is a list of famous people who have or had disabilities. Try to match each name with the descriptions that follow. Work in teams. The team that gets the most correct matches is the winner.

a. Walt Disney	c. Andrea Bocelli	e. Tom Cruise
b. Beethoven	d. Marlee Matlin	

1. This Hollywood actor has dyslexia, difficulty with reading. He learns his lines by listening to a tape recorder.
2. This Italian opera singer is blind.
3. This man composed nine famous symphonies and many more classical compositions even though he was deaf. He is one of the most famous and beloved composers of all time.
4. This woman is a well-known Hollywood actress. She is deaf.
5. This man had a learning disability and was slow in school. Later he became a well-known movie producer and cartoonist. He was the creator of Mickey Mouse.

Chapter 8

Tastes and Preferences

IN THIS CHAPTER

Lecture: Baby Boomers
Note-Taking Focus: Recognizing Paraphrases
Focused Listening: Review of Yes/No Questions with Do or Did
Using Language: Talking about Likes and Dislikes
Expressing Approval and Disapproval

Did You Know?

- The country with the most TV sets is China, with 227.5 million. The country with the most VCRs is the United States. 81% of U.S. households own at least one.[1]
- The most valuable painting in the world is *Portrait of Dr. Gachet* by Vincent Van Gogh. It was bought by a Japanese businessman for $82.5 million in 1990.[1]
- The most popular sports in the United States are:
  1. swimming
  2. walking
  3. bicycling
  4. bowling
  5. fishing

  On a list of 30 sports, playing basketball was number 8. Running was number 14, and playing soccer was number 24.[2]
- The Beatles are the most successful rock group of all time.[1]

PART 1

Listening to Conversations

Jeff and his friend Dan play in a rock band. Last night Anna went to a club to hear them play. Today Dan has stopped by the house for a visit. In the following conversation, Anna and Dan try to find out what they have in common.

[1] *Guinness Book of World Records.*

[2] Sporting Goods Manufacturers Association, <http://www.sgma.com/press_room/2000_releases/m2000-012.html>.

Before You Listen

1 Prelistening Questions. Discuss these questions with your classmates.

1. Do you like to listen to music? What kind of music do you prefer? Do you like to go to clubs to listen to music?
2. In your opinion, is it important for two people to have the same tastes in order to be happy together?
3. What are some ways of asking about people's likes and dislikes in English?

2 Vocabulary Preview. These sentences contain expressions from the conversation. Use the context to match the underlined words and expressions with their definitions.

Sentences	Definitions
1. *A:* Did you have a good time last night? *B:* Not really. The movie was boring.	a. _____ doesn't like
2. *A:* What do you think of this painting? *B:* I'm crazy about it!	b. _____ hate
3. *A:* I can't stand that old shirt. When are you going to throw it out? *B:* Sorry, I like it.	c. _____ to enjoy oneself d. _____ agree
4. These tomatoes have been in the refrigerator for two weeks. They're disgusting.	e. _____ I love it.
5. Ellen and Howard don't see eye to eye on anything, but they are very happily married.	f. _____ awful, horrible
6. John doesn't care for sports. He prefers to read and listen to music.	

Listen

3 Listening for Main Ideas.

1. Close your book as you listen to the conversation. Listen for the answers to these questions.
    1. Compare Dan and Anna's tastes in the following areas:
        music
        art
        food
        sports
        movies
    2. At the end of the conversation, what do Dan and Anna agree to do together?
2. Compare answers with a partner.

Stress

4 Listening for Stressed Words.

1. Now listen to part of the conversation again. Some of the stressed words are missing. During each pause, repeat the phrase or sentence; then fill in the missing stressed words.

Dan: What did you think of our band?

Anna: Well, your music is ___________ for ___________, but to tell you the truth, it was kind of ___________. I guess I really prefer ___________.

Dan: Do you go to ___________ much?

Anna: No, not very often. I ___________ ___________ it. They're ___________expensive here!

Dan: So, what do you like to do for ___________?

Anna: Well, I ___________ to ___________! And there are so many interesting ___________ restaurants around here!

Dan: What's your ___________ kind of food?

Anna: Well, ___________, of course. What about you?

Dan: Believe it or not, I'm ___________ ___________ about pasta. But I really like ___________ food.

Anna: Oo, I ___________ ___________ beans. Uh . . . What about ___________ food?

Dan: I don't ___________ for it. Too ___________. How about American food? You know, hamburgers, hot dogs, french fries . . .

Anna: ___________! All that fat and salt and sugar . . . We don't see eye to eye on ___________, do we?

Dan: Well, let's see. How do you feel about ___________ art? There's a ___________ exhibit at the county ___________ right now.

Anna: To be ___________, I don't ___________ the modern stuff. I ___________ 19th century art, you know, Monet, Van Gogh, Renoir.

Dan: Hmm. How about ___________? Are you interested in ___________?

Anna: __________ football? I __________ it!

Dan: Baseball?

Anna: It's okay.

Dan: How about tall musicians with __________ hair?

Anna: It __________.

Dan: OK, I got it. How about __________ musicians with curly hair who __________ you to a movie?

Anna: Science fiction?

Dan: Sounds __________!

Anna: At least we agree on __________!

2. Compare answers and read the conversation with a partner. Pay attention to the stressed words.

Reductions

The following exchange is from the conversation:

Dan: Are you interested in football?
Anna: American football? I hate it!
Dan: Baseball?

Note the form of Dan's second question. The complete question should be "Do you like baseball?" However, Dan drops the subject and the verb because his meaning is clear to Anna from the context of the first question. This kind of reduction is common in rapid, informal speech.

5 **Listening for Reductions.** Listen to the following short exchanges. Write the full questions instead of the reduced ones.

1. Do you like Japanese food?
2. ____________________
3. ____________________
4. ____________________
5. ____________________

After You Listen

6 **Vocabulary Review.** Work in pairs to practice the new vocabulary. Student A should look at page 261. Student B should look at page 271.

Using Language

Talking about Likes and Dislikes

Like very much

It's fantastic / wonderful / great / terrific / cool* / super* / awesome*

I love it.

I'm crazy about it.

Cool!*

Dislike very much

It's terrible / horrible / disgusting / awful / gross*

It stinks.*

I can't stand it.

I hate it.

Yuck!*

Ick!*

Like a little

It's nice / OK / all right / not bad

I like it.

I prefer[1] ________________.

Dislike a little

I don't care for it.

I don't like it.

I'm not crazy about it.

Neutral

It's OK.

It's so-so.

I don't care one way or another.

I can take it or leave it.

---

* These expressions are slang.

[1] Use "prefer" only when you have a choice. For example:
Q: Do you prefer coffee or tea?
A: I prefer coffee.

7 **Expressions for Asking about Likes and Dislikes.** Read the tapescript of the conversation on page 322 and fill in the chart with the questions that Dan asks to find out about Anna's likes and dislikes.

1. *What did you think of (our band)?*
2.
3.
4.
5.
6.
7.

Additional expressions:

Do you like ______________________________?

What's your opinion of ______________________________?

Language Tip: The following exchange is from the conversation:

Anna: Oo, I can't stand beans . . . Uh, what about Indian food?

Dan: I don't care for it. Too spicy. How about American food? You know, hamburgers, hot dogs, french fries . . .

There is not much difference between "What about . . ." and "How about . . ." to ask if someone likes something.

[Note: "How about verb + ing" is also used for giving suggestions.

8 Talking about Likes and Dislikes. Here is a list of the topics and examples mentioned in the conversation. Work with a partner. First, add other examples of each topic. Then take turns asking and answering questions about each other's likes and dislikes. Use the language from the explanation chart or Activity 7.

Examples

Q: How do you feel about heavy metal?
A: I don't care for it much.

Q: What's your opinion of American fast food?
A: Yuck! It's disgusting.

Topics	Examples
Music	rock, jazz
Food	Italian, Mexican, Indian, American
Art	modern, 19th century
Sports	baseball, American football
Movies	science fiction

Talk It Over

Giving an Impromptu Speech.

1. Write one specific question about people's tastes and preferences. Use an expression from the explanation chart on page 158 or Activity 7. You may choose a topic from the following list or pick your own, but be sure your question is specific.

   Too general: How do you feel about sports?
   Specific: Are you interested in golf?

cars	animals
sports	flowers
music	person to have dinner with
food (fruits, vegetables, drinks)	day of the week
place to take a vacation	season
time of the day	things to do on a Saturday night
TV shows	colors
writers, artists, actors, singers	place to be alone
cities	

2. Your teacher will collect all the questions and put them in a hat (or box).
3. Students will take turns picking a topic and speaking about it for about one minute. In your speech, you can:
   - give your opinion about the topic, using expressions for talking about likes and dislikes
   - give reasons for your opinion
   - talk about your experience

PART 2

Listening to Lectures

Before You Listen

You are going to hear a radio interview with Dr. Stuart Harris, a professor of marketing, about a part of the U.S. population known as the "baby boom generation," or "baby boomers."

1 Prelistening Discussion. Discuss these questions in small groups.

1. As far as you know, which part of the U.S. population is the largest: young, middle-aged, or old?
2. Which part of the population is the largest in your community? In general, is the population getting older or younger or staying the same? Is this a problem?
3. What do you know about the baby boom generation? If your teacher is from the United States, do you think he or she is a baby boomer?

2 **Vocabulary Preview.** The following terms appear in the lecture. With your classmates, define the words you already know. Mark the words you do not know.

____ boom	____ stock market crash	____ fad
____ birthrate	____ Great Depression	____ gadgets
____ huge	____ housing	____ fat free
____ age group	____ appliances	____ to be concerned
____ not only . . . but also	____ station wagon	____ physical fitness

Listen

Recognizing Paraphrases

There are several differences between written and spoken English. One important difference is that the spoken language contains a great deal of paraphrases. This means that speakers often say the same thing twice, but they use different words. When you are taking notes, you need to be able to recognize paraphrases so that you don't write the same thing twice in your notes.

The following phrases signal that a speaker is paraphrasing:

in other words
that is (abbreviated as "i.e.")
I mean
to put it another way
what I'm trying to say is

3 **Recognizing Paraphrases.** Listen to the following pairs of sentences. Decide whether their meaning is similar or different and write S or D in the spaces.

1. ____
2. ____
3. ____
4. ____
5. ____

4 **Predicting Note Organization.** In this chapter you are going to hear an interview, not a lecture. An interview consists of questions and answers. With your teacher and classmates, discuss the form your notes might have.

5 **Taking Draft Notes.** Listen to the interview and take notes in the best way you can. Use your own paper.

U.S. Birthrate 1930-1995

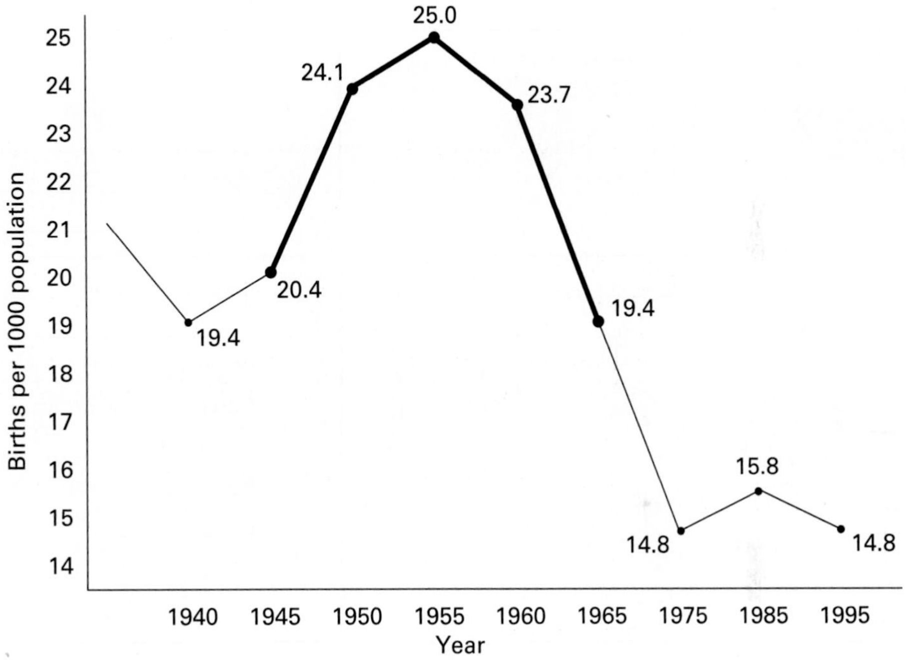

After You Listen

6 **Rewriting Your Notes.** Look at the following sample notes. They are in the form of two columns. Use your notes from Activity 5 to fill in the missing information. Remember to use abbreviations and symbols. Listen to the interview again if necessary.

The Baby Boom Generation

Questions / Topics	Answers
A. ______________________ ______________________ ______________________ ______________________	1. boom = ______________ 2. Between end of WW2 & early 1960s, U.S. birthrate ______________ 3. Today: 76 mil. boomers age = ________
B. Age of baby boomers—important?	Yes. Reasons: 1. ______________ 2. ______________ Result: ______________ ______________
C. Diffs. between ____________ and ____________.	1. Parents grew up ______________ ______________ → poor 2. Boomers grew up after ____________. U.S. econ = ____________. Results: a. ______________ b. ______________ c. ______________
D. ______________________ ______________________ ______________________	1. ____________ (biggest expense) 2. ______________ 3. ______________ 4. ______________
E. Prod. created spec. for boomers	1. ______________ 2. ______________ 3. ______________
F. New ______________________ ______________________	Ex.: 1. diet centers 2. tanning salons 3. ______________ 4. ______________ Reason: ______________ ______________

7 Defining New Vocabulary. With a partner, look back at the words you marked as unknown in Activity 2 and discuss the meaning of each new term. Your teacher may ask you to write sentences with these new words.

8 Discussing the Lecture. Discuss the following questions about the interview and your own experience. Refer to your notes as necessary. Use the new vocabulary as you talk.

1. What is the meaning of the word "boom"?
2. Who are the baby boomers in the United States, and why do they have great economic and political power?
3. In what three ways are the baby boomers different from their parents?
4. What are the biggest expenses for baby boomers?
5. What are some specific examples of products and industries that were created to serve the tastes and preferences of the baby boomers?
6. Do you think that middle-aged people around the world are similar to or different from American baby boomers? For example, are middle-aged people everywhere concerned about their looks and their health?

Talk It Over

Talking about Fads. In the interview, Dr. Harris spoke about SUVs, or sport utility vehicles, as a fad. The automobile industry provides many examples of fads. For example, in the 1980s, small cars were in style in the United States. In contrast, now many Americans are buying huge cars that have room for seven or eight people.

Saying That Something Is Popular

popular	in style
fashionable	trendy
be "in"	

FYI

Fad (noun) */fad/*
a temporary fashion, notion, manner of conduct, etc., esp. one followed enthusiastically by a group.

This chart gives examples of fads and popular items in the United States in the 1990s and 2000s. Work in small groups. Answer these questions:

1. Are these popular in your community or school?
2. Who follows them? Do you?
3. For each category, give other examples of fads or people that are popular.

Example

SUVS are trendy cars. They are in style now. However, during the 1980s, small cars were fashionable.

Categories	United States	Other fads
Clothing	bell bottoms, platform shoes	
Hair	"buzz" haircuts (very short, like a soldier); different-colored hair (like purple or blue)	
Body decoration and art	body piercing; tattoos; tinted contact lenses	
Food	fat-free and sugar-free foods; high-protein diets	
Pets	large dogs	
Colors to wear	black	
Musicians	Ricky Martin, Britney Spears, Christina Aguilera, Green Day	
Cars	SUVs	
Sports	rollerblading; dirt bikes; snowboarding	
Actors	Jackie Chan; Jennifer Aniston; Will Smith; Jennifer Lopez	

PART 3

Focused Listening and Speaking

Focused Listening

Review of Yes/No Questions With Do or Did

It can be difficult to hear the difference between "do" and "did" in questions with pronoun subjects. Listen to the long and short forms in the chart. Notice the linking and reductions.

	Long	Short
1.	Do I look tired?	d'way look tired?
2.	Did I look tired?	did-ay look tired?
3.	Do you live with your parents?	d'yuh live with your parents?
4.	Did you live with your parents?	didjuh live with your parents?
5.	Does he own a car?	duzee own a car?
6.	Did he own a car?	didee own a car?
7.	Does she need any help?	dushee need any help?
8.	Did she need any help?	ditshe need any help?
9.	Do we have any homework?	duwee have any homework?*
10.	Did we have any homework?	diwee have any homework?*
11.	Do they live together?	d'they live together?*
12.	Did they live together?	dit-they live together?*

1 **Distinguishing between *Do* and *Did*.** Listen to pairs of sentences. Circle the first item you hear in each pair.

1.	Do you	Did you
2.	Did he	Does he
3.	Did they	Do they
4.	Do I	Did I
5.	Did she	Does she
6.	Do we	Did we
7.	Do they	Did they
8.	Do we	Did we

*It may be almost impossible to hear the difference between Nos. 9 and 10 and between Nos. 11 and 12. You may need to rely on context to tell you if the question is present or past.

2 ***Do* and *Did* in WH-questions.** Listen to the questions and write the missing words.

1. ________ ________ ________ decide to do?
2. ________ ________ ________ eat?
3. Why ________ ________ ________ ________ copy my notes?
4. Where ________ ________ park our car?
5. Where ________ ________ put my keys?
6. ________ ________ ________ leave class early?
7. Where ________ ________ leave your bag?
8. ________ ________ ________ ________ ________ do?

Getting Meaning from Context

3 **Using Context Clues.** The following conversations are about people's tastes and preferences.

1. Listen to each conversation.
2. After each conversation, you will hear a question. The tape or CD will pause.
3. Read the answer choices and circle the letter of the best answer.
4. Then listen to the next part of the conversation to hear the correct answer.

1. a. a car
   b. a painting
   c. a television set
   d. a movie

2. a. a T-shirt
   b. a tie
   c. a suit
   d. a wallet

3. a. swim
   b. dance
   c. water-ski
   d. jump out of an airplane

4. a. She likes it.
   b. She is not sure.
   c. She thinks it's funny.
   d. She's angry.

5. a. She likes it.
   b. She is not sure.
   c. She thinks it's funny.
   d. She's angry.

Using Language

Expressing Approval and Disapproval

"To approve / disapprove" means that you think a behavior or product is socially or morally acceptable or unacceptable. As an example, many parents approve of tattoos for older people, but they may disapprove of them on teenagers.

The following expressions are used to express approval and disapproval.

Approval

to approve of
+ [noun / verb + ing]

to be in favor of + noun

to be for + noun

Disapproval

to disapprove of
+ [noun / verb + ing]

to be against + noun

On the Spot!

1. The following chart lists behaviors and fashions that are popular among some young people in some cultures. In the You column, write "+" if you approve of these things and "–" if you disapprove. Do the same thing in the column marked Your Parents.

Behavior / product	You	Your parents
pierced ears		
body piercing (nostril, lips, tongue, eyebrows)		
tattoos		
smoking		
living away from home before marriage		
living with roommates of the same sex		
living with roommates of the opposite sex		
interracial dating		
living together before marriage		
teenage couples going out alone		

2. Discuss your choices with your classmates. Use the expressions in the explanation box.
   1. Why do you approve or disapprove of an item?
   2. In which cases do you agree with your parents? Disagree?
   3. Are there items where your opinion is different for males and females?

PART 4

Listening and Speaking in the Real World

In this section you will hear about David, a 35-year-old professional man. For the past year he has been dating two women, Katherine and Jean. He likes both of them very much. David would like to get married and start a family soon, so he feels it's time to choose one woman and "get serious." Both women are interested in him, but David is having a hard time choosing between them.

Before You Listen

1 **Describing Your Ideal Partner.** On a piece of paper, list at least five qualities you desire in a romantic partner. Then share your list with one or more classmates. Complete the following sentence:

(For unmarried people) "My ideal partner / wife / husband would be (intelligent, kind) / have (a good job, a lot of money) . . ."

(For married people): "The qualities I admire most in my partner / wife / husband are his or her (intelligence / kindness . . .)"

Listen

2 **Comparing People's Qualities.** Listen as David describes Katherine and Jean. Take notes on their positive and negative qualities.

	Katherine	Jean
Positive qualities		
Negative qualities		

After You Listen

3 **Discussion.** Compare your notes from Activity 2 with a partner. Discuss the qualities that David mentions.

1. Do you agree that the positive qualities are important for a person to have?
2. Would the negative qualities bother you?
3. What other positive qualities do you want in a partner?
4. What other qualities would you want to avoid?
5. What do you think David should do?

Talk It Over

Reading and Writing Personal Ads.

1. Read the ads. Then choose the ad from the person who sounds the most interesting to you. Tell the members of your group which ad you chose and why.

...ance & more. Box 385.

180 FROM WOMEN:

Tall, attractive brunette, enjoys music, dancing, hiking, travel. Seeks good-looking, honest, secure man with sense of humor for friendship, possible relationship. Box 192.

Elegant, petite blond grad student, marriage-minded, seeks professional man to share tennis, skiing, reading, sailing, opera. Box 120.

Artistic, bookish elementary school teacher, vegetarian. Seeks marriage with witty man who loves classical music, kids, pets. Box 239.

European wild thing, 5'6", seeks fun-loving man to achieve perfect relationship. Box 923.

Sexy redhead with brains and class seeks ski companion with refined taste and great sense of humor. Box 329.

Fun-...oing, 23, college

share tennis, ... 112

181 FROM MEN:

Average guy, 33, college grad, good-looking, mature; seeks foreign-born woman, slim, educated, for romance & more. Box 385.

Want to laugh? Talkative male, 24, seeks partner for dating fun. I'm smart, handsome, educated & hip. Into rock music, dancing & partying. Box 127.

Stockbroker 5'11", attractive, spontaneous, traveler; seeks attractive, fit, honest Asian female. Box 383.

Police officer, athletic, attractive, 28, seeks woman for companionship & adventure. Must enjoy life. Race/religion/age not important. Box 472.

Poetic, marriage-minded professional pilot, 6'3", seeks non-smoking, energetic, adventurous woman for serious relationship. Box 489.

2. Write an ad about yourself. Follow the instructions in the following explanation box. However, don't write your name on your ad!
3. Your teacher will collect and type all the ads and post them on the bulletin board.
   1. Read all the ads and try to guess which classmate wrote each one.
   2. Your teacher may ask you to choose *one* ad and respond to it in writing. Tell the class which ad you chose and why.
   3. Finally, each person in the class should say which ad he or she wrote!

How to Write an Interesting Personal Ad

1. Begin your ad by describing yourself. You may choose to include some of the following information:
   - your age
   - nationality
   - profession
   - religion
   - what you look like ("tall, nice-looking man")
   - what you enjoy doing ("loves intelligent conversation")
   - what kind of person you are ("honest, caring man")
   - something unique about you ("bird lover")
2. In the second part of the ad, write about the person you would like to meet. List the characteristics that are important to you.
3. State what you want from a relationship: marriage? a good time? a serious relationship? friendship? someone to share a hobby with? a tennis partner?

The Language of Personal Ads

1. Do not write complete sentences. Notice that the ads on page 172 begin with adjectives or descriptive phrases.
2. Use the word "seeks" (meaning "looking for") when you describe the person you would like to meet.
3. Use commas to separate a series of adjectives ("honest, attractive, funny guy")
4. Use adjective clauses ("seeks woman who loves golf") and prepositional phrases ("lawyer with great sense of humor")

Video Activities: The Coffee Lover

Before You Watch. Discuss the following questions in small groups.

1. Do you like to drink coffee? Why?
2. How would you feel if you drank ten cups of coffee every day?
3. As far as you know, does coffee cause health problems for some people?

Watch. Discuss the following questions with your classmates.

1. How many cups of coffee does Kat drink each day?
2. Does she plan to stop drinking coffee?

Watch Again. Read the statements below. Decide if they are true (T) or false (F). Then watch the video again to check your answers.

1. _____ Kat has worked in the same place for 45 years.
2. _____ Kat doesn't drink coffee in the evening.
3. _____ Scientists now believe that coffee raises cholesterol levels.
4. _____ If you drink too much coffee, it can make your hands shake.
5. _____ If your heart is weak, drinking coffee will make it stronger.

After You Watch. Use the survey below to interview three students in your class. Add one more question.

1. What is your favorite drink: coffee, tea, or something else?
2. How many times a day do you drink it?
3. What is your favorite time of day to drink this drink?
4. How do you drink it (with milk or sugar, hot or cold, etc.)?
5. ____

In class, everyone should share the results of the survey.

Chapter 9

New Frontiers

IN THIS CHAPTER

Lecture:	The Moon's Effect on Human Behavior
Note-Taking Focus:	Supporting a Position with Evidence
Pronunciation:	Pronunciation of the /*th*/ Sound
Focused Listening:	-*ed* Endings
Using Language:	Introducing Surprising Information Expressing Interest or Surprise

Did You Know?

- The first person to walk on the moon was Neil Armstrong (USA). His historic walk took place on July 24, 1969.
- Alfred Nobel, the Swedish inventor who invented dynamite in 1866, created an organization to give awards each year to people who help the world. These awards are the Nobel Prizes for physics, chemistry, physiology, medicine, literature, and peace.
- In a survey about space travel, 44% of Americans said they would want to travel in space if they had the chance. 54% of American men and 33% of American women said they believe there is intelligent life on other planets.[1]
- The human immunodeficiency virus (HIV), which causes AIDS, was first identified in 1983.[2]

PART 1

Listening to Conversations

Before You Listen

In the following conversation Jeff, Nancy, and Anna talk about space exploration.

1 **Prelistening Questions.** Discuss these questions with your classmates.

1. What are the advantages and disadvantages of space exploration?
2. If you had a chance to live in space, would you do it?

[1] *USA Today,* <http://www.usatoday.com/snapshot/news/nsnap006.htm>.

[2] *Guinness Book of World Records.*

2 **Vocabulary Preview.** The words on the left are used in the conversation. Match them with their definitions.

Words	Definitions
1. footprints	a. ____ a settlement that people build in a new land or territory
2. disease	b. ____ once each year
3. annual	c. ____ referring to the sun
4. satellite	d. ____ sickness, bad health
5. gravity	e. ____ the force that pulls everything toward the center of the earth
6. pollution	f. ____ the shapes left on the ground after a person has walked on it
7. colony	g. ____ dirt in the air or water
8. solar	h. ____ a natural or artificial body that travels around a planet such as the earth
9. pioneer	i. ____ the first person to find, do, or create something important (e.g., a new land or a new medical procedure)

Listen

3 **Listening for Main Ideas.**

1. Close your book as you listen to the conversation. Listen for the answers to these questions.
    1. What benefits of the space program did Nancy and Jeff mention?
    2. What is an advantage of living in a space colony?
    3. What is a pioneer? Can you give any examples?
2. Compare answers with a partner.

Stress

4 **Listening for Stressed Words.**

1. Now listen to part of the conversation again. Some of the stressed words are missing. During each pause, repeat the phrase or sentence; then fill in the missing stressed words.

Jeff: Anna! Nancy! Come out to the ____________! You've got to see this ____________!

Nancy: ____________! Look how big and ____________ it is!

Anna: It looks as if you could reach out and ____________ it.

Jeff: Do you ____________ that it's been more than ____________ years since the first ____________ walked on the moon? And would you believe their ____________ are still there?

Anna: Really? How ____________?

Jeff: There's no ____________ on the moon, so there's no wind to blow them away.

Anna: That's ____________. But you know, I've always ____________ why some governments spend so much ____________ on space exploration. I mean, there are so many ____________ problems on earth, like ____________, hunger, disease . . .

Nancy: Well, you may be ____________ to know that the ____________ spends less than ____________ percent of its annual budget on the space program. And ____________, you have to consider the technological and scientific ____________of space exploration.

Anna: Like what?

Jeff: Well, to give just one example, ____________ were invented only about ____________ years ago, and now they're used for ____________ prediction, ____________ phones, satellite TV. . .

Nancy: Also, a lot of ____________ discoveries have come out of space research. ____________ it or not, that's how soft ____________ lenses were developed. Also, some ____________ can be produced more ____________ and cheaply in space, where there's no ____________.

Jeff: Just ____________—pretty soon we'll be able to buy ____________ labeled "Made in Space" instead of "Made in Indonesia" or "Made in the USA."

2. Compare answers and read the conversation with a partner. Pay attention to the stressed words.

After You Listen

5 **Vocabulary Review.** These questions use the vocabulary from this section. Answer the questions with a partner and see how much you know. (The answers are on page 275, but don't look now!)

1. Which of the following bodies has the strongest force of gravity?
   a. Earth
   b. Mars
   c. the sun
   d. the moon

2. In the United States, which of the following people has the highest annual salary?
   a. a professional (NBA) basketball star
   b. a brain surgeon
   c. the president
   d. a scientist working for the space program

3. Which of the following animals has the largest footprint?
   a. a camel
   b. a grizzly bear
   c. an elephant
   d. a walrus

4. What is the English name of a childhood disease in which the skin is covered with red spots?
   a. pneumonia
   b. chicken pox
   c. influenza
   d. hepatitis

5. Which of the following is a natural satellite of the earth?
   a. the sun
   b. the moon
   c. the stars
   d. a space colony

6. Which of the following countries was once a colony of Great Britain (England)?
   a. The Philippines
   b. Mozambique
   c. The United States
   d. Venezuela

7. The Wright brothers were pioneers in the field of ___________.
   a. medicine
   b. computers
   c. biology
   d. aviation

8. Which of the following large cities has the worst air pollution?
   a. Tokyo, Japan
   b. Los Angeles, California, USA
   c. Frankfurt, Germany
   d. Mexico City, Mexico

9. If you can use solar energy to make your food, you are probably a _____.
   a. jellyfish
   b. tree
   c. bird
   d. spider

Pronunciation

The */th/* Sound

The English language has two sounds that are written with the letters "th." The two sounds are almost the same, except that one of them is voiced, as in the word *there,* and the other is voiceless, as in the word *think.*

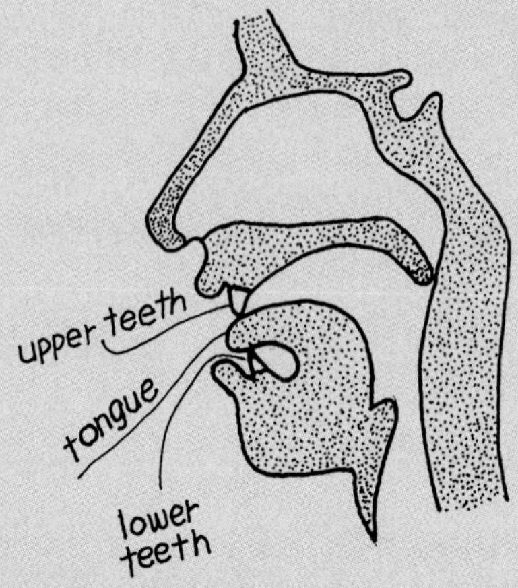

To pronounce both sounds, follow these steps:

1. Place the tip of your tongue between your top and bottom teeth. Keep your lips relaxed.
2. Hold your mouth in this position as you exhale air from your lungs.
3. Make your vocal cords vibrate as you exhale to produce the voiced /th/ sound.
4. Be sure to do steps 1 to 3 all at the same time.

6 **Pronouncing Voiced and Voiceless */th/*.** Listen to two lists of words. The words in the first list have a voiceless */th/* sound. The words in the second list have the voiced sound. Repeat the words after the speaker.

voiceless */th/*	**voiced */th/***
think	this
thought	that
thumb	those
author	rather
nothing	other
mouth	father
both	breathe
throat	smooth

7 **Distinguishing between Voiced and Voiceless** */th/.* Now listen to the following sentences from the conversation. Repeat them after the speaker. Put a slash (/) through every voiceless /*th*/ you hear. Put a circle around every voiced /*th*/.

Examples: there think

1. Their footprints are still there.
2. There's no weather on the moon.
3. If the living conditions are the same as on earth, then why not?
4. Don't you think it would be exciting to be a pioneer?
5. What's that?
6. You know, someone who does something first.
7. I'm going to stay right here on earth and finish college.

Using Language

Introducing Surprising Information

Sometimes special phrases are used to introduce information that may be surprising or unexpected to the listener. The expressions below are used for introducing surprising information.

It's weird / strange / funny, but . . .

Surprisingly

Oddly enough

8 Identifying Ways to Introduce Surprising Information. Read the tapescript of the conversation on pages 327 and 328 and fill in these blanks with the expressions that introduce surprising information. The answers are on page 275.

1. ______________________________ that it's been more than 30 years since the first astronauts walked on the moon?

2. ______________________________ their footprints are still there?

3. ______________________________ that the United States spends less than one percent of its annual budget on the space program.

4. A lot of medical discoveries have come out of space research. ________________________, that's how soft contact lenses were developed.

5. The article said that, ______________________________, life in these communities might be even nicer than on earth because they'll be smaller, without the problems we have in big cities today.

9 Truth or Lie Game.

1. Your teacher will hand out a card to each student in the class. The card will say "truth" or "lie." Don't show your card to anyone.
2. Prepare to tell the class something surprising or unexpected about yourself. If your card says "truth," your story must be completely true. If it says "lie," you must make something up, but it should sound true.
3. Take turns telling your stories. When it is your turn, begin with one of the expressions for introducing surprising information. After you are finished, the teacher will ask the class to vote on whether you told the truth or not. Your purpose, of course, is to fool your classmates!

Talk It Over

Solving a Science Problem. Imagine you are a member of a space crew. Your spaceship has crash-landed on the lighted side of the moon. Another spaceship will pick you up about two hundred miles away. Because you will have to walk there, you can take only a limited number of items with you.

1. Below are 14 items your crew will have to choose from. Read the items and use your dictionary if necessary to understand their meanings.
2. Decide which items are the most important and which are the least important. Place the number "1" by the most important item, the number "2" by the second most important, and so on.
3. When you have finished, compare your rankings with those of your classmates. Explain the choices you made.

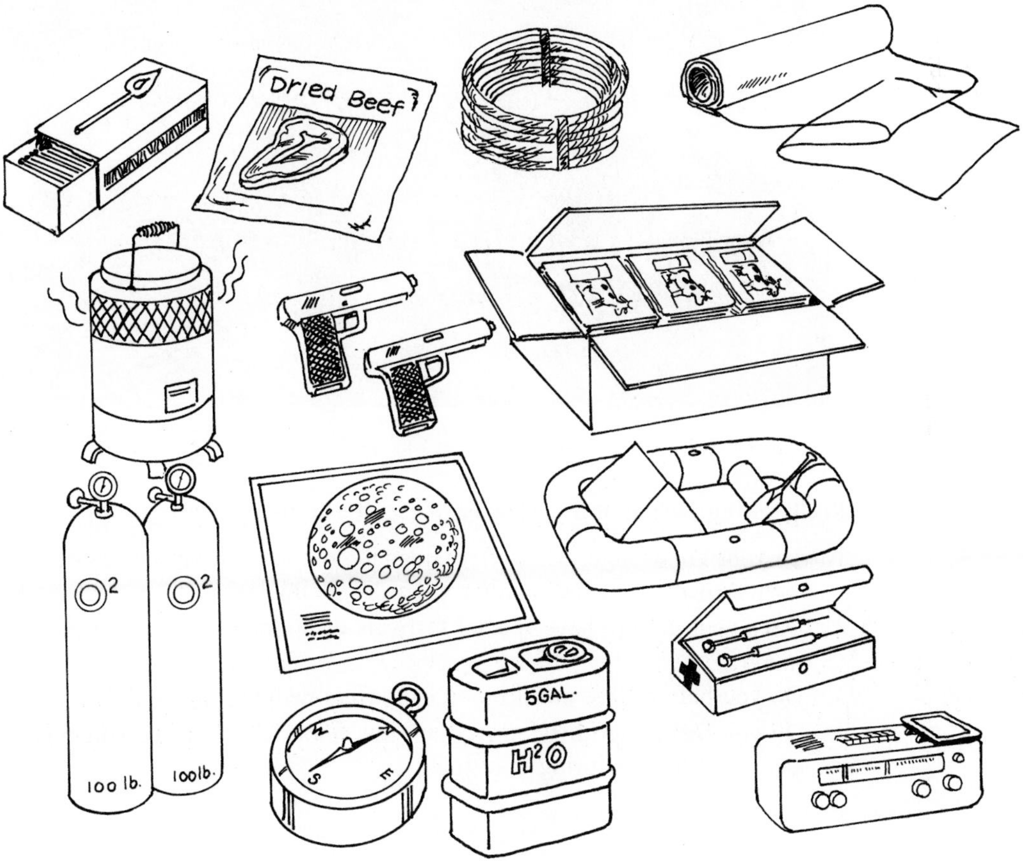

_____ box of matches
_____ dried food
_____ 50 feet of nylon rope
_____ parachute silk
_____ portable heating unit
_____ two pistols
_____ one case of dehydrated milk
_____ two 100-pound tanks of oxygen
_____ map of the moon's surface and rock formations
_____ life raft
_____ magnetic compass
_____ five gallons of water
_____ first aid kit containing injection needles
_____ solar-powered FM receiver-transmitter

PART 2

Listening to Lectures

Before You Listen

In this lecture two students have a debate about the effects of the moon on human behavior.

1 Prelistening Discussion. Discuss these questions in small groups.

1. To your knowledge, what effect does the moon have on the physical environment (e.g., the weather, the tides, animals)?
2. Does your culture have special festivals or holidays at the time of the full moon?
3. Do you believe that a full moon can affect people's behavior?
4. Do you feel or act differently when the moon is full? Have you ever done anything strange during that time?

2 **Vocabulary Preview.** The following terms appear in the lecture. With your classmates, define the words you already know. Mark the words you do not know.

____ to regulate	____ to commit suicide	____ a hypothesis
____ ocean tides	____ poison	____ proof
____ unpredictable	____ a mental hospital	____ link
____ loony	____ weird	____ a coincidence
____ an assault	____ to make up one's mind	

3 **Discussing Note-Taking Forms.** You are going to hear two students debate the following question: Does the full moon cause people to behave strangely? One student will argue in favor of the question, and the other will argue against it.

With your classmates, discuss different ways of setting up your page of notes. Draw them on the board.

Listen

Supporting a Position with Evidence

A debate is a formal argument between two speakers who have different opinions about a question or issue. In a debate, each speaker states a position and then tries to *prove* it with supporting *evidence* such as facts and statistics, quotations from experts, or references to other published works. The "winner" of a debate is the person who convinces the audience that he or she is right.

Information in a debate is normally organized from general to specific. The following paragraph illustrates this type of organization:

> Americans watch too much television, and they watch too many violent programs. According to the *Los Angeles Tribune* of November 5, 1999, Americans spend an average of 2,300 hours per year watching TV. Thomas Lear, a psychiatrist at the University of Illinois, states in his book *Watching the Tube* that between 90 and 95 percent of all adult programs contain violence, "bad" language, or hostile sexual relations. Lear explains that when people see these behaviors repeated thousands of times, they start to think that such behaviors are normal and acceptable.

Here are sample notes for this paragraph. Notice that the supporting details are indented and numbered, and each piece of evidence is written on a separate line.

A. Amer. watch too much TV & violent progs.
   1. 2300 hrs/yr. (LA Tribune)
   2. 90–95% of progs. have violence, bad lg., hostile sex (T. Lear)]

4 Taking Notes on a Position and Supporting Evidence. Listen to one position about the full moon and three pieces of supporting evidence. Take notes as in the example.

Dr. Lieber: ______________________________

1. 1977: ______________________________
2. 1980 study: ______________________________
3. in mental hospitals: ______________________________

Compare your notes with those of a classmate.

5 Taking Draft Notes. Listen to the lecture and take notes in the best way you can. Use your own paper. As you listen and take notes, refer to the two speakers' handouts shown here.

Joshua's handout

Is the Full Moon Associated with Violent or Self-Destructive Behavior in Humans? YES!

- 11,613 cases of aggravated assault in a five-year period: assaults occurred more often around the full moon. (1978)
- 34,318 crimes in a one-year period: crimes occurred more frequently during the full moon. (1976)
- 841 cases of "self-poisonings" in a four-year period: self-poisonings did occur more often on the day of the full moon. (1980)

Dana's handout

Is the Full Moon Associated with Violent or Self-Destructive Behavior in Humans? NO!

- 58,527 police arrests in a seven-year period: no difference in the number of arrests made during any phase of the moon. (1977)
- 361,580 calls for police assistance in a three-year period: no relationship to the phase of the moon. (1983)
- 1,289 aggressive "incidents" by hospitalized psychiatric patients in a 105-week period: no significant relationship between the severity or amount of violence/aggression and phase of the moon. (1998)
- The rate of agitation in 24 nursing home residents in a three-month period: no significant relationship to moon phase. (1989)
- 4,190 suicides in a 58-year period: suicides had no relationship to the phase of the moon. (1991)
- 3,468 emergency room visits and hospital admissions by people who intentionally took poison; visits and admissions were not different on days with full moons. (1983)
- 4,835 traffic accidents in a four-year period: no relationship to the phase of the moon. However, there was an increase in the number of accidents that occurred in the summer and on weekends. (1993)

After You Listen

6 **Outlining the Lecture.** Use your notes from Activities 4 and 5 to complete these outlines. Remember to use abbreviations and symbols. Listen again if necessary.

Joshua: Full moon causes unusual behavior

In English, "loony" = crazy < Latin *luna* (moon)

I. Full moon → ________________

  A. 1977 book "The Lunar Effect" said

  ____

    1. Ex.: woman tried to kill Gerald Ford

    2. 2 research studies showed ________

    ____

    3. ________________

II. ________ → ________

  A. ________________

    1. 9 people jump off Gold. Gate Bridge

  B. People who poison themselves ________

  ____

  C. Wkrs. in mental hosp: patients more diff. during full moon

Dana: Full moon does NOT cause unusual behavior

-No scientific support

-Someone's opinion $\neq$ proof

-20 studies show ________________

____

I. Studies show no relat. bet. behav. & full moon

  A. Study of 60,000 arrests:

  ____

  B. Studies of suicide:

    1. 7 studies showed ________

    ____

    ____

    2. Study of self-poisonings showed

    ____

  C. Studies in mental hospitals:

  ____

  D. People in nursing homes:

  ____

  E. Studies of people in emerg. rooms:

  ____

III. Many prof. say moon has weird effect.

Ex.: ______________________

____

____

IV. Cause? ______________________

____

____

____

II. Conclusion: ______________________

____

____

____

____

____

____

____

7 Defining New Vocabulary. With a partner, look back at the words you marked as unknown in Activity 2 and discuss the meaning of each new term. Your teacher may ask you to write sentences with these new words.

8 Discussing the Lecture. Discuss the following questions about the lecture. Refer to your notes as necessary. Use the new vocabulary as you talk.

1. How does the full moon regulate the physical world?
2. What is the first speaker's hypothesis?
3. According to the first speaker, which behaviors may be caused by the full moon?
4. According to the second speaker, what is the difference between scientific proof and coincidence?
5. Which speaker "won" the debate, in your view? Why?
6. After listening to the two speakers, has your opinion about the effects of the full moon changed?

Talk It Over

Expressions for Citing Evidence. As you learned, one way to support a position is to give evidence from experts or scientific studies. Special verbs and phrases are used to cite (name) the *source* of the supporting evidence. These include:

According to (*Time*)
As (this study) shows
Research shows that
Dr. Baker points out / reports / states / explains

Debate. Now that you have heard a debate in English, you are ready to plan and conduct a debate in your class.

1. Choose one of these topics for your debate, or think of one of your own.

   Topics
   1. Should smoking be illegal in restaurants?
   2. Should governments spend money on space programs?
   3. Should college entrance examinations be abolished?
   4. Should voting in government elections be mandatory or voluntary?
   5. Should army service be required for women if it is required for men?
2. Divide the class into teams. One team will argue in favor of the question. The other will argue against the question.
3. Work in pairs or small groups and make a list of arguments and facts you will use to support your position. If possible, find information and research to support your position. *Note*: Do *not* give your opinion. Remember that a debate is based on *facts.*
4. Compare your supporting statements with other students who share your position. Modify or add to your supporting statements if necessary. Together, create one "master" page of supporting evidence to be used during the debate.
5. Each side should select one person as its speaker. These two speakers should then debate the topic.
6. The teacher will decide which side has "won" the debate.
7. After the debate you may discuss your *real* opinion about the topic.

PART 3

Focused Listening and Speaking

Getting Meaning from Context

1 **Using Context Clues.** You are going to hear five short talks about discoveries.

1. Listen to each talk.
2. After each talk, you will hear a question. The tape or CD will pause.
3. Read the answer choices and circle the letter of the best answer.

1. a. Discoveries and inventions usually happen at the same time.
   b. An invention helped Columbus to make an important discovery.
   c. All discoveries depend on inventions.
   d. Columbus invented ships because he hoped to discover a new land.

2. a. It requires expensive technology.
   b. It is very old.
   c. It will decrease in the future.
   d. It began in ancient Rome.

3. a. Uranus was discovered almost 2,000 years ago.
   b. Telescopes were invented by the Romans.
   c. Uranus was not named after a Roman god.
   d. Sir William Herschel did not know about the discoveries of the Roman astronomers.

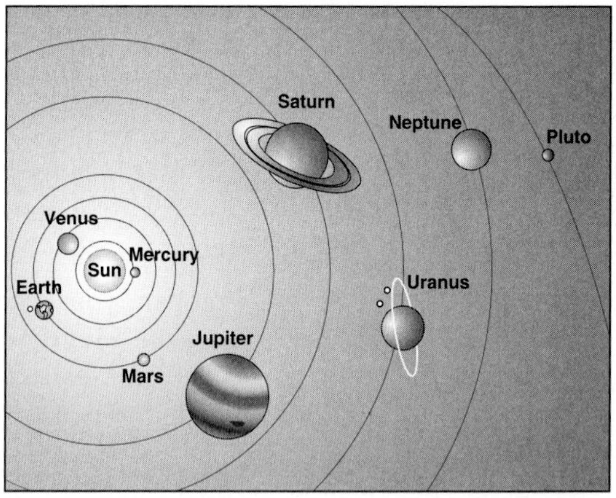

4. a. It was the greatest accomplishment of the ancient Chinese.
   b. It led to improvements in people's health.
   c. It was accidental.
   d. It was a big mistake.

5. a. Columbus used rubber to build his boats.
   b. Rubber comes from a tree.
   c. "Rubber" was originally a French word.
   d. Rubber was discovered in Europe.

2 **Talking about Inventions and Discoveries.** The following discoveries and inventions were discussed in Activity 1. What role, if any, do they play in your life?

1. solar energy
2. the planets
3. tea
4. rubber

Focused Listening

Pronunciation of *-ed* Endings

The *-ed* ending is found on regular past tense verbs and the past participle. For example:

- We finished the work at 8 P.M. (Past tense verb)
- We're very excited about your visit. (Participle used as adjective)
- The papers were corrected by the TA. (Passive voice)

The *-ed* ending has three different pronunciations in English.

1. In words ending with */t/* or */d/,* it is pronounced as a separate syllable, */id/.*

   Examples

   wait; waited — decide; decided

2. In words that end with a voiceless consonant, it is pronounced as */t/.*

   Examples

   step; stepped — wish; wished
   talk; talked — watch; watched

3. In words that end with a voiced consonant or a vowel, it is pronounced as */d/.*

   Examples

   live; lived — die; died
   turn; turned — use; used
   enjoy; enjoyed — call; called

3 **Practicing the Past Tense Endings.** Listen and repeat the following words after the speaker.

/t/	/d/	/id/
passed	discovered	directed
camped	jogged	wanted
crashed	agreed	started
looked	closed	
asked	breathed	

4 **Distinguishing between Past Tense Endings.** Listen to the following past tense verbs and check the pronunciation that you hear. You'll hear each word twice.

	/t/	/d/	/id/
1.			
2.			
3.			
4.			
5.			
6.			
7.			
8.			
9.			
10.			
11.			
12.			
13.			
14.			
15.			

5 **Pronouncing the Past Tense Endings.** With a partner, decide on the *-ed* pronunciation of these words. In the blanks write */t/, /d/,* or */id/.* Then say the words.

1. _____ pointed
2. _____ dreamed
3. _____ traveled
4. _____ kissed
5. _____ thanked
6. _____ waited
7. _____ explored
8. _____ interested
9. _____ judged
10. _____ moved

Using Language

Expressing Interest or Surprise

In Chapter 1, page 7, you learned several ways of showing that you are interested in what someone is saying. Here are some additional expressions you can use:

That's (really) interesting.
That's an interesting / great / nice story.

If you are surprised by something you hear, you can say:

(That's) incredible!
(That's) unbelievable!
(That's) amazing!
I can't believe it.
I'm shocked.

6 Talking about Discoveries. We discover things that are already there, just waiting for us to find them. Most discoveries are quite ordinary. For example, think of a baby discovering his or her toes.

Work in small groups and tell your classmates about discoveries that you have made in your life. It may help you to think in terms of categories. Use expressions to express surprise, as appropriate, to respond to your classmates' comments.

Discoveries

Categories	Examples
A skill you found you have	the ability to sing, to make bread perfectly
A place	a new restaurant, a vacation spot
A new form of entertainment	jazz, bungee jumping
Something you never noticed before about something familiar	Your dog has different-colored eyes. There is a funny noise in your house.
Something unusual about another country or its people	You cannot negotiate the prices of items in stores.

PART 4

Listening and Speaking in the Real World

In this section you are going to listen to a game show called Explorations, Inventions, and Discoveries. You will play along with the contestants on the tape.

Before You Listen

1 **Prelistening Questions.** Discuss the following questions with your classmates.

1. Are game shows popular in your community? Do you enjoy watching them?
2. Do you enjoy watching English-language game shows? Which one(s) in particular?
3. Are game shows different in different languages?
4. Would you like to be a contestant on a game show? Which one?

Listen

2 **Listening to a Game Show.** You are going to listen to a game show with questions about explorations, inventions, and discoveries. As you hear each question, you should circle *your* answer in the column below marked Your Answer. Then you will hear the answer given by this week's contestant, Roger Johnson. Finally, the host, Ronnie Perez, will provide the correct answer. (Also found on page 275.)

Question	Your answer	Roger's answer
1	a. Apple	a. Apple
	b. Microsoft	b. Microsoft
	c. Intel	c. Intel
2	a. Mt. Everest in Nepal	a. Mt. Everest in Nepal
	b. Mt. Fuji in Japan	b. Mt. Fuji in Japan
	c. Mt. Whitney in the United States	c. Mt. Whitney in the United States
3	a. Spain	a. Spain
	b. Portugal	b. Portugal
	c. Italy	c. Italy
4	a. Christopher Columbus	a. Christopher Columbus
	b. Leif Eriksson	b. Leif Eriksson
	c. Ferdinand Magellan	c. Ferdinand Magellan
5	a. Italy	a. Italy
	b. Egypt	b. Egypt
	c. China	c. China
6	a. penicillin	a. penicillin
	b. aspirin	b. aspirin
	c. ginseng	c. ginseng
7	a. the motion picture	a. the motion picture
	b. the telephone	b. the telephone
	c. the lightbulb	c. the lightbulb
8	a. Isaac Newton	a. Isaac Newton
	b. Galileo Galilei	b. Galileo Galilei
	c. Nicolaus Copernicus	c. Nicolaus Copernicus

After You Listen

3 **Reviewing the Listening.**

1. How many questions did you answer correctly? Which student got the most correct answers?
2. Using the answers as cues, try to reconstruct the questions. Turn to page 275 to see if you are right.

Talk It Over

Ordering Events in a Story.

The Travels of Marco Polo

Marco Polo was born in Venice in the year 1254. With his father and uncle, he traveled to Asia and eventually reached China, where he met the famous emperor Kublai Khan. Late in his life Marco Polo spent some time in prison. There he wrote a book about his travels in Asia, which became a valued source of information about the lands of the East. Marco Polo died in 1324.

The following paragraphs give information about Marco Polo's travels. This information is not in the correct order. Your task will be to put the events in the correct sequence.

1. Divide into groups of seven students each, if possible.
2. Each person in the group should choose one of the paragraphs. (If your group has only six people, one person should select two paragraphs.)
3. Read your paragraph. If necessary, use a dictionary to understand all the important information. On the map, mark the part of Marco Polo's voyage that is described in your paragraph.
4. When everyone has finished preparing,
   a. Listen to each person tell his or her part of the story. Use the map on page 197 for illustration as you speak. *Do not read your classmate's paragraphs.* If you do not understand something, ask for repetition or clarification.
   b. Decide what the correct order of the story is.
   c. Draw the missing parts of Marco Polo's voyage on your map. Using the map for illustration, explain your part of the story to the group.
5. Check the correct order on page 275.

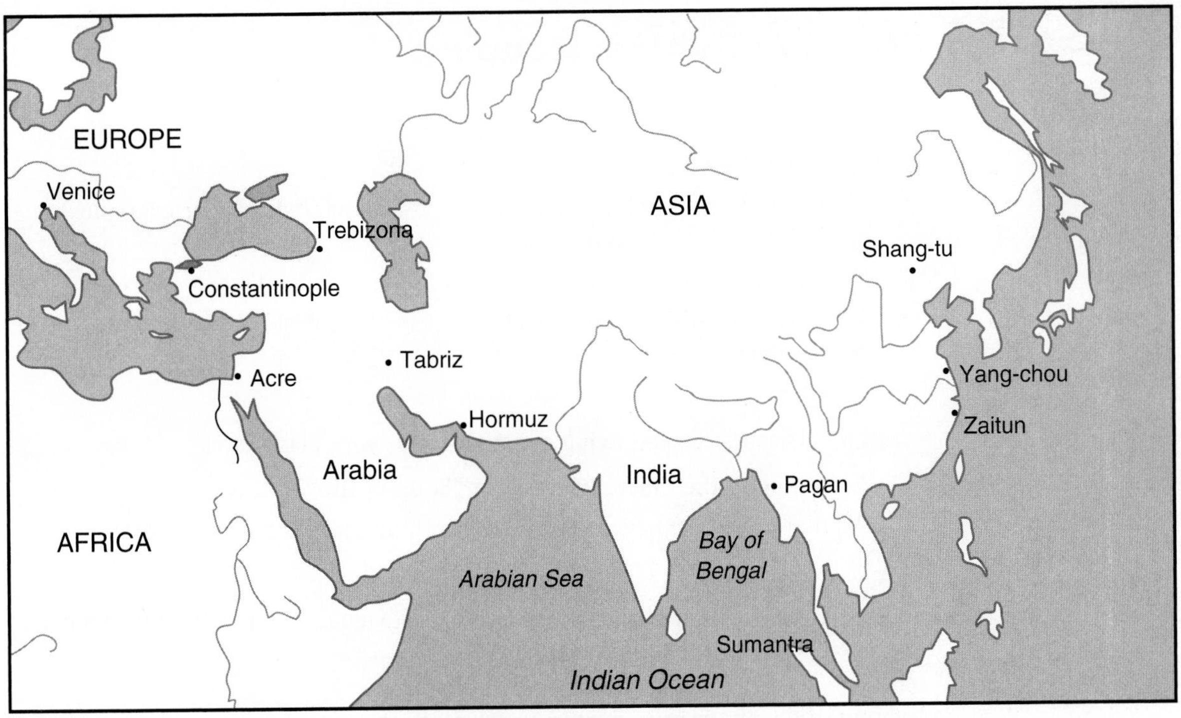

Story

A. The Polos finally left China in 1292. They sailed south from Yang-chou, through the Straits of Sumatra, and around the tip of India.

B. More than three years after leaving Venice, they finally arrived at the palace of the emperor Kublai Khan in Shang-tu, China.

C. Marco Polo, his father, and his uncle sailed on their famous voyage to the Orient in 1271. First they traveled to the port city of Acre in Palestine. From there they traveled by camel to the Persian port of Hormuz.

D. They then sailed up the western coast of India and across the Arabian Sea, returning to the port of Hormuz. After that they traveled by land to Tabriz, Trebizona, and Constantinople.

E. They arrived back in Venice in the year 1295 after traveling more than 15,000 miles.

F. The Polos stayed in China for 17 years. During that time, Marco traveled to Southeast Asia and India and back. After that, he became a government official in the Chinese city of Yang-chou.

G. They wanted to sail from Hormuz to China, but they could not find a ship. Therefore, they continued traveling by camel across the deserts and mountains of Asia.

Video Activities: Mapping the Human Genome

Before You Watch.

1. What determines each person's inherited characteristics—for example, eye color, height, or blood type?
2. Define the following terms: *gene, DNA.*
3. Tell what you know about research that is being done on the human genetic code.

Watch. Discuss the following questions with your classmates.

1. According to the video, what is the "book of life"?
2. What are the scientists in the video working on? What is their goal?

Watch Again. What are the benefits and disadvantages of mapping the human genetic code? Complete the chart.

Mapping the genetic code	
Benefit	**Disadvantage**

After You Watch. Discuss these questions in small groups.

1. Which is greater, in your opinion: the benefit or the disadvantage of mapping the genetic code?
2. Can you think of additional advantages and disadvantages, besides the ones mentioned in the video?
3. Do you believe this kind of research should continue? Who should pay for it?

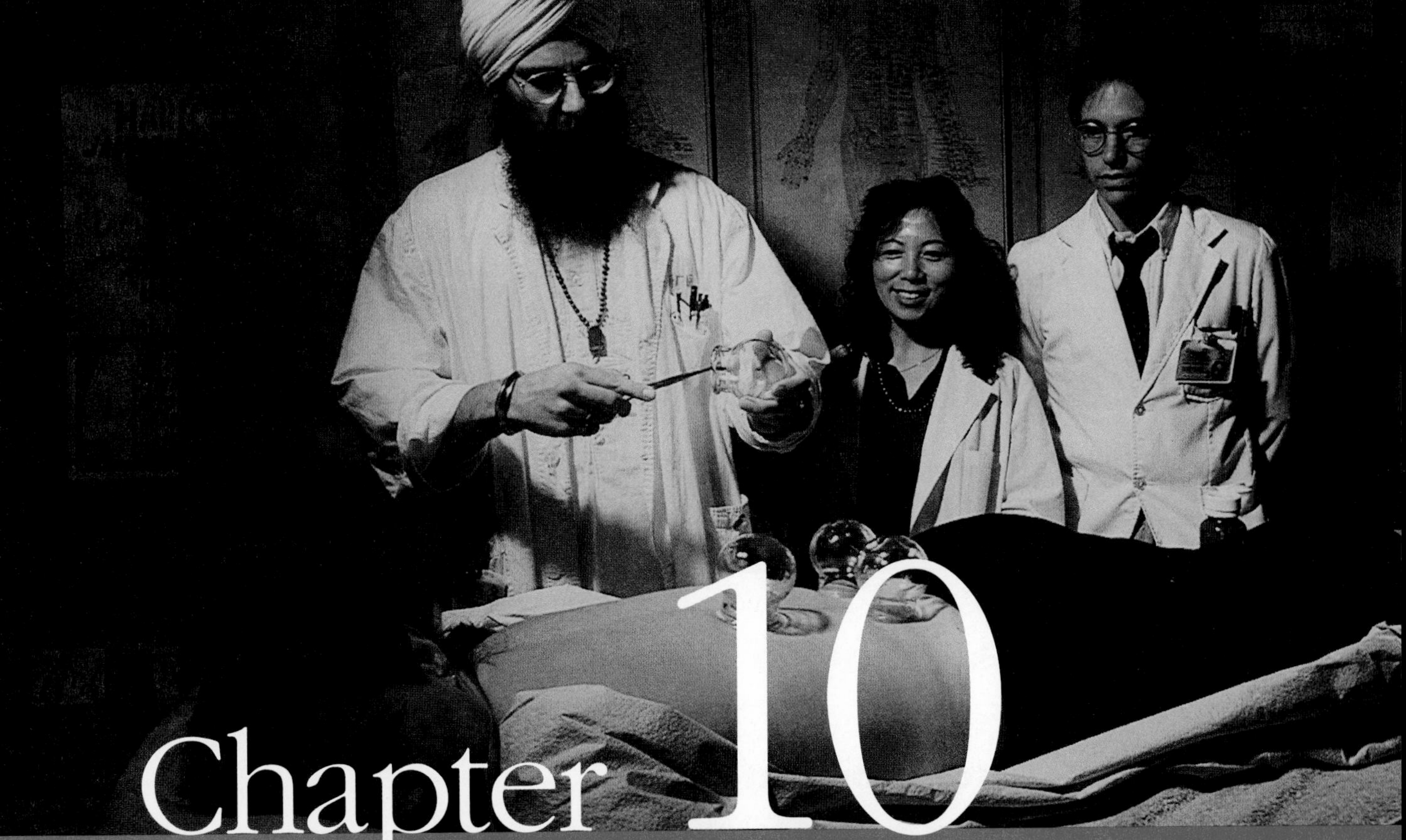

Chapter 10

Medicine, Myths, and Magic

IN THIS CHAPTER

Lecture: Sleep Disorders
Note-Taking Focus: Digressing and Returning to the Topic
Focused Listening: Negative Tag Questions
Using Language: Expressing Disbelief or Skepticism
Answering Negative Tag Questions
Talking about Appearances and Reality

Did You Know?

- Many people believe that cold weather, hot weather, or changes in the weather can cause someone to catch a cold. All these beliefs are wrong. In fact, colds are caused by more than 200 different viruses, which are passed from person to person through close contact.
- 500 million people alive today will eventually be killed by tobacco.[1]
- Each year, between 300 and 500 million people become ill with malaria, and several million die.[2]
- A common English saying is, "An apple a day keeps the doctor away." That is because apples contain vitamin C, which is necessary for fighting disease.

PART 1

Listening to Conversations

Before You Listen

Nancy and Anna come home from school and find Jeff in bed watching television. It's the middle of the afternoon.

[1] *Time Almanac 2000.*

[2] <http://www.malaria.org/>.

1 Prelistening Questions. Discuss these questions with your classmates.

1. Have you ever had the flu (influenza)?
2. What were your symptoms?
3. Did you take medicine to feel better? What kind?
4. When you are sick, do you usually prefer to take medicine from a doctor or to use natural products?

2 Vocabulary Preview. These sentences contain expressions from the conversation. Use the context to match the underlined words and expressions with their definitions.

Sentences	Definitions
1. *A:* Where were you last night? *B:* I was out partying until 3 A.M.	a. ____ I don't believe it. / That's ridiculous (slang)
2. *A:* I've got a fever and a runny nose. My whole body hurts. *B:* It sounds like you've got the flu.	b. ____ a superstition c. ____ "nonscientific" treatments used by traditional people
3. *A:* I failed my math test today. *B:* Cheer up. I'm sure you'll do better next time	d. ____ to eliminate; make something go away
4. *A:* What's the best way to get rid of a headache? *B:* Take two aspirin.	e. ____ attending parties (slang) f. ____ wet (when someone has a cold or the flu)
5. *A:* Do you think the full moon causes some people to act crazy? *B:* Give me a break.	g. ____ Don't feel sad.
6. My grandmother never went to doctors. She always used folk remedies when she was sick.	
7. *A:* Do you think it's bad luck to see a black cat? *B:* Of course not. That's an old wives' tale.	

Listen

3 Listening for Main Ideas.

1. Close your book as you listen to the conversation. Listen for the answers to these questions.
   1. What are Jeff's symptoms?
   2. What treatments do Nancy and Anna suggest?
   3. What does Jeff prefer to do?
2. Compare answers with a partner.

Stress

4 Listening for Stressed Words.

1. Now listen to part of the conversation again. Some of the stressed words are missing. During each pause, repeat the phrase or sentence; then fill in the missing stressed words.

Anna: Herbal tea? Well, I _______________ that makes sense. When I was sick as a _______________, my mother used to give me _______________ _______________ with lemon. And for a _______________, a spoonful of _______________.

Nancy: That reminds me of our grandmother's cure for a _______________. Talk about an old wives' tale! She came from a small _______________ in Russia, and in the _______________ days, people used to have these special glass _______________. They'd _______________ them and put them on the sick person's _______________. That was supposed to get _______________ of a cough. Can you _______________ it?

Anna: Why not? You know, _______________ of times I think home remedies _____________ work because people _______________ in them. We say they're _______________, because we think everything has to be scientific. But there are lots of things that science _______________ explain. Sometimes the best doctor is _______________, don't you agree?

Nancy: Yes, I do. So what do you _______________, Jeff? Do you want to try the _______________?

Jeff: _______________ me a _______________. Why don't you just bring me some _______________ juice? And could you _______________ me find the TV _______________?

TV Announcer: Cold-Aid contains _______________ _______________ more of the pain reliever doctors recommend _______________. Next time _______________ have a cold or the flu, try Cold-Aid—the new _______________ formula cold medicine that really works!

Jeff: _______________ the herbal tea, Nancy! Just _______________ me some Cold-Aid!

2. Compare answers and read the conversation with a partner. Pay attention to the stressed words.

Stress in Compound Phrases

Compound phrases combine two nouns or an adjective and a noun to form new words, phrases, or idioms that can usually be found in the dictionary.

For example: orange + juice = orange juice.

Whether the compound is written as one word or as two words, the first word is almost always stressed.

5 **Pronouncing Compound Phrases.** Listen to examples of compound nouns from the conversation. Notice which syllables are stressed as you repeat each phrase after the speaker.

grándmother	oránge juice	cóld medicine
fólk remedy	páin reliever	

Adjective + Noun Combinations

Words in adjective + noun combinations are stressed equally. These phrases are not found in the dictionary because they are not idioms.

6 **Predicting Stress in Adjective + Noun Combinations.** The following table contains both compound phrases and adjective + noun combinations. Following the rules you have just learned, mark the stressed word(s) in each item. Then listen to the tape to check your answers.

1. old mother	stepmother
2. coffeepot	large pot
3. cigarette lighter	broken lighter
4. flashlight	green light
5. white house	White House
6. hair dryer	dry hair
7. playboy	tall boy
8. fast reader	mind reader
9. black fly	butterfly

After You Listen

7 **Vocabulary Review.** Work in pairs to practice the new vocabulary. Student A should look at page 261. Student B should look at page 271.

Using Language

Expressing Disbelief or Skepticism

In the conversation, Nancy asks Jeff if he would like to try their grandmother's home remedy for a cough. Jeff replies, "Give me a break." This idiomatic expression means that Jeff does not believe in the home remedy. He thinks it is foolish.

The following phrases are used to express disbelief or skepticism.

That's hard to believe.	**More Polite**
I don't believe that.	↓
You're joking / Are you joking?	
You're kidding / Are you kidding?	
Nonsense!	
(That's) baloney! (slang)	
Give me a break. (slang)	
That's ridiculous / absurd / crazy / silly.	**Less Polite**

8 **Talking about Superstitions.**

1. Discuss the following questions with your classmates.
    1. Are you, or is anyone in your family, a superstitious person?
    2. Every culture in the world has some superstitious beliefs. How do superstitions begin, and why do people believe in them?
2. The chart gives examples of common American and Canadian superstitions in several categories.
    1. Tell if you or someone you know has a similar belief. Write about it in the chart.
    2. Give other examples of superstitions.
    3. To express disbelief, use the expressions from the explanation box. To express surprise, use the vocabulary from Chapter 9, page 193.

FYI

superstition (noun)
a belief, not based on reason or knowledge, that some objects or actions are lucky and some are unlucky

Finding a four-leaf clover brings good luck.

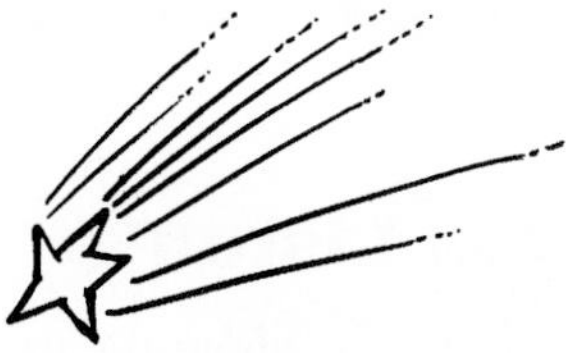

If you see a falling star, you can make three wishes, and they will come true.

Walking under a ladder or seeing a black cat cross your path is bad luck.

The number 13 is bad luck.

When your nose itches, it means that company is coming.

American and Canadian superstitions	Similar beliefs
Numbers: The number 13 is bad luck, and Friday the 13th is an unlucky day.	
Objects: It is good luck to hang a horseshoe on the wall. It is bad luck to walk under a ladder. You should not open an umbrella indoors.	
Animals: It is bad luck if a black cat crosses your path.	
Nature / weather / seasons: If you see a falling star, you should make a wish.	
Food / health: It's bad luck to spill salt.	
Marriage / family: It's bad luck for a bride and groom to see each other the day before the wedding.	
Other:	

PART 2

Listening to Lectures

Before You Listen

The following lecture is about the causes and treatments of sleeping problems in adults.

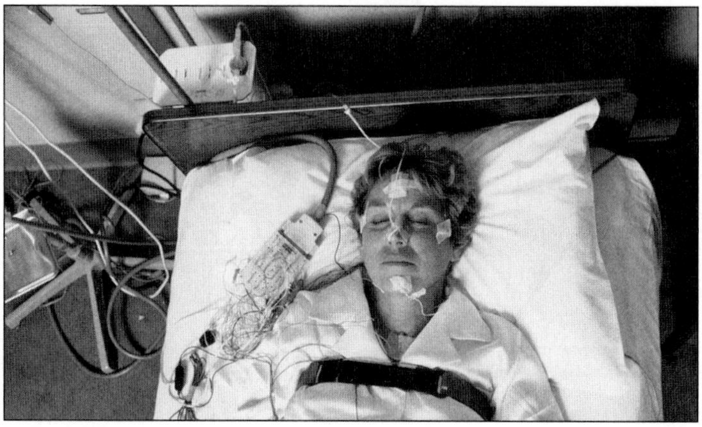

1 Prelistening Discussion. Discuss these questions in small groups.

1. How many hours of sleep do you need each night in order to feel rested?
2. How do you feel when you sleep too little or too much?
3. Do you ever have trouble sleeping? When?
4. What remedies do you know for sleep problems? Have you used any of them?

2 Vocabulary Preview. The following terms appear in the lecture. With your classmates, define the words you already know. Mark the words you do not know.

____ rested	____ a mask	____ stimulants
____ a disorder	____ regulate	____ addictive
____ breathing	____ diagnose	____ hypnosis
____ a symptom	____ insomnia	____ to lower
____ snoring	____ chronic	____ therapy, a therapist
____ a treatment		____ a clinic

Listen

Digressing (Going off) and Returning to the Topic

Lecturers often include personal stories, jokes, or other information that is not directly related to the main topic. When speakers "go off the subject" (digress) like this, you do not need to take notes. However, you need to start taking notes again when the speaker signals a return to the main subject. Study the expressions below.

Going off the topic	**Returning to the topic**
By the way	As I was saying
That reminds me	Anyway
Before I forget	Back to our topic
	Where was I?

3 **Predicting Lecture Organization.** This lecture is about three types of sleep disorders. Use the information in the Language Tip box to predict what an outline of the lecture will probably look like. Write it on paper and then compare your outline with that of your classmates.

Language Tip: Medical Conditions

When medical conditions are described, you can expect the following language and information:

- the symptoms
- the cause
- the treatment
- the cure (if there is one)

For example, if a person has a cold, the symptoms include a runny nose, a sore throat, a fever, and weakness. The cause is a virus. The treatment is to rest and drink a lot of liquids. There is no cure.

4 **Recognizing Digressions.** Listen to information on one type of sleep disorder. Listen carefully for the place where the speaker goes off and then returns to the topic. Remember that you do not need to take notes on digressions.

After you listen, look at the following notes and cross out any unnecessary information.

narcolepsy

- symptom: sudden attack of sleep (no control)
- usually happens to students in 8 a.m. classes
- cause: high levels of chemical in brain
- treatment: medication

5 **Taking Draft Notes.** Listen to the lecture and take notes in the best way you can. Use your own paper.

After You Listen

6 Rewriting Your Notes.

1. Review the notes from Activity 5 with one or two classmates. Fill in any information that you missed. Listen again if necessary.
2. Rewrite your notes in outline form.

7 Defining New Vocabulary. With a partner, look back at the words you marked as unknown in Activity 2 and discuss the meaning of each new term. Your teacher may ask you to write sentences with these new words.

8 Discussing the Lecture. Discuss the following questions about the lecture and your own experience. Refer to your notes as necessary. Use the new vocabulary as you talk.

1. Name the three sleep disorders discussed in the lecture. For each disorder, review

    the symptoms

    the cause

    the treatment(s)
2. What are some unsafe treatments for insomnia? Why are they dangerous?
3. Which of the techniques for treating insomnia have you used? What additional treatments do you recommend?
4. Do you think that a therapist or a psychologist could help someone suffering from stress or another psychological problem?

Talk It Over

Discussing Medical Conditions. Here is a list of common medical problems. Work in groups. For each problem, list the symptoms, cause, and treatments. Include old wives' tales. Note: Some of the items on the list are symptoms, not illnesses. In that case, discuss the cause and the treatment.

a cold	baldness	a burn	high blood pressure
a cough	a toothache	dandruff	diabetes
hiccups	an itchy eye	dry skin	chicken pox
a sore throat	bad breath	warts	food poisoning

PART 3

Focused Listening and Speaking

Getting Meaning from Context

1 Using Context Clues. You are going to hear five short conversations.

1. Listen to each conversation.
2. After each conversation, you will hear a question. The tape or CD will pause.
3. Read the answer choices and circle the letter of the best answer.
4. Then listen to the next part of the conversation to hear the correct answer.

1. a. She has diabetes.
   b. She is overweight.
   c. She smokes too much.
   d. She is pregnant.

2. a. an astrologer
   b. a language professor
   c. a magician
   d. a doctor

3. a. He fell down.
   b. He got some money.
   c. His tooth fell out.
   d. He fell asleep.

4. a. a doctor
   b. a scientist
   c. the woman's father
   d. the woman's son

5. a. The man is eating too much.
   b. She forgot the man's birthday.
   c. The food is too expensive.
   d. The man is going to die.

Focused Listening

Negative Tag Questions

In Chapter 4, you learned how to ask and answer affirmative tag questions. These questions can have two meanings, depending on the intonation of the question. English also has negative tag questions. The first part of the question has a negative verb, and the tag is affirmative. For example:

- George isn't married, is he?

With rising intonation, this question is a request for information. The speaker isn't sure if George is married.

With falling intonation, this question means the speaker is almost sure that George is not married. The tag is used as a way of making conversation. It is not a real question.

A negative tag question with rising intonation can also express a hope:

- You're not going to wear that shirt, are you?

The speaker hopes that the listener is not going to wear "that" shirt. We can infer that the speaker does not like or does not approve of the shirt.

2 **Recognizing the Meaning of Negative Tag Questions.** Listen to negative tag questions and decide the speaker's meaning.

Question		The speaker . . .
1.	a.	is sure Maria didn't call
	b.	is not sure if Maria called
2.	a.	is sure there's no homework
	b.	is not sure if there is homework
3.	a.	hopes it will not rain
	b.	is certain that it will not rain
4.	a.	hopes the listener is not going out
	b.	is sure the listener is not going out
5.	a.	is asking a question
	b.	is making an observation
6.	a.	hopes the ice cream is not finished
	b.	is certain the ice cream is not finished
7.	a.	understands that James is not coming for dinner
	b.	hopes James is not coming for dinner
8.	a.	hopes the bus hasn't arrived
	b.	knows the bus hasn't arrived

Answering Negative Tag Questions

Many English learners are confused about the correct way to answer negative tag questions. Look at these examples:

Question	Answer	Meaning
1. It's not your birthday today, is it?	No, it's not.	It is not the listener's birthday. The speaker was correct.
2. It's not your birthday today, is it?	Yes, it is.	It is the listener's birthday. The speaker was wrong.

3 **Asking and Answering Negative Tag Questions.** Work in pairs to ask and answer negative tag questions. Student A should look at page 262. Student B should look at page 272.

Using Language

Talking about Appearances and Reality

If a person tells you a surprising fact about his or her character, you can politely respond by saying that the person does not seem that way to you. For example:

A: I always feel nervous around strangers.

B: Really? I don't think of you like that. You always seem so confident.

Here are some other ways of talking about appearances:

You seem / appear (confident).

You don't seem (nervous).

I don't think of you like that.

You don't seem like that to me.

You're not (really) like that, are you?

1951, 1963, 1975
Luckiest of all the signs, you are also talented and articulate. Affectionate yet shy, you seek peace throughout your life. Marry a Sheep or a Boar. Your opposite is the Cock.

1952, 1964, 1976
You are eccentric and your life is complex. You have a very passionate nature and abundant health. Marry a Monkey or Rat late in life. Avoid the Dog.

1953, 1965, 1977
Wise and intense with a tendency towards physical beauty. Vain and high tempered. The Boar is your enemy. The Cock or Ox are your best signs.

1954, 1966, 1978
Popular and attractive to the opposite sex. You are often ostentatious and impatient. You need people. Marry a Tiger or a Dog early, but never a Rat.

1955, 1967, 1979, 1991
Elegant and creative, you are timid and prefer anonymity. You are most compatible with Boars and Rabbits, but never the Ox.

CHINESE ZODIAC

The Chinese Zodiac consists of a 12-year cycle, each year of which is named after a different animal that imparts distinct characteristics to its year. Many Chinese believe that the year of a person's birth is the primary factor in determining that person's personality traits, physical and mental attributes and degree of success and happiness throughout his lifetime. To learn about your Animal Sign, find the year of your birth among the 12 signs running around the border. If born before 1924 or after 1971, add or subtract 12 to find your year.

1956, 1968, 1980
You are very intelligent and able to influence people. An enthusiastic achiever, you are easily discouraged and confused. Avoid Tigers. Seek a Dragon or a Rat.

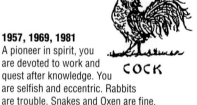

1957, 1969, 1981
A pioneer in spirit, you are devoted to work and quest after knowledge. You are selfish and eccentric. Rabbits are trouble. Snakes and Oxen are fine.

1962, 1974, 1986
Tiger people are aggressive, courageous, candid, and sensitive. Look to the Horse and Dog for happiness. Beware of the Monkey.

1961, 1973, 1985
Bright, patient, and inspiring to others. You can be happy by yourself, yet make an outstanding parent. Marry a Snake or Cock. The Sheep will bring trouble.

1960, 1972, 1984
You are ambitious yet honest. Prone to spend freely. Seldom makes lasting friendships. Most compatible with Dragons and Monkeys. Least compatible with Horses.

1959, 1971, 1983
Noble and chivalrous. Your friends will be lifelong, yet you are prone to marital strife. Avoid other Boars. Marry a Rabbit or a Sheep.

1958, 1970, 1982
Loyal and honest, you work well with others. Generous yet stubborn and often selfish. Look to the Horse or Tiger. Watch out for Dragons.

4 **Talking about the Chinese Zodiac.**

1. Alone:
   1. In what year were you born? According to the Chinese zodiac, what is your animal sign?
   2. Read the description of your sign. If necessary, use a dictionary so that you will understand all the words. According to the description, what are your good and bad qualities? Make a list.

      Example

Good qualities	Bad qualities
honest	aggressive

2. In groups of three or four:
   1. Tell your classmates your sign. Then tell about your good and bad qualities. Define new words for your classmates.
   2. Your classmates should respond, where appropriate, with expressions from the explanation box on page 211.

PART 4

Listening and Speaking in the Real World

In the United States everyone is encouraged to learn first aid, which means how to take care of people who are injured or sick in an emergency. First aid courses are offered regularly at community centers, high schools, and medical offices. One technique that is always part of first aid training is rescue breathing. In this section, you will learn the steps in rescue breathing.

Before You Listen

1 **Prelistening Questions.**

1. Have you ever had a life-threatening emergency? What happened? Who helped you?
2. Have you ever seen a serious accident or medical emergency? Did you do anything to help the victim(s)?
3. Have you ever taken a first aid course? Do you think it's important for everyone to know first aid?

2 **Predicting.** With a partner, look at the pictures in Activity 3. Describe each one. Try to predict the correct order of the steps.

Listen

3 **Identifying the Steps in Rescue Breathing.** Listen as a first aid instructor explains the steps in rescue breathing. Write numbers under the pictures to show the correct order. Note: One of the steps is performed twice.

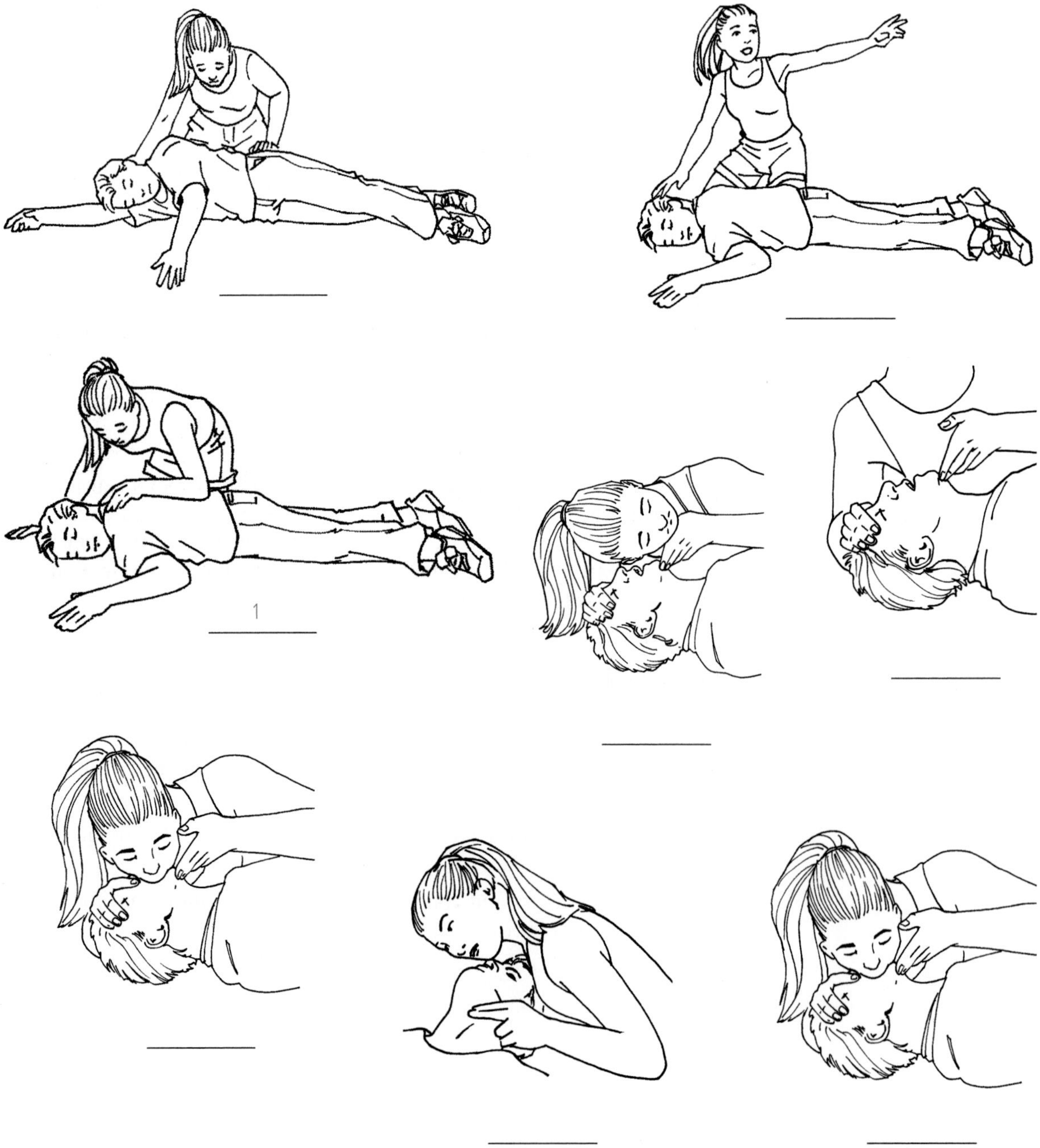

After You Listen

4 Reviewing the Steps in Rescue Breathing. Work with a partner.

1. Compare your answers to Activity 3.
2. Use the pictures to describe the steps in rescue breathing.

On the Spot!

How much responsibility do we have to try to save another person's life? In small groups, discuss the following situations. Try to imagine what you would do in each case.

1. Would you perform rescue breathing on the following people? Why or why not?
   a. a member of your family, male or female
   b. a friend or acquaintance of your own sex
   c. a friend or acquaintance of the opposite sex
   d. a stranger, male or female

2. Imagine that one of the following fell into a rapidly moving river. Would you jump in and try to rescue them? Why or why not?
   a. your child
   b. your parent
   c. your sister or brother
   d. your husband or wife
   e. your friend
   f. a stranger
   g. your dog

3. One of the people below needs a kidney transplant. Would you be willing to donate one of your kidneys to them? Why or why not?
   a. your child
   b. your parent
   c. your sister or brother
   d. your husband or wife
   e. your friend
   f. a stranger

Video Activities: A New Treatment for Back Pain

Before You Watch.

1. In your culture, is there a difference between "scientific" and "alternative" types of medicines and treatments?
2. What are some ways you know to treat back pain?
3. The following words refer to the human nervous system. Review their meanings: *nerve, spinal cord, brain.* Share what you know about the way information from the body reaches the brain.

Watch. Read the following statements. Write (T) if they are true and (F) if they are false.

1. _____ The procedure uses electricity to reduce the patients' pain.
2. _____ The treatment takes place in a doctor's office.
3. _____ The treatments are painful.
4. _____ The pain relief from the procedure is immediate.

Watch Again. Take notes on the two patients before and during/after the needle treatment.

Patient	Before treatment	During/After treatment
Doris Dorry	• *had back pain for 25 years* • *pain level was a "10"*	
Judy Ellis		

After You Watch. Below is a list of well-known alternative treatments in the United States.

1. Put a check in the "You" column next to every treatment you have tried.
2. Ask two other students if they have tried these treatments. Put checks in the appropriate columns.

Treatment	You	Student 1	Student 2
Acupuncture to relieve pain			
Acupressure (shiatsu)			
Massage to reduce pain and stress			
Hypnosis to reduce stress, pain, or anxiety			
Eating garlic, soybeans, mushrooms, or other plants to reduce blood pressure			
Meditation to reduce stress			
Vitamin C pills to prevent colds			

Chapter 11

The Media

IN THIS CHAPTER

Lecture: Marketing and Advertising
Note-Taking Focus: Taking Notes on Advantages and Disadvantages
Focused Listening: Stress in Noun/Verb Pairs
Using Language: Arguing and Conceding
Summarizing and Concluding

Listen

3 Listening for Main Ideas.

1. Close your book as you listen to the conversation. Listen for the answers to these questions.
    1. How do Dan and Anna feel about the movie they saw?
    2. How does each of them feel about censorship?
    3. What is Jeff's opinion?
    4. With whom do you agree?
2. Compare answers with a partner.

Stress

4 Listening for Stressed Words.

1. Now listen to part of the conversation again. Some of the stressed words are missing. During each pause, repeat the phrase or sentence; then fill in the missing stressed words.

Jeff: Well, __________ don't believe in __________ censorship, especially not for __________. But _____ the other day I was reading that there __________ be a connection between __________ violent films and __________ violently.

Dan: For __________ people that may be true, but not for __________ people. I mean, __________ just saw the film and __________ not about to do anything violent, __________ we?

Anna: No, but what if some __________ person in the audience __________ it and got some __________ ideas from it?

Dan: I think that __________ or __________, a person like that is __________ going to do something strange or violent __________. Seeing a __________ doesn't cause people to go off the __________ end unless there is something __________ with them in the __________ place.

Anna: Maybe you're right. But what about those __________ in the audience? That was an R-__________ movie, so what were they __________ there?

Dan: OK, you've got a __________ there. I __________ that kids __________ be allowed to see violent films. I think __________ need to supervise their kids better, and theaters should be ___________ about enforcing the ratings. But that's ___________ from total censorship, which is what ___________ were talking about before, Anna.

Anna: OK Dan, ___________ ___________. But ___________ time, can we please see a ___________?

2. Compare answers and read the conversation with a partner. Pay attention to the stressed words.

After You Listen

5 **Vocabulary Review.** Work in pairs. Student A should look at page 262. Student B should look at page 272.

Using Language

Arguing and Conceding

In the conversation, Anna and Dan have opposite opinions about movie censorship.

Reread the script of the conversation and notice the structure of their discussion:

- One person states an opinion; for example, violent movies should be censored.
- The other person disagrees.
- Both speakers support their positions with facts and reasons.
- Sometimes one speaker *concedes* that the other person is right. This means that the speaker agrees, after much discussion, that the other person's point of view is correct. It is like saying that the other person has "won" the argument.

Here are other expressions that English speakers use to argue and concede.

Conceding a point and continuing the discussion	**Conceding finally**	**Ending the discussion without conceding**
Maybe you're right, but . . .	You win.	I respect your opinion, but I don't agree.
I see your point, but . . .	I give up.	We just don't see eye to eye on this.
You've got a point there, but . . .	You're right.	I just don't see it that way.
That may be true.		
Yeah, but . . .		

6 Recognizing Expressions of Concession.

1. In the chart, read each summary of Anna and Dan's arguments. Then write a summary of the other person's response using expressions of concession.

Argument	Response
1. *Jeff:* There may be a connection between watching violent films and acting violently.	*Dan:* For some people that may be true, but not for ordinary people.
2. *Dan:* Violent films don't make ordinary people do anything violent.	*Anna:*
3. *Anna:* Violent films might make a disturbed person do something violent.	*Dan:*
4. *Anna:* Teenagers shouldn't see violent films.	*Dan:*
5. *Dan:* Theaters should enforce the ratings, but we shouldn't have total censorship.	*Anna:*

7 Using Expressions of Concession.

You are going to discuss two sides of a controversial question and practice using the expressions of concession.

1. Here is a list of controversial topics related to the media. As a class, choose *one* of these topics for discussion.

   Topics

   a. Watching violent movies causes people to act violently.
   b. The media should not report on the private lives of politicians.
   c. Watching television is bad for young children.
   d. Pornography and sex sites should be banned on the Internet.

2. Divide into pairs. Some pairs of students are to agree and other pairs are to disagree with the topic.

   In the spaces below, make of list of facts or reasons that support your position.

   Support 1: ______________________________

   Support 2: ______________________________

   Support 3: ______________________________

3. Compare your supporting statements with other pairs who share your position. Modify or add to your supporting statements if necessary.

4. Now discuss the topic with a pair that disagrees with your position. Use your supporting statements to try to persuade the other team that your position is correct.
   Begin your discussion like this: "Our position is that . . . We believe this because . . ."
   In your discussion, use expressions for agreeing, disagreeing (see Chapter 5, page 105), and conceding. You may use language from the explanation box on page 221.
5. Your teacher will tell you when to conclude your discussion. At that point, you will have five minutes to tell your real opinion about the topic.

PART 2

Listening to Lectures

Before You Listen

The following lecture is from an introductory course in marketing. It describes several types of media used in advertising and talks about the advantages and disadvantages of each type.

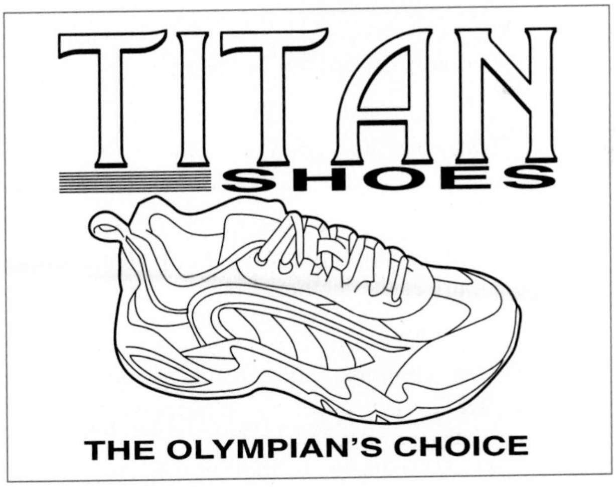

1 Prelistening Discussion. Discuss these questions in small groups.

1. What are "the media"? How many different types can you list?
2. Give an example of an advertisement from each type of media you listed. For example, did you listen to the radio this morning? What advertisements did you hear?
3. Do you pay attention to advertisements, or do you usually ignore them?
4. In your opinion, what are the characteristics of a good advertisement? Tell about an ad you like. Why do you like it? Did the ad convince you to buy the product?

2 **Vocabulary Preview.** The following terms appear in the lecture. With your classmates, define the words you already know. Mark the words you do not know.

____ advertise	____ category	____ specialized
____ advertising	____ billboard	____ to direct
____ advertisement ("ad")	____ print (media)	____ permanent
____ advertiser	____ local	
____ to make a profit	____ memorable	

Listen

Taking Notes on Advantages and Disadvantages

Lecturers often present the advantages and disadvantages of various topics or issues. The following are some phrases from the lecture. They will help you recognize when the lecturer is about to introduce advantages and disadvantages.

Introducing advantages	**Introducing disadvantages**
There are several advantages of . . .	However, there are some disadvantages.
The advantage(s) of . . . is/are . . .	On the other hand, the disadvantage(s) of . . . is/are . . .
These are the advantages of . . .	The disadvantage(s) is/are . . .

3 **Taking Notes on Advantages and Disadvantages.** Here are abbreviated notes from one part of the lecture. Listen to the passage and rewrite the notes in two forms:

1. an outline
2. two columns, with advantages on one side and disadvantages on the other

Topic: The Media Used in Advertising
Print media
newspaper advert.
adv.
everybody reads
cheap
published every day
local (bus. can reach customers directly)
disadv
no color → not exciting

4 **Taking Draft Notes.** Listen to the whole lecture and take notes in the form of an outline, a two-column chart, or a combination of the two. Use your own paper.

After You Listen

5 Rewriting Your Notes.

1. Review the notes from Activity 4 with one or two classmates. Fill in any information that you missed. Listen again if necessary.
2. Rewrite your notes.

6 Defining New Vocabulary. With a partner, look back at the words you marked as unknown in Activity 2 and discuss the meaning of each new term. Your teacher may ask you to write sentences with these new words.

7 Discussing the Lecture. Discuss the following questions about the lecture and your own experience. Refer to your notes as necessary. Use the new vocabulary as you talk.

1. Explain the difference among the following terms: advertise, advertising, advertisement ("ad"), advertiser.
2. What is the purpose of advertising, for advertisers?
3. What are the three categories of media used in advertising? Which types of media belong in each category?
4. What are the advantages and disadvantages or each type of media described in the lecture?
5. Have you ever used an ad to buy or sell something? What did you buy or sell? Where did the ad appear?

8 Designing a Magazine Ad. Pretend that you and your classmates work for an advertising agency. Your assignment is to design a magazine ad for a new toothpaste called "ToothBrite." With the members of your design team, use the following questions to plan and create your ad.

1. Which type of person is most likely to be interested in your product?
2. In which magazine (or type of magazine) will you place your ad? Why?
3. Write your ad copy. "Copy" in this context means the words or sentences that will appear in the ad. Usually the ad copy consists of a short, memorable *slogan*. For example, the slogan for Coca-Cola used to be "It's the real thing."
4. Design your ad:

   Pick a background.

   Choose the main images for your ad: people? animals? objects?

   Will your ad be photographed or drawn?

   Where will the name of the product appear? How large will it be?

   Where will you place the ad copy?

   What colors will you use?

On the Spot!

Discuss this situation in small groups.

Situation

You are the owner-publisher of a small magazine. You depend on money from advertising to stay in business. There have been months where you made almost no profit at all.

One day you receive a phone call from a potential new advertiser who wants to take out an expensive full-page ad about his political group. You need the money from the ad, but you hesitate to accept it for one reason: it comes from a hate group whose members advocate violence against people who don't agree with them.

Question: What would you do if you were the owner of the magazine? Why?

PART 3

Focused Listening and Speaking

Getting Meaning from Context

1 **Becoming Familiar with an English-Language Newspaper.** Newspapers in large cities have many sections. Bring an English-language newspaper to class. Look at the different sections. In the following list, check off the sections that your paper has. Add sections that are not on the list.

_____ world news	_____ sports
_____ local news	_____ entertainment
_____ travel	_____ weather
_____ business	_____ family / society
_____ editorials (opinions)	

_____ Other: ____

2 Using Context Clues. Listen as a man reads selections from the newspaper out loud. Decide which part of the newspaper the selections probably appeared in. Write the letters in the blanks.

a. travel	1. ____
b. business	2. ____
c. editorials / opinion page	3. ____
d. sports	4. ____
e. entertainment	5. ____
f. world news	6. ____
g. weather	7. ____

Focused Listening

Stress in Noun/Verb Pairs

Many nouns and verbs are spelled alike but pronounced differently. In these pairs, the nouns are stressed on the first syllable, and the verbs are stressed on the second.

For example:

Permít (verb): to allow. "The teacher permitted the students to leave early."

Pérmit (noun): a license or certificate allowing someone to do a certain activity. "You need a special permit to park your car here."

3 Pronouncing Noun/Verb Pairs.

1. Listen and repeat the noun/verb pairs in the chart.

Nouns	Verbs
1. cóntrast	1. contrást
2. désert	2. desért
3. éxport	3. expórt
4. ímport	4. impórt
5. íncrease	5. incréase
6. ínsult	6. insúlt
7. pérmit	7. permít
8. présent	8. presént
9. próduce	9. prodúce
10. récord	10. recórd

2. Use a dictionary to check the meanings of the words you do not know.

4 **Discriminating between Nouns and Verbs Spelled Alike.** Listen to sentences containing the following words. Place a mark above the stressed syllable you hear.

1. permit
2. export
3. present
4. produces
5. desert
6. insult
7. increased
8. recorded
9. contrasts
10. import

5 **Pronouncing Noun/Verb Pairs in Context.** Work in pairs. Student A should look at page 263. Student B should look at page 273.

Language Tip: Summarizing and Concluding

The following expressions are used to summarize or conclude a story.

to make a long story short
the bottom line is
in short
so
to conclude

6 **Summarizing a News Story.**

1. At home

   Find a news article in an English-language newspaper. Read it carefully and study the vocabulary. Then prepare a short (two to three sentences) summary of the story *in your own words.*

2. In class

   In small groups, take turns telling the news stories you prepared. As one person speaks, the others may interrupt to ask questions about the details of the story. (See Chapter 6, page 119, to review expressions for interrupting.)

Example

Student 1: I read a story in *USA Today* about the possible health risks of using cell phones.

Student 2: Excuse me, what are the risks?

Student 1: Some studies suggest that the radio waves from cell phones can damage the brain, especially in children. But other studies conclude that there is no danger. Anyway, the article said that the U.S. government is going to do a scientific study with the phone industry about the effects of cell phone use.

Student 3: May I interrupt? How much will the study cost?

Student 1: About $1 million.

Student 2: Does that mean we shouldn't use cell phones?

Student 1: No, but the bottom line is that if you're concerned, you should use cell phones only for short calls.

PART 4 Listening and Speaking in the Real World

Companies often take telephone surveys of customers and potential customers. The information from these surveys helps companies make decisions about marketing and new products. In this section you are going to hear one such telephone survey.

Before You Listen

1 **Prelistening Discussion.** Discuss these questions with your classmates.

1. Have you ever participated in a telephone survey? If yes, what was it about?
2. Look at the survey form in the next activity. Read the questions. What do you think this survey is about?

Listen

2 **Listening to a Telephone Survey.** Before listening to the phone survey, look at the questionnaire. What do you think the purpose of the survey is? As you listen, take the role of the caller and complete the form based on the information you hear.

SURVEY

I. Respondent's Biographical Data

Age: 25–35 ______
36–45 ______
46–55 ______
56 and above ______

Marital status: Single ____
Married ____
Divorced ____

Occupation: ________________________________

Yearly income: $15,000–20,000 ______
21,000–30,000 ______
31,000–40,000 ______
41,000–50,000 ______
above 50,000 ______

II. Newspapers

Name(s):	Subscribe?	
________________________	Yes ______	No ______
________________________	Yes ______	No ______
________________________	Yes ______	No ______

Hours read per week: ____________

III. Magazines

Name(s):	Subscribe?	
________________________	Yes ______	No ______
________________________	Yes ______	No ______
________________________	Yes ______	No ______

Hours read per week: ____________

IV. Books

Types of books read: biographies ______
mysteries ______
science fiction ______
novels ______
self-help books ______
textbooks ______
other ______

Amount of time spent reading per week ____________

Book club member: Yes ______ No ______

V. Television

Number of TV sets in household: ____________

Hours per week watched: ____________

After You Listen

3 **Surveying People's Reading Habits.** Work with a partner. Use the survey form from Activity 2 to interview each other about your reading habits. Discuss the differences between you and your partner and add questions that are not on the survey form.

Talk It Over

Surveying People's Television-Viewing Habits.

1. As a class, make up a survey about people's television-viewing habits. Include at least five questions. You may use the survey from Activity 2 as a model. Do not write open-ended questions. Rather, provide answer choices or blanks that can be filled in.

   Example

   Poor question: What kind of television program do you like to watch?

   Better: Which of the following types of television programs do you like to watch?

   _____ soap operas

   _____ news

   _____ sports

   etc.

2. Use your questionnaire to interview one or more people. If possible, interview people who are not in your class.
3. After the interviews, work in small groups and compare your findings. On a blank survey form, compile your group's answers to each question. Then summarize your findings.

   Example

   "In short, none of the people we interviewed like to watch the news in English."

   "So, the most popular TV show among the people we interviewed was _________________."

   "To conclude, the people we interviewed had an average of two television sets per family."

4. Discuss your own answers to the survey questions.

Video Activities: Bye, Bye, Charlie Brown

Before You Watch. Discuss the following questions in a group.

1. Have you ever seen or read "Peanuts"? (In some countries it is called "Snoopy.") Tell what you know about this comic strip. Do you have a favorite character?
2. What other comic strips do you know?

Watch. Write answers to the following questions.

1. What did Charles Schultz think of the name "Peanuts"?

   ____

2. Why did Charles Schultz retire?

   ____

3. What unusual event happened on the day this video was made?

   ____

   ____

Watch Again. Fill in the missing details.

1. For nearly __________ years, the comic strip Peanuts appeared in more than __________ newspapers in __________ different countries. It had approximately __________ readers. It was first published in __________.
2. Charles Schultz never liked the name "Peanuts" because it doesn't have __________________. He would have preferred to call the strip __________________.
3. The woman at the end of the video will miss the character called __________________.

After You Watch. Discuss these questions in small groups.

1. Why do you think Peanuts is such a popular comic strip?
2. Do you have a favorite comic strip? Describe it.
3. Why do people in every culture love comics?

Chapter 12

With Liberty and Justice for All

IN THIS CHAPTER

Lecture: The Universal Declaration of Human Rights
Note-Taking Focus: Review of Note-Taking Skills
Focused Listening: Stress in Word Families
Using Language: Acknowledging a Mistake

Did You Know?

- The percentage of children who are poor in selected countries:*

Mexico	26%
United States	22.4%
Italy	20.5%
Britain	19.8%
Turkey	19.7%

- Women all over the world earn less money than do men with the same level of education. For example, American men with a bachelor's degree earned an average of $51,405 in 1998. In contrast, women earned $36,559.
- According to Anti-Slavery International, the world's oldest human rights organization, there are currently over 200 million people worldwide living in slavery. Most of them are women and children.
- A survey taken in February 2000 found that 66% of Americans support the death penalty. Though the death penalty was abolished in the United States for a time, it was reinstated in 1976.

PART 1 Listening to Conversations

Before You Listen

Jeff applied for a job as an office assistant in a doctor's office. In the following conversation, he is being interviewed by the office manager.

* United Nations Children's Fund.

1 Prelistening Questions. Discuss these questions with your classmates.

1. What skills does an assistant in a doctor's office need to have?
2. Do you think it is unusual for a man to apply for a job as an office assistant?
3. What questions will the office manager probably ask Jeff?
4. Look up the word "discrimination" (against someone) in a dictionary. Write the meaning here:

____

____

2 Vocabulary Preview. These sentences contain expressions from the conversation. Use the context to match the underlined words and expressions with their definitions.

Sentences	Definitions
1. It's hard to make a living as an actor.	a. ____ anxious, nervous
2. *A:* I forgot to buy milk. *B:* It's no big deal. You can buy it tomorrow.	b. ____ felt comfortable together
3. *A:* How did you do on the test? *B:* I blew it. I couldn't remember anything.	c. ____ Good luck!
4. My best friend and I hit it off from the first moment we met.	d. ____ not important; not a problem
5. *A:* Why are you so uptight today? *B:* My car broke down and my mother is sick.	e. ____ He's clever; smart
6. *A:* Do you think you'll get into National University? *B:* It's a long shot. My grades aren't that good.	f. ____ I failed.
7. *A:* How's your new secretary? *B:* He's polite and he has a good head on his shoulders.	g. ____ to get a good salary
8. *A:* My driving test is this afternoon. *B:* Break a leg!	h. ____ The chances aren't good; probably not

Listen

3 Listening for Main Ideas.

1. Close your book as you listen to the conversation. Listen for the answers to these questions.
    1. What questions did the office manager ask Jeff? How did she feel about hiring him?
    2. How did Jeff feel about the interview?
    3. Why was Jeff surprised in the end?
2. Compare answers with a partner.

Stress

4 Listening for Stressed Words.

1. Now listen to part of the conversation again. Some of the stressed words are missing. During each pause, repeat the phrase or sentence; then fill in the missing stressed words.

Jeff: Hi, Nancy.

Nancy: Hi, how did your ___________ go?

Jeff: I ___________ it, Nancy. The office manager and I didn't hit it ___________ very well. First of all, she seemed very ___________ when I told her I was a ___________. And you should have ___________ her face when I told her I lived with two ___________! Maybe if I'd been a ___________ I would have had a ___________, but I really think it's a ___________ shot.

Nancy: That's not ___________. It's ___________ to discriminate against people because of their ___________. If you're the ___________ person for the job, she has to ___________ you.

Jeff: I know, but . . .

Jeff: Hello?

Manager: Can I speak to Jeff Evans, please?

Jeff: ___________.

Manager: This is Marla Graham from Dr. Erickson's office. I'm calling to tell you that if you're ___________ interested in working for us, well, we'd be ___________ to have you.

Jeff: You're ___________. I got the job?

Manager: Yes, Mr. Evans, you got it. You've got a good head on your ___________. Besides, we decided that we need a ___________ touch around this office. Can you start on ___________ at 1:00?

Jeff: I'll be there.

Manager: Okay. See you then.

Jeff: Great. Bye. I don't ___________ it! I got the job!

Nancy: Congratulations! Break a ___________!

2. Compare answers and read the conversation with a partner. Pay attention to the stressed words.

Reductions

Past Forms of Modals

In rapid, informal speech, past forms of modals are reduced:

would have come	→	would've come	or	would'a come
should have said	→	should've said	or	should'a said
could not have been	→	couldn't 've been	or	couldn'a been

5 Comparing Long and Reduced Forms. The sentences on the left side contain reduced forms. Listen and repeat them after the speaker. Note: You will hear the reduced forms only.

Reduced form	Long form
1. If I'd been a woman, I <u>mighta</u> gotten it.	If I had been a woman, I might have gotten it.
2. You <u>shoulda</u> seen her face.	You should have seen her face.
3. I <u>coulda</u> passed the test if I'd studied.	I could have passed the test if I had studied.
4. You <u>should'na</u> said that.	You shouldn't have said that.
5. You <u>musta</u> been tired after working for ten hours.	You must have been tired after working for ten hours.

6 Listening for Reductions.

1. Listen to the following conversation. It contains reduced forms. Write the long forms in the blanks.

A: What's wrong?

B: I'm sure I flunked my test in Chinese history.

A: Didn't you study?

B: Yeah, but I guess I _________ _________ studied more. I _________ _________ watched that basketball game on TV last night. Then maybe I _________ _________ done better.

A: The test _________ _________ been really hard.

B: Yeah, and it was too long. There wasn't enough time to answer all the questions.

2. Check your answers. Then read the dialogue with a partner for pronunciation practice.

After You Listen

7 Vocabulary Review. Work in pairs. Student A should look at page 263. Student B should look at page 273.

Using Language

Acknowledging a Mistake

In the conversation, Nancy asks Jeff how his job interview went. He replies, "I blew it," meaning that he failed or made a mistake. The following expressions are ways that people acknowledge making a mistake:

I goofed (up) (on something)

I screwed up (something)

I messed up

The following expressions have special meanings:

I put my foot in my mouth = I said something rude or improper

I made a fool of myself = I embarrassed myself by acting foolishly

8 **Talking about Mistakes.** Tell your classmates about mistakes you have made. Use the expressions from the explanation box. Also, say what you should have done or could have done instead.

Examples

I blew it when I decided to get married when I was 18. I should have waited until I was more mature.

I screwed up when I forgot to return my books to the library. I had to pay eight dollars in overdue fines. I should have written myself a note to return them on time.

Once I was at a party and I made a rude remark about a girl across the room. Then I realized that her brother was standing right next to me. I really put my foot in my mouth that time! I shouldn't have opened my big mouth.

On the Spot!

1. In small groups, read the following four situations, which involve possible discrimination. For each situation, discuss the following questions:
    1. What does each person want, and why?
    2. What, if anything, could have been done to prevent the conflict?
    3. What can be done now to resolve the conflict?
    4. What would <u>you</u> do if you were in this situation?
2. Your teacher may ask you to do one of the following extension activities:
    1. With a partner, choose one of the situations and role-play it.
    2. Choose one case. Write an imaginary letter to the newspaper about your experience. Then your partner will pretend to be the other party in the conflict and write a rebuttal letter.

Situations

Situation 1

Mr. Berkowitz, an apartment manager, refuses to rent an apartment to Barry and Frank. They are students at the university and both have part-time jobs. They can easily afford the rent, and they have good references. However, Mr. Berkowitz claims that he would prefer to rent to a married couple.

Situation 2

Brian Lund, a 54-year-old bank manager, says he was fired from his job because of his age. Ms. Thayer, the supervisor, says that she let the manager go because he came to work late three times in the last month. However, Mr. Lund claims that he was late only two times and that was due to his wife's illness. He points out that the bank has hired a much younger manager at a much lower salary.

Situation 3

Rosita, a student and waiter, says she didn't get a job in an expensive restaurant because of her appearance. She has a pierced eyebrow and tongue. The restaurant manager says the reason Rosita wasn't hired was that she was not experienced enough. However, the following week, the restaurant hired a man who was even less experienced than Rosita.

Situation 4

Karen McDowell, a history teacher, feels she was refused a teaching job at a private high school because of her disability. Ms. McDowell is a paraplegic and uses a wheelchair to get around. According to school officials, not all the buildings at the high school have elevators; accommodating Ms. McDowell would be too difficult and too costly for the school. The teacher they hired was able-bodied but much less experienced than Ms. McDowell.

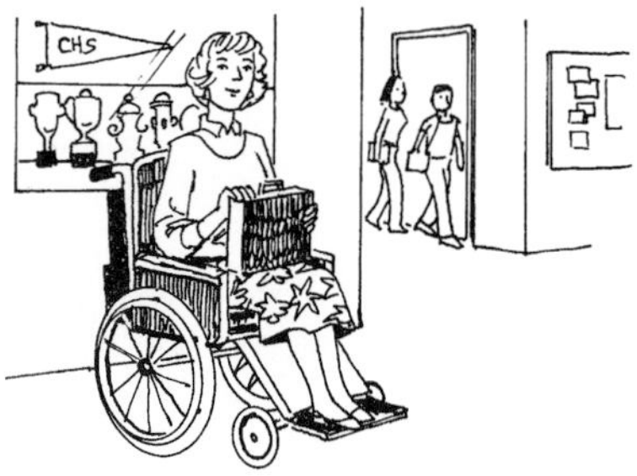

PART 2

Listening to Lectures

Before You Listen

The lecture in this section is about the Universal Declaration of Human Rights.

1 **Prelistening Discussion.** Discuss these questions in small groups.

1. What are human rights? Give examples.
2. Give examples of human-rights violations around the world.
3. Have you ever heard of the Universal Declaration of Human Rights? Share what you know about this document.

2 **Vocabulary Preview.** The following terms appear in the lecture. With your classmates, define the words you already know. Mark the words you do not know.

____ document(s)	____ torture, to torture	____ to violate
____ civil rights	____ minority groups	____ refugee(s)
____ (to be) arrested	____ to mistreat	____ a vision
____ to prohibit	____ to abolish	
____ slave(s), slavery	____ apartheid	

Listen

Review of Note-Taking Skills

As you take notes on the final lecture in this book, use the techniques of writing key words, abbreviating, and indenting that you learned in Chapter 1. As you listen, you will hear that this lecture contains many of the organizational features that were presented in previous chapters. For example:

causes and effects (Chapter 4)
examples (Chapter 5)
classifying (Chapter 7)
paraphrasing (Chapter 8)
digressing (Chapter 10)

If necessary, review these elements by referring to the chapters listed.

3 **Taking Draft Notes.** Listen to the lecture and take notes in the best way you can. Use your own paper.

After You Listen

4 **Rewriting Your Notes.**

1. Review the notes with a classmate. Make sure you have included all the important information. Listen again if necessary.
2. Then copy your notes neatly using the techniques you have learned in this book.

5 **Defining New Vocabulary.** With a partner, look back at the words you marked as unknown in Activity 2 and discuss the meaning of each new term. Your teacher may ask you to write sentences with these new words.

6 **Discussing the Lecture.** Discuss the following questions about the lecture and your own experience. Refer to your notes as necessary. Use the new vocabulary as you talk.

1. What is the Universal Declaration of Human Rights? When was it passed?
2. Give examples of human rights in each of the following categories:
   a. civil and political rights
   b. economic rights
   c. social rights
   d. cultural rights
3. How do you, personally, benefit from each of the rights listed in this lecture? How would your life be different if you didn't have these rights?
4. If someone is arrested, what rights should they have? For example, should they be allowed to speak to a lawyer?
5. Did you ever have slavery in your country's history? If yes, when was it abolished?
6. How are minority groups treated around the world? In general, do they have the same civil rights as people in the majority?

Talk It Over

Discussion. Look at the drawing of Lady Justice and discuss the following questions.

1. What is she holding in each hand?
2. What do these items symbolize?
3. Why is she wearing a blindfold?
4. What does this drawing tell us about justice in a perfect world?

A Perfect World. As a class, create a picture, or vision, of a perfect world. To do this, each student should state one thing that would make the world a better place. Then go around the room, and each person will state his or her idea. Use the following language; notice that you must use the conditional verb tense.

For me, the world would be a better place if . . .

PART 3

Focused Listening and Speaking

Focused Listening

Stress in Word Families

Word families are groups of words that have the same base form but different grammatical endings; for example *happy* (adjective), *happiness* (noun), *happily* (adverb).

The following general rules apply to the pronunciation of words in families:

- In general, when a suffix is added to a word, the new form is stressed on the same syllable as the base word; for example: *care, careful, caring, careless.*
- Words ending in *-tion, -sion, -ic, -ical, -ity, -ety, -al, -ian* almost always have primary stress on the syllable *before* the suffix. Thus, the base word and the form ending in these suffixes may be stressed differently. For example:

biólogy; biológical	áble; abílity
expláin; explanátion	áccident; accidéntal
pópular; populárity	

1 Pronouncing Word Families. Listen and repeat the following word families. Place a mark over the stressed syllable in each word. The first item is done as an example.

1. respónsible	responsibílity	
2. apply	applying	application
3. manage	manager	management
4. free	freedom	
5. social	society	
6. culture	cultural	
7. educate	educated	education
8. universe	universal	university

2 Predicting Stress. In the following word families, the stress is marked for the first word. Predict where the stress will fall on the other words. Then listen to the tape and check your answers.

1. art	artist	artistic
2. scíence	scientist	scientific
3. respéct	respected	respectful
4. hístory	historical	historian
5. pérson	personal	personality
6. discríminate	discrimination	

Getting Meaning from Context

3 **Using Context Clues.** You are going to hear five short talks.

1. Listen to each talk.
2. After each talk, you will hear a question. The tape or CD will pause.
3. Read the answer choices and circle the letter of the best answer.

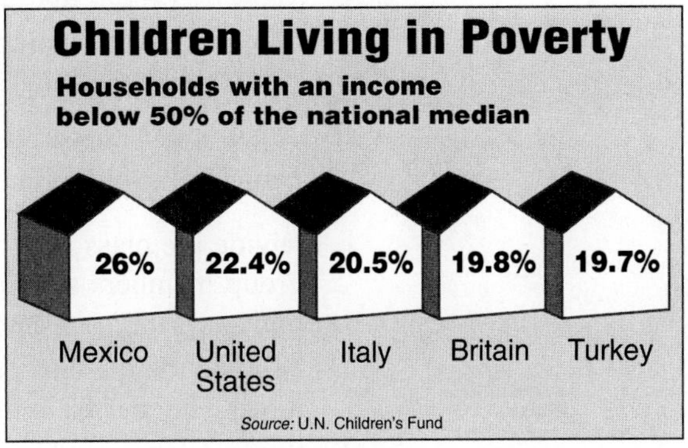

1. a. Employers and workers have different ideas about e-mail privacy.
   b. Companies that check workers' e-mail are breaking the law.
   c. Most companies don't believe in freedom of speech.
   d. 40% of American companies have e-mail.

2. a. More than half the countries in the world no longer practice capital punishment.
   b. Death is the punishment for all major crimes in the United States.
   c. Research proves that the existence of the death penalty helps to prevent crime.
   d. In the year 2000, 108 people were executed in the United States.

3. a. Children who work will receive higher pay.
   b. More and more children will work in industrialized countries.
   c. Fewer children will work.
   d. Factory work will become less dangerous.

4. a. Most Americans are vegetarians.
   b. Animals have the same rights as people in the United States.
   c. Many Americans are opposed to violence against animals.
   d. Animals are always hurt in the production of movies.

5. a. It is almost impossible for a disabled person to find a job.
   b. It is illegal to fire a person with AIDS from a job.
   c. 50 million Americans use wheelchairs.
   d. There are more people with disabilities in America than in other countries.

Talk It Over

Discussion. The items in Activity 3 deal with the following topics:

Topic 1: E-mail and privacy
Topic 2: Capital punishment
Topic 3: Child labor
Topic 4: Treatment of animals
Topic 5: People with disabilities

1. Divide the class into five groups. Each group is assigned one topic. The group members should write at least three discussion questions for their topic.
2. Now divide the classroom into five "discussion stations," one for each topic. The discussion questions should be placed or posted at the station.
3. Students should choose the topic they want to discuss and go to that station. They should discuss the questions posted at the station.
4. After 15 or 20 minutes, your teacher may instruct you to choose a different station with a different discussion topic.

PART 4

Listening and Speaking in the Real World

In this section you will hear statistical information about three groups that have suffered or are suffering from discrimination today: women, minority groups in the United States, and refugees.

Before You Listen

1 **Prelistening Discussion.**

1. What percentage of women work in your community? What kinds of jobs do they usually have? How much are they paid, compared to men?
2. In every country, some groups (ethnic, economic, religious, or national) get a better education than others. Why do you think this occurs?
3. What is a *refugee*? Where do refugees come from?
4. Look at the incomplete graphs in the next activity. Read the titles. What information does each graph contain?

Listen

2 Completing Graphs. Listen to the tape or CD and complete the following graphs.

1. Women's Earnings as a Percentage of Men's

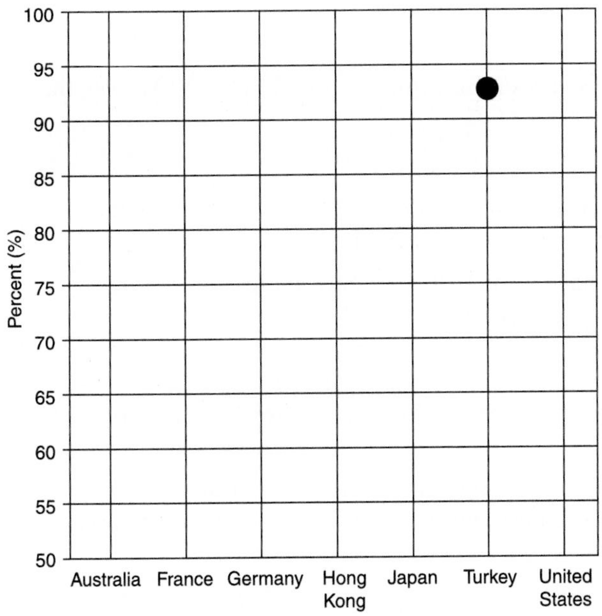

Source: International Labor Organization, 1995

2. Difference in Educational Attainment by Race and Age

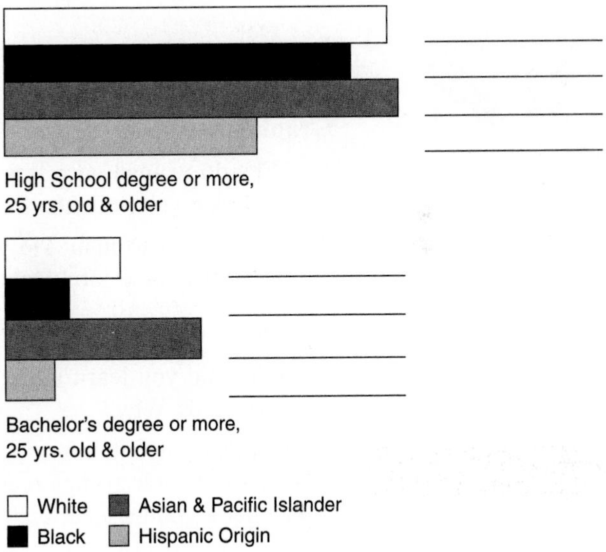

Source: Department of Education, National Center for Education Statistics

3. Refugees around the World

Source: UNHCR, 1998 statistic overview.

After You Listen

3 **Reviewing the Language of Statistics.** With a partner, compare your answers for Activity 2. Speak in complete sentences. For example:

In Australia, women earn 90 cents for every dollar that men earn. (You can also say: Women earn 90% of what men earn.)

In 1997, 25% of white Americans graduated from college.

23% of the world's refugees are found in Europe.

4 **Discussion.** In small groups, discuss the information in Activity 2. Answer the following questions.

Graph 1

1. Why do women earn less money than men for doing the same job? Is this fair? Are governments trying to change this situation?
2. If you are a woman: Do you have a job? Do men earn more than you for doing the same job? How do you feel about this?

Graph 2

1. What did you learn about the United States from this graph? Were you surprised? Why?
2. Compare the situation in other countries with the situation in the United States. Which groups receive the best education? Which groups must struggle to get a good education?
3. Compare how people in different countries can get a good education if they don't have much money.

Graph 3

1. When refugees are forced to escape to a new place, what problems do they have?
2. In your opinion, do the countries of the world have a responsibility to take in and help refugees?
3. What problems exist for countries that take in large numbers of refugees?

Talk It Over

Peacemakers Report. As your final project in this course, you will do an oral report on a peacemaker, that is, a person who has won the Nobel Peace Prize.

1. Select your peacemaker from the people below and on the next page.
2. Do some research on this person. Use an encyclopedia or the Internet.
3. Prepare a three- to four-minute oral report. Include the following information:
    - the person's name and country
    - the year in which the person won the Nobel Prize
    - the person's life, work, and accomplishments
    - how this person made his or her country a better place
4. If possible, use props or audiovisual aids representing the peacemaker. For example:
    - dress in a costume from that person's country
    - bring a map and show where the country is
    - bring an example of art, music, or food from that country
    - bring stamps or postcards from that country

John Hume and David Trimble, Northern Ireland, 1998

Carlos Filipe Ximenes Belo *(left)* and Jose Ramos-Horta *(below)*, East Timor, 1996

Joseph Rotblat *(right)*, UK, 1995

Rigoberta Menchu,
Guatemala, 1992

Yasir Arafat *(left)*, Palestine, Shimon Peres *(center)* and Yitzhak Rabin *(right)*, Israel, 1994

F.W de Klerk *(left)* and Nelson Mandela *(right)*,
South Africa, 1993

Daw Aung San Suu Kyi,
then-Burma, 1991

Mikail S. Gorbachev,
then-USSR, 1990

Video Activities: Justice and Racism

Before You Watch. Discuss the meanings of the following words in small groups. Check the meanings in a dictionary if necessary.

Justice Jury Defendant Guilty Verdict Convict (verb) Testimony

Watch. Discuss the following questions in small groups.

1. At the beginning of the video, the announcer says, "Justice is supposed to be blind, including color blind, but is it?" What is the answer to this question, according to the video?
2. Who is more racist, judges or juries? Why?
3. According to Judge Danielson, what is the solution to the problem of racism in the justice system?

Watch Again. Below are incomplete statements from the video. Try to guess the missing words. Then watch the video again and check your answers.

a. "Because racism still exists in our society, we see it in our court __________________."

b. "__________________ may say they're impartial, but sometimes they make comments to other __________________ about the defendant."

c. "Each judge knows that he or she has an ethical __________________ to deal with (racism) when it occurs in the courtroom."

d. "Racism is going to be __________________ with us right on into the millennium, even in our criminal justice system."

After You Watch. Read the following section from the video transcript.

Announcer: Jurors may say they say they're impartial, but sometimes they make comments to other jurors about the defendant. Comments like . . .

Attorney: *Those people* . . . They don't mind being in jail, or even if we make a mistake on this verdict, people from *that* community . . . They don't mind doing time.

a. What is the meaning of "*Those* people . . . *that* community"?
b. Why is this a biased way of talking?

Appendices

Pairwork Activities for Student A

Chapter 1 Part 4, page 21

5 **Reading Maps for Locations.** Ask your partner for the locations of the places listed under your map. Ask "Where is ________?" Your partner will use expressions of location. Then ask your partner to repeat the description. Write the name of the place on the map. When you are finished, your two maps should be the same.

Example

Student A: Where is the Undergraduate Library?

Student B: It's on Campus Road, up the street from the Administration Building.

Student A: Is it north or south of College Boulevard?

Student B: North.

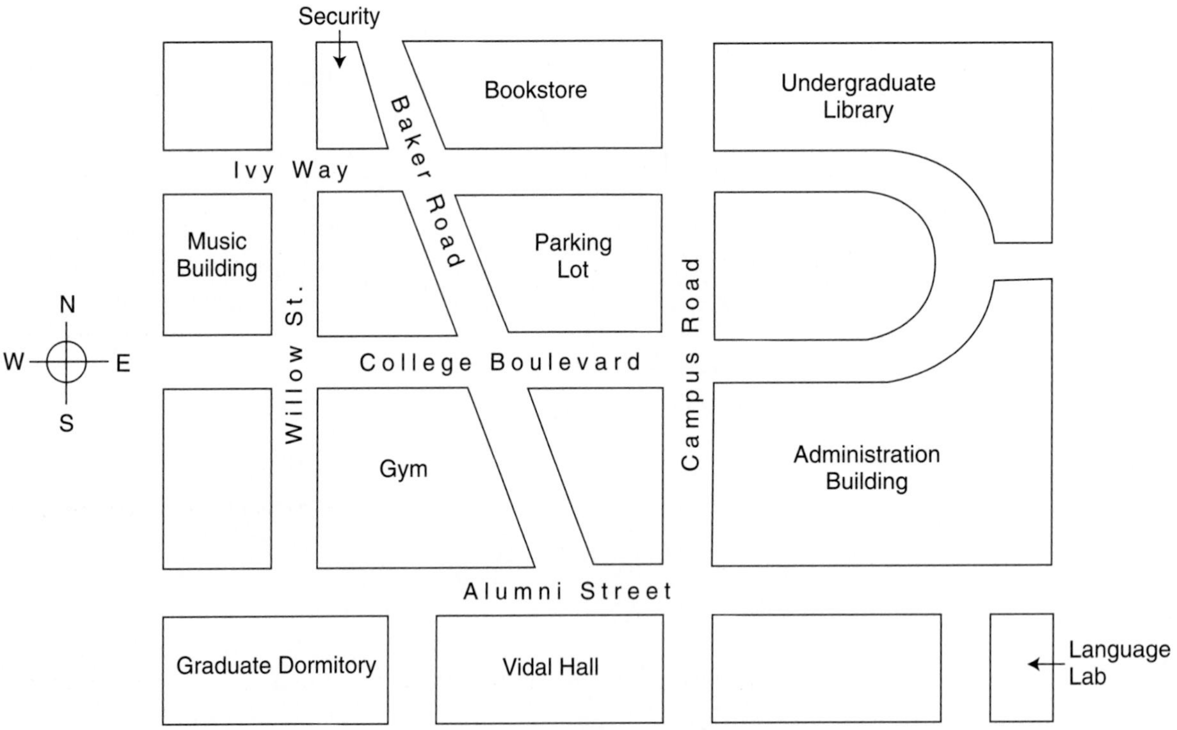

Engineering Building
President's House
Graduate Library
Cafeteria
Law School
Art Museum

Chapter 2 Part 1, page 30

8 **Role-Play.** Role-play these phone conversations. Take turns playing Student A and Student B. Read the information for your role and be sure to use the expressions for opening and closing a phone conversation.

Student A

Situation 1

You are a student. Your friend told you about a very nice room for rent with an American family. Call the family to get information about the room. Then make an appointment to go see it.
You can ask about the following things (choose three or four):

- who lives in the house
- number of bathrooms
- use of the kitchen
- parking
- rent and utilities
- furniture, telephone
- any restrictions (smoking, visitors, pets, etc.)

Situation 2

You are the manager of an apartment building. You have a vacant apartment. It has two bedrooms, one bathroom, air conditioning, and parking for two cars. It is fully furnished in a security building. The rent is $800 a month. It is 30 minutes away from the local college. You will only rent to someone serious and mature. A smoker is OK, but pets are not. A student calls and asks about the apartment.

Chapter 2 Part 3, page 38

3 **Role-Play.** Role-play situations in an apartment building.

Student A

Situation 1

You are a tenant in a large apartment building. Your refrigerator has broken for the third time in less than six months. Call the manager to express your frustration and to tell him or her you also want the refrigerator replaced.

Situation 2

You are a music major in college. You love to play your CDs while you do your homework at night. The problem is that your downstairs neighbor goes to bed early and does not like your music. This neighbor complained once, and since then you have tried to be quieter at night. However, you refuse to stop listening to music. Now it is 12:30 A.M., and someone is knocking on your door.

Chapter 2 Part 4, page 41

3 **Requesting and Giving Directions.** Look at the map. Ask your partner for directions to the places listed at the bottom of your map. When you find the place, write its name on your map. Then give your partner directions to the places that he or she asks about, from where it says, "Start here each time." At the end of this activity, your two maps should look the same.

Example

Student A: How do I get to the print shop?

Student B: That's easy. Go two blocks north on Maple Street. Turn left and go one block west on 8th Street. The print shop will be on your left, in the middle of the block, next to the hardware store.

Student A: Thanks!

MAP A

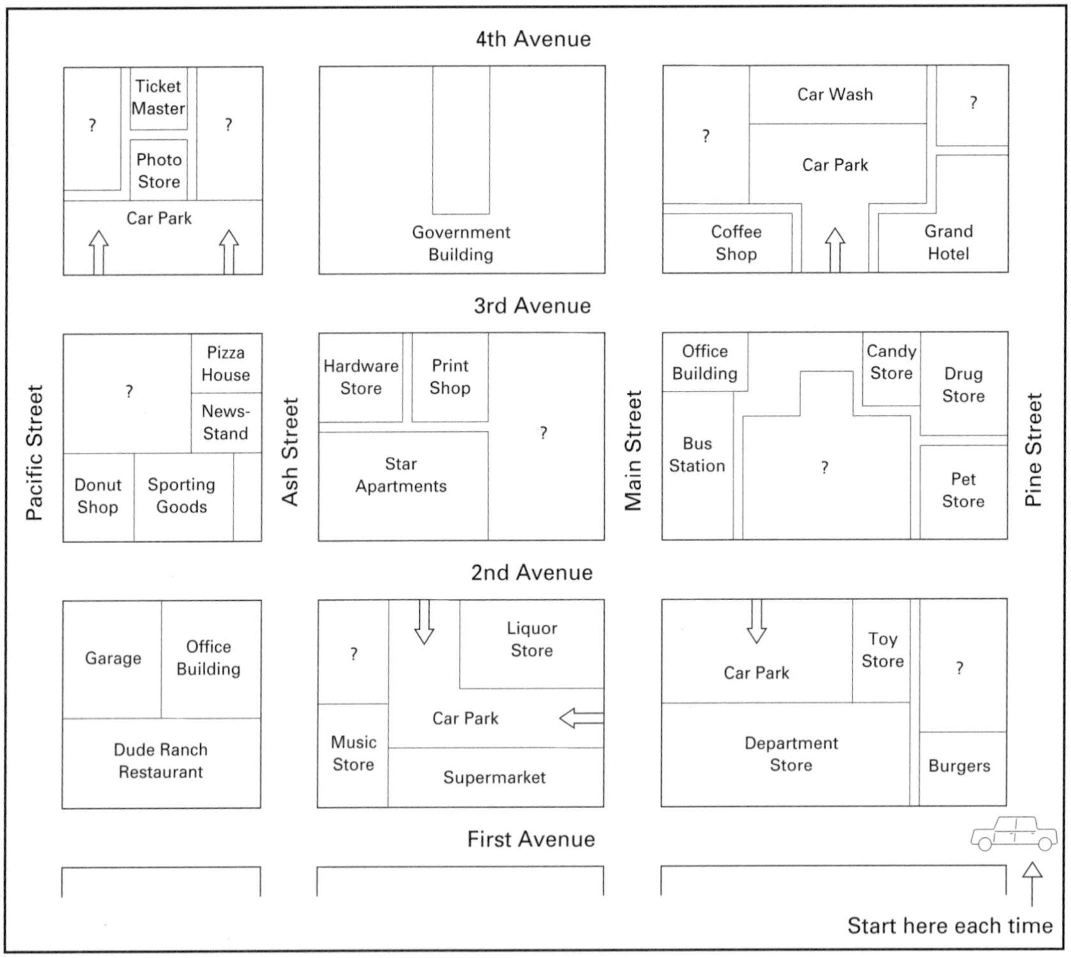

Where is . . . ?

the bank	the laundromat	the public library
the post office	the gas station	the movie theater
the Chinese restaurant	the bakery	Trinity College

Chapter 3 Part 1, page 49

8 **Review of Idioms.** The following box contains statements using the idioms from this section. Read an item from your box. Student B will select the appropriate response from his or her box.

Student A

1. You look worried. What's wrong?
2. I can't make ends meet on $600 a month. I need more money!
3. My father won't give me any more money this month.
4. What's the secret to living on a budget?
5. Why didn't you go to the concert?

Chapter 3 Part 3, page 58

5 **Pair Practice with Teens and Tens.**

Student A

1. Your partner will read some sentences with numbers to you. Circle the numbers you hear.

1.	13	30
2.	115	150
3.	$14.05	$40.05
4.	$16.60	$60.60
5.	1919	1990
6.	7040	7014
7.	1.14	1.40

2. Now read the following sentences to your partner.
    1. I pay $70 a month for parking.
    2. She is 160 centimeters tall.
    3. The president's house has 19 rooms.
    4. She paid $50.50 for a haircut.
    5. Her family has lived here since 1830.
    6. Please deliver the package to 1670 Loyola Street.
    7. That cookie contains only 114 calories.

Chapter 4 Part 1, page 71

7 **Vocabulary Review.** The following box contains statements using the new vocabulary from this section. Read an item from your box. Student B will select the appropriate response from his or her box.

Student A

1. How was your trip to New York last December?
2. What on earth happened to your arm?
3. Do you want to go to the beach this afternoon?
4. I heard your mother got a full-time job.
5. What's your brother doing these days?

Chapter 4 Part 3, page 83

4 **Asking and Answering Affirmative Tag Questions.** Use the statements in the box to make affirmative tag questions. Decide if the intonation should rise or fall. Then ask your partner the questions.

Student A

1. You're from _____________ (name of country, city, or area) . . . , *aren't you?*
2. Last night's homework was _____________ (hard, easy, boring, confusing, etc.) . . .
3. This _____________ (book, pen, etc.) is yours . . .
4. It's _____________ (cold, hot, pleasant) today . . .
5. Our next test is _____________ (day or date) . . .
6. This classroom is _____________ (comfortable, too small, etc.) . . .

Chapter 5 Part 1, pages 94 and 95

6 **Vocabulary Review.** The following box contains statements using the new vocabulary from this section. Read an item from your box. Student B will select the appropriate response from his or her box.

Student A

1. It's 3 o'clock in the morning! Why aren't you sleeping?
2. Are you leaving?
3. Wake up, Sally. It's 7 A.M.
4. Hello? Is anybody home?
5. Who takes care of your kids while you're working?
6. What's wrong with this light? It's not working properly.
7. How's the baby doing?
8. Why did George quit his job?

7 **Asking for a Favor.** Read the situations in the following box and ask your partner for help or for a favor. Your partner must give an appropriate response.

Example

It's Thursday. Your library books are due tomorrow. Ask your partner to return the books to the library for you.

A: My library books are due tomorrow. Could you please return them to the library for me?

B: I'm sorry, but I'm not going there today.

Student A

1. Your arms are full of books. Ask your partner to open the door for you.
2. It's raining and you don't have a car. Ask your partner to drive you home after class.
3. You're trying to concentrate. Ask your partner to speak on the phone more quietly.

Chapter 7 Part 1, page 140

6 **Vocabulary Review.** The following box contains statements using the new vocabulary from this section. Read an item from your box. Student B will select the appropriate response from his or her box.

Student A

1. Do you understand tonight's homework assignment?
2. You look really stressed out.
3. I have an appointment with Dr. Brown at 3 P.M.
4. Jerry is a two-faced liar. He told my girlfriend I was seeing another woman!
5. I like Claudette. She's very friendly.
6. I've known my best friend since we were three years old.
7. I've told John six times that I don't want to go out with him, but he keeps asking me.
8. Why is it so hard to make friends with Americans?

Chapter 7 Part 3, page 148

3 **Using Interjections.** Work in pairs to practice using interjections.

Student A

1. Say the following sentences to your partner and wait for a response.
    1. Did you understand last night's homework?
    2. Oops! I forgot my listening book at home.
    3. Ouch! My leg!
    4. The teacher looks really annoyed.
2. Now listen to your partner and choose the proper response from the following list.
    a. Huh? Could you repeat that?
    b. Uh-huh. Let's go home before it starts.
    c. Let's go see if it's still there.
    d. I'll pick it up.

Chapter 8 Part 1, page 158

6 **Vocabulary Review.** The following box contains statements using the new vocabulary from this section. Read an item from your box. Student B will select the appropriate response from his or her box.

Student A

1. What is this disgusting stuff?
2. Sally has a new boyfriend. She's crazy about him!
3. What do you think of action movies?
4. Did you have a good time last weekend?
5. Why did you break up with your girlfriend?
6. I don't care for this new chair you bought.

Chapter 10 Part 1, page 204

7 **Vocabulary Review.** The following box contains statements using the new vocabulary from this section. Read an item from your box. Student B will select the appropriate response from his or her box.

Student A

1. I think I saw a UFO last night![1]
2. My girlfriend broke up with me last night.
3. Do you know a good way to get rid of a sore throat?
4. I have a runny nose and a cough.
5. Do you think the number 13 is bad luck?
6. Were you out partying last night?
7. What's a folk remedy for a burn?
8. My grandmother says it's bad luck to give someone an umbrella as a gift.

[1] UFO = "unidentified flying object." This term refers to a vehicle used by visitors from outer space.

Chapter 10 Part 3, page 211

3 **Asking and Answering Negative Tag Questions.** Use the statements in the box to make negative tag questions with rising intonation (asking for information). Your partner should answer truthfully.

Example

You read:	You're not from France.
You ask:	You're not from France, are you?
Your partner answers:	Yes, I am (if he or she is from France). *or* No, I'm not (if he or she is not from France).

Student A

1. You don't smoke . . .
2. There's no homework tonight . . .
3. It isn't raining . . .
4. You don't have children (grandchildren, sisters, brothers) . . .

Chapter 11 Part 1, page 221

5 **Vocabulary Review.** The following box contains statements using the new vocabulary from this section. Read an item from your box. Student B will select the appropriate response from his or her box.

Student A

1. What's the matter? You look sad.
2. Do you believe in ghosts?
3. The show is about to start.
4. I don't see the point of this painting. What does it mean?
5. You had no right to take my book without my permission!
6. Hurry up! We're going to miss the bus!
7. Is the test finished?
8. We haven't heard from Joey in a month.
9. I hate my job! The stress is killing me!
10. If people want to smoke, that's their business. But no one should smoke around children.

Chapter 11 Part 3, page 228

5 **Pronouncing Noun/Verb Pairs in Context.**

Student A

1. Read these sentences to your partner; be careful to stress the underlined word correctly. Your partner will check your pronunciation.
   1. The school does not have a complete <u>record</u> of your grades.
   2. The company is going to <u>present</u> an award to Mr. Jackson.
   3. A <u>desert</u> is a place with very little water.
   4. The United States <u>exports</u> food all over the world.
   5. You will <u>insult</u> your hosts if you are late for dinner.
2. Now your partner will say some sentences. Check your partner's pronunciation of these words:
   1. próduce
   2. íncrease
   3. contrást
   4. pérmit
   5. impórt

Chapter 12 Part 1, page 238

7 **Vocabulary Review.** The following box contains statements using the new vocabulary from this section. Read an item from your box. Student B will select the appropriate response from his or her box.

Student A

1. My brother is a professional dancer.
2. Do you think it's going to rain tonight?
3. Why are you so uptight today?
4. Didn't you hit it off with your new boss?
5. Guess what! I got the job at the television station!
6. I'm really sorry, but I need to change our lunch appointment.
7. Your son has a good head on his shoulders.
8. I totally blew my history exam.

Pairwork Activities for Student B

Chapter 1 Part 4, page 21

5 **Reading Maps for Locations.** Ask your partner for the locations of the places listed under your map. Ask "Where is ________?" Your partner will use expressions of location. Then ask your partner to repeat the description. Write the name of the place on the map. When you are finished, your two maps should be the same.

Example

Student B: Where is the Undergraduate Library?

Student A: It's on Campus Road, up the street from the Administration Building.

Student B: Is it north or south of College Boulevard?

Student A: North.

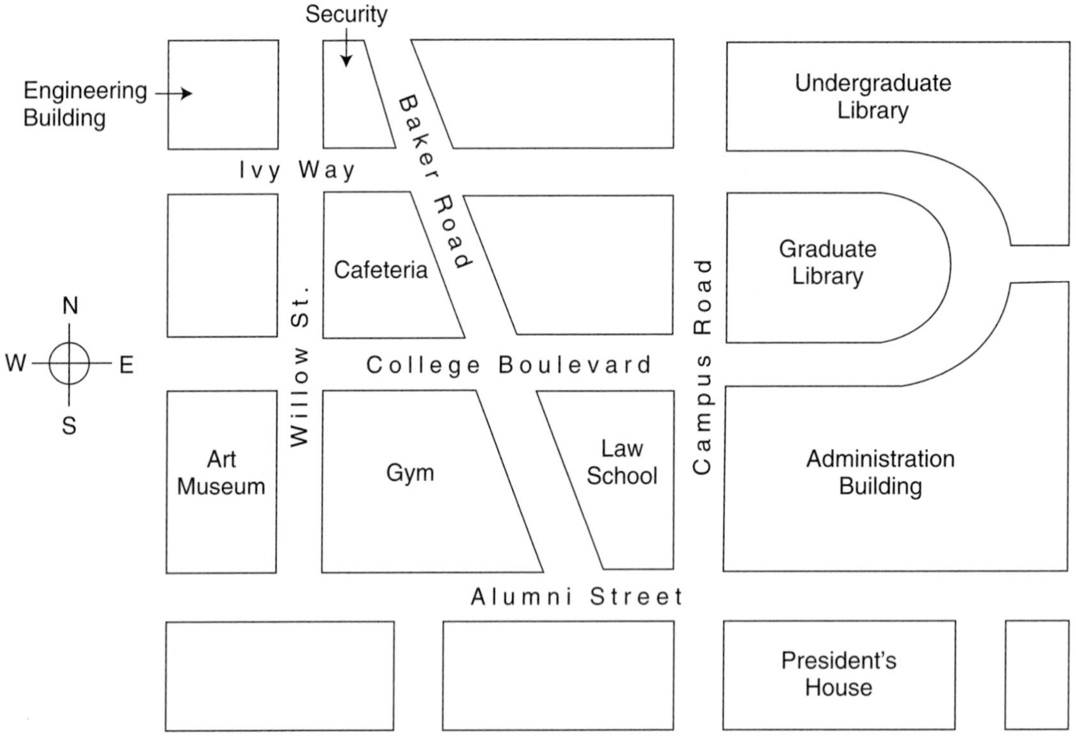

Music Building	Parking Lot	Bookstore
Graduate Dormitory	Vidal Hall	Language Lab

Chapter 2 Part 1, page 30

8 **Role-Play.** Role-play these phone conversations. Take turns playing Student A and Student B. Read the information for your role and be sure to use the expressions for opening and closing a phone conversation.

Student B

Situation 1

You live in a large house with your husband or wife and two children. You have an extra bedroom that you want to rent to a student. The room is furnished. It has a private phone and bath. The rent is only $300, but the student must agree to do ten hours a week of babysitting. Also, you have two large dogs, so the student cannot have any pets. You definitely do not want a smoker. A student calls and asks about the room.

Situation 2

You are a university student looking for a place to live. You saw the following ad in the campus housing office. You can afford to spend $900 a month on rent, and you don't have a car. Therefore, it's important for you to rent an apartment close to the college. Call the owner and get more information about the apartment. Decide if you want to see the place or not. If so, make an appointment with the manager.

> Beautiful 2br. 11/2 ba. apt.
> A/C, Stv/Frg, sec. 2 car garg.
> 555-3672

Chapter 2 Part 3, page 38

3 **Role-Play.** Role-play situations in an apartment building.

Student B

Situation 1

You are the manager of a large apartment building. You have one tenant who frequently complains about problems in his or her apartment. This takes up a lot of your time. Now the tenant calls you with a new complaint. You feel that this tenant should pay for the repairs because you think the tenant doesn't take good care of the apartment.

Situation 2

The neighbor above you plays loud music late at night. You wrote this neighbor a polite note about it, but the problem has not stopped. Now it is 12:30 A.M. and you cannot sleep because of the music. You are very frustrated. You go upstairs, knock on the neighbor's door, and tell the neighbor you want the problem to stop.

Chapter 2 Part 4, page 41

3 **Requesting and Giving Directions.** Look at the map. Ask your partner for directions to the places listed at the bottom of your map. When you find the place, write its name on your map. Then give your partner directions to the places that he or she asks about, from where it says, "Start here each time." At the end of this activity, your two maps should look the same.

Example

Student A: How do I get to the print shop?

Student B: That's easy. Go two blocks north on Maple Street. Turn left and go one block west on 8th Street. The print shop will be on your left, in the middle of the block, next to the hardware store.

Student A: Thanks!

MAP B

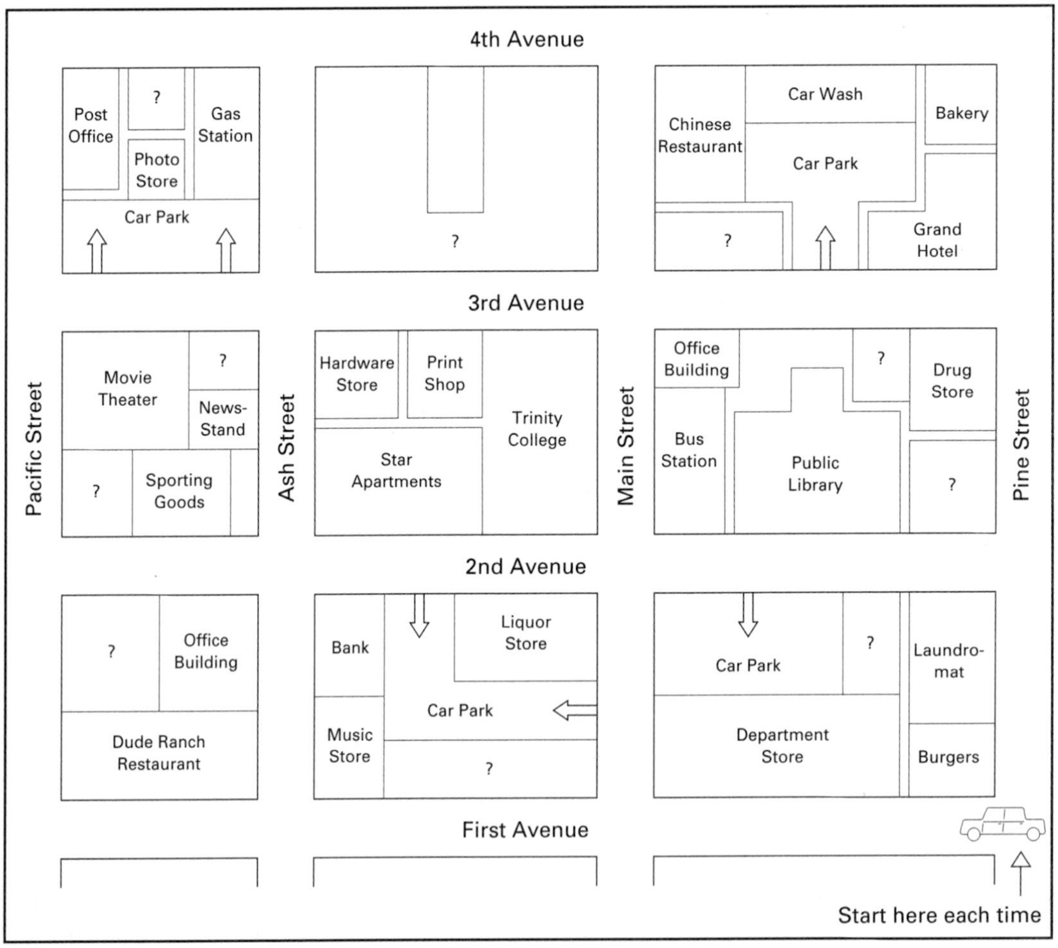

Where is . . . ?

the coffee shop	the pet store	the donut shop
the pizza house	the garage	the toy store
the government building	the supermarket	the candy store

Chapter 3 Part 1, page 49

8 **Review of Idioms.** The following box contains statements using the idioms from this section. Student A will read an item from his or her box. Select the appropriate response from your box.

Student B

a. Don't spend more than you earn.
b. Because the tickets cost an arm and a leg.
c. I'm broke again. I can't pay my rent.
d. Maybe you should get a part-time job.
e. My dad is a tightwad too.

Chapter 3 Part 3, page 58

5 **Pair Practice with Teens and Tens.**

Student B

1. Read the following sentences to your partner.
   1. I have only 30 cents in my wallet.
   2. She weighs 115 pounds.
   3. The sweater cost $40.05.
   4. Your change is $60.60.
   5. She was born in 1919.
   6. Our business office is at 7040 Adams Street.
   7. Today one U.S. dollar traded for 1.14 Euro.
2. Now listen as your partner reads sentences with numbers to you. Circle the numbers you hear.

1.	$17	$70
2.	160	116
3.	90	19
4.	$15.50	$50.50
5.	1813	1830
6.	1617	1670
7.	140	114

Chapter 4 Part 1, page 71

7 **Vocabulary Review.** The following box contains statements using the new vocabulary from this section. Student A will read an item from his or her box. Select the appropriate response from your box.

Student B

1. I fell down the stairs and broke it.
2. Yeah. She's supporting me while I finish my B.A.
3. It was the worst. It snowed for five days straight.
4. He spends all his time studying. I almost never see him.
5. No thanks. I'm not in the mood.

Chapter 4 Part 3, page 83

4 **Asking and Answering Affirmative Tag Questions.** Use the statements in the box to make affirmative tag questions. Decide if the intonation should rise or fall. Then ask your partner the questions.

Student B

1. You speak ____________ (language) . . . ,*don't you?*
2. ____________ (an actor or actress) is from England . . .
3. The verb tenses in English are difficult to understand . . .
4. The textbook for this class is (expensive, useful, etc.) . . .
5. The capital of Canada is Toronto* . . .
6. The ____________ (type of food) at ____________ (name of restaurant) is ____________ (delicious, terrible, etc.) . . .

* The capital of Canada is not Toronto; it's Ottawa.

Chapter 5 Part 1, pages 94 and 95

6 **Vocabulary Review.** The following box contains statements using the new vocabulary from this section. Student A will read an item from his or her box. Select the appropriate response from your box.

Student B

a. Yeah, come on in.
b. I have to finish this paper by 10 A.M. Time is running out.
c. I just checked up on her. She's sleeping.
d. I'm tired! I don't want to go to school today!
e. He decided to stay home for a couple of years and bring up his kids.
f. My mother.
g. Yes, it's getting dark. I'd better take off.
h. I know. I told the manager, and he's going to look into it.

7 **Asking for a Favor.** Read the situations in the following box and ask your partner for help or for a favor. Your partner must give an appropriate response.

Example

It's Thursday. Your library books are due tomorrow. Ask your partner to return the books to the library for you.

B: My library books are due tomorrow. Could you please return them to the library for me?

A: I'm sorry, but I'm not going there today.

Student B

1. Your partner speaks English very well. Ask your partner to read your composition and check the grammar.
2. Ask your partner to help you paint your bathroom on Saturday.
3. You need to move a heavy table. Ask your partner to help you.

Chapter 7 Part 1, page 140

6 **Vocabulary Review.** The following box contains statements using the new vocabulary from this section. Student A will read an item from his or her box. Select the appropriate response from your box.

Student B

a. It sounds like he's a little slow to catch on.
b. Please have a seat. The doctor is with another patient right now.
c. Really? You're lucky to have such a close friendship.
d. No, I'm in the dark too.
e. I am. It's really hard to study and have a job at the same time.
f. You have to be patient. Friendships don't happen overnight.
g. He did? I thought he was your best friend!
h. I agree. She's very nice.

Chapter 7 Part 3, page 148

3 **Using Interjections.** Work in pairs to practice using interjections.

Student B

1. Listen to your partner and choose the proper response from the following list.
   a. Oh-oh, I wonder what's wrong.
   b. What happened? Are you hurt?
   c. Uh-uh. The directions were too confusing.
   d. You can share mine.
2. Now say the following sentences to your partner and wait for a response.
   1. Do you think it's going to rain tonight?
   2. You need the past participle here, not the present.
   3. Oh-oh, I left my wallet in the restroom!
   4. Here's your dictionary . . . oops!

Chapter 8 Part 1, page 158

6 **Vocabulary Review.** The following box contains statements using the new vocabulary from this section. Student A will read an item from his or her box. Select the appropriate response from your box.

Student B

a. I can't stand them.
b. It's peanut butter. Don't you like it?
c. No. It rained all day Saturday and Sunday, so I stayed home.
d. Really? What's his name?
e. OK, I'll take it back to the store.
f. Because we didn't see eye to eye on anything.

Chapter 10 Part 1, page 204

7 **Vocabulary Review.** The following box contains statements using the new vocabulary from this section. Student A will read an item from his or her box. Select the appropriate response from your box.

Student B

a. No, I stayed home and watched TV.
b. Give me a break. I don't believe in aliens.
c. Rub butter on it.
d. The best way is to drink hot tea with honey.
e. Cheer up. I'm sure you'll meet someone new.
f. You'd better not go to school today.
g. Really? I wonder where she got that idea.
h. No, I think that's an old wives' tale.

Chapter 10 Part 3, page 211

3 **Asking and Answering Negative Tag Questions.** Use the statements in the box to make negative tag questions with rising intonation (asking for information). Your partner should answer truthfully.

Example

You read:	You're not from France.
You ask:	You're not from France, are you?
Your partner answers:	Yes, I am (if he or she is from France). *or* No, I'm not (if he or she is not from France).

Student B

1. You don't eat meat . . .
2. There's no test tomorrow . . .
3. You don't have a computer (cell phone) . . .
4. Milk isn't good for adults . . .

Chapter 11 Part 1, page 221

5 **Vocabulary Review.** The following box contains statements using the new vocabulary from this section. Student A will read an item from his or her box. Select the appropriate response from your box.

Student B

a. Hold on, I can't find my jacket.
b. No, I'm not superstitious.
c. You should take a vacation before you go off the deep end.
d. I don't know, but I think the colors are beautiful.
e. I'm just tired.
f. Don't worry. He'll call us sooner or later.
g. We'd better find our seats.
h. Yes. You're free to leave.
i. You've got a point there. Cigarette smoke is dangerous for children.
j. I'm sorry. I didn't think you'd mind. Next time I'll ask first.

Chapter 11 Part 3, page 228

5 **Pronouncing Noun/Verb Pairs in Context.**

Student B

1. Your partner will say some sentences. Check your partner's pronunciation of these words:
   1. récord
   2. presént
   3. désert
   4. expórt
   5. insúlt
2. Now read these sentences to your partner. Be careful to stress the underlined word correctly. Your partner will check your pronunciation.
   1. That store has the freshest <u>produce</u> in town.
   2. A large <u>increase</u> in a country's birthrate is called a baby boom.
   3. We should compare and <u>contrast</u> those two cars before we decide which one to buy.
   4. If you want to go fishing in this park, you need to get a <u>permit</u>.
   5. My father's company <u>imports</u> shoes from Italy.

Chapter 12 Part 1, page 238

7 **Vocabulary Review.** The following box contains statements using the new vocabulary from this section. Student A will read an item from his or her box. Select the appropriate response from your box.

Student B

a. Because I've got two final exams this afternoon.
b. That's too bad. Maybe the next test will be easier.
c. No big deal. What day is good for you?
d. I knew you'd be the most qualified person for the job. Break a leg!
e. Thank you. I hope he'll do well in college.
f. Really? It must be hard for him to make a living.
g. Not at all. I don't think she likes me.
h. It's a long shot. It doesn't rain in June very often.

Chapter 4 Part 2, page 79 On the Spot! Job Applicants

Read about your background and qualifications before the interview.

A. Applicants for Manager

1A. *Education*: High school graduate
Experience: Two years as the night manager at another supermarket
Skills: Well-organized; good communication skills with the workers

2A. *Education*: B.A. in management
Experience: Managed a fast-food restaurant in London for five years; good recommendations
Skills: None specifically related to managing a supermarket, but you're highly motivated and eager to learn

3A. *Education:* B.A. in chemistry
Experience: Four years managing another supermarket; you had some trouble communicating with the workers there
Skills: Have also worked as a checker, stock clerk, butcher, and truck driver

B. Applicants for Butcher

1B. *Education*: High school graduate and completed trade school for butchers
Experience: None
Skills: Know how to cut and prepare every kind of meat

2B. *Education*: High school graduate
Experience: Worked in parents' butcher shop during the summers since age 12
Skills: Know how to cut and prepare most kinds of meat

3B. *Education:* Master's degree in sociology
Experience: Worked as a butcher's helper at another supermarket for four years
Skills: Know how to cut and prepare most kinds of meat; speak three languages

C. Applicants for Stock Clerk

1C. *Education*: High school graduate
Experience: None
Skills: You are honest and willing to work hard; you need this first job in order to get experience

2C. *Education*: Tenth grade
Experience: Worked as a stock clerk in another supermarket; your work was good but sometimes you were late
Skills: Nothing special

3C. *Education:* High school graduate
Experience: Worked in an office for six months; excellent references
Skills: Can read and follow directions very well

D. Applicants for Checker

1D. *Education*: Eighth grade
Experience: Worked as a checker at another market for 15 years
Skills: Know how to operate cash register; polite and helpful

2D. *Education*: High school graduate
Experience: None in a supermarket
Skills: Learned how to operate cash register while working in a department store; received Employee of the Month award for outstanding customer service

3D. *Education:* B.A. in English
Experience: Worked at another market as a stock clerk and bagger* for four years
Skills: You don't know how to use a cash register yet, but you learn quickly

* This is the person who puts groceries in bags after the checkout clerk has entered the price in the cash register.

Answers

Chapter 5 Part 2 On the Spot!

"The Tokyo District Court . . . rejected the husband's demand for damages but did ask the woman to return her wedding rings and a cash gift of $8,000."

Chapter 7 Part 3

4 **Guessing Meanings of Slang Expressions.**

Slang Expressions	Meanings
1. freaked out	to become extremely upset
2. to shoot some hoops	play basketball
3. cheesy	tacky
4. goofy	silly
5. to lose it	to lose control, or lose one's temper
6. pig out	to overeat
7. blabbermouth	someone who talks too much and tells secrets
8. bummed out	discouraged, depressed
9. wiped out	exhausted
10. chickened out	to back out of something because of fear

Chapter 9 Part 1

5 **Vocabulary Review.**

1. c
2. a
3. c
4. b
5. b
6. c
7. d
8. d
9. b

8 **Identifying Ways to Introduce Surprising Information.**

1. Do you realize
2. Would you believe
3. You may be surprised to know
4. Believe it or not
5. Surprisingly

Chapter 9 Part 4

2 **Listening to a Game Show.**

1. a. Apple
2. a. Mt. Everest in Nepal
3. c. Italy
4. b. Leif Eriksson
5. c. China
6. a. penicillin
7. b. the telephone
8. c. Nicolaus Copernicus

Talk It Over

Correct order: C, G, B, F, A, D

Nobel Peace Prize Winners between 1970 and 2000

1970	Norman E. Borlaug (U.S.)
1971	Willy Brandt (West Germany)
1973	Henry A. Kissinger (U.S.); Le Duc Tho (North Vietnam)*
1974	Eisaku Sato (Japan); Sean MacBride (Ireland)
1975	Andrei D. Sakharov (U.S.S.R.)
1976	Mairead Corrigan and Betty Williams (both Northern Ireland)
1977	Amnesty International
1978	Menachem Begin (Israel) and Anwar el-Sadat (Egypt)
1979	Mother Teresa of Calcutta (India)
1980	Adolfo Pérez Esquivel (Argentina)
1981	Office of the United Nations High Commissioner for Refugees
1982	Alva Myrdal (Sweden) and Alfonso García Robles (Mexico)
1983	Lech Walesa (Poland)
1984	Bishop Desmond Tutu (South Africa)
1985	International Physicians for the Prevention of Nuclear War
1986	Elie Wiesel (U.S.)
1987	Oscar Arias Sánchez (Costa Rica)
1988	U.N. Peacekeeping Forces
1989	Dalai Lama (Tibet)
1990	Mikhail S. Gorbachev (U.S.S.R.)
1991	Aung San Suu Kyi (Burma)
1992	Rigoberta Menchú (Guatemala)
1993	F. W. de Klerk and Nelson Mandela (both South Africa)
1994	Yasir Arafat (Palestine), Shimon Peres, and Yitzhak Rabin (both Israel)
1995	Joseph Rotblat and Pugwash Conference on Science and World Affairs (U.K.)
1996	Carlos Filipe Ximenes Belo and José Ramos-Horta (East Timor)
1997	International Campaign to Ban Landmines and Jody Williams (U.S.)
1998	John Hume and David Trimble (Northern Ireland)
1999	Médecins Sans frontières (Doctors Without Borders; French-based global organization)
2000	Kim Dae Jung (South Korea)

* Le Duc Tho refused prize, charging that peace had not yet really been established in South Vietnam.

Sample Abbreviations and Symbols to Use in Taking Notes

Mathematical symbols to use in expressing relationships among ideas:

=	is like, equals, means (in defining a term)
	is unlike, not the same as
#	number
<	is smaller than
>	is larger than
+	plus, in addition, and

Other useful symbols:

&	and
%	percent
$	dollars
@	at
?	question, something unclear
~	approximately
↑	increase, go up
↓	decrease, go down
→	causes (as in A → B)
♂	male
♀	female
″	same as above (repeated or used again)
∴	therefore, as a result

Some common abbreviations:

a.m.	morning	w/o	without
p.m.	afternoon or evening	yr.	year
e.g.	for example	mo.	month
i.e.	that is, in other words	wk.	week
re:	concerning or regarding	no.	number
etc.	and so on	pd.	paid
vs.	versus	ft.	foot
ch.	chapter	lb.	pound
p., pp.	page, pages	cm	centimeter
w/	with	km	kilometer

Tapescript

Chapter 1 **Education and Student Life**

PART 1

Listening to Conversations

Listen

3 **Listening for Main Ideas.** page 3. Close your book as you listen to the conversation.

Listen for the answers to these questions.

Anna: Excuse me. Could you tell me where Kimbell Hall is?
Nancy: Oh, you mean Campbell Hall?
Anna: Oh yeah, right.
Nancy: Do you see that brown building over there?
Anna: Uh, behind the fountain?
Nancy: Yeah, that's it. Come on, I'm going there too. Are you here for the English placement test?
Anna: Yes, I am. How about you?
Nancy: Actually, I'm one of the English teachers here.
Anna: Oh really? Maybe I'll be in your class!
Nancy: It's possible. What's your name?
Anna: Anna Maria Cassini, but most people call me Anna. And you?
Nancy: I'm Nancy Anderson. So, where are you from?
Anna: From Italy.
Nancy: Aha. And, uh, how long have you been here?
Anna: Just three weeks.
Nancy: Really? Your English sounds great!
Anna: Thanks. That's because my family used to come here every summer when I was little. I can speak pretty well . . .
Nancy: Mmm - hmmm.
Anna: . . . but now I want to go to college here, so I need to improve my skills, especially grammar and writing. That's why I signed up for this English program.
Nancy: I see. Uh, what do you want to major in?
Anna: International business. My father has an import-export company, and he has a lot of business here. And I also want to take art classes, because I'm really into art.
Nancy: Can't you study those things in Italy?
Anna: Of course, but you have to speak good English these days to get ahead in business. It's better for my career if I go to college here.
Nancy: Well, here's Campbell Hall. Good luck on the placement exam. It was nice meeting you, Anna.
Anna: Thanks. You too.
Nancy: Bye now.
Anna: Bye bye.

Stress

4 Listening for Stressed Words. page 4.

1. Now listen to the conversation again. Some of the stressed words are missing. During each pause, repeat the phrase or sentence; then fill in the missing stressed words.

   See conversation.

Reductions

5 Comparing Long and Reduced Forms. page 6. The sentences on the left side are from the conversation. They contain reduced forms. Listen and repeat them after the speaker. Note: You will hear the reduced forms only.

See student text.

6 Listening for Reductions. page 6.

1. Listen to the following conversation between an international student and a school office assistant. You'll hear the reduced forms of some words. Write the long forms in the blanks.

   A: Could you help me, please? My name is Kenji Takamoto. I used to be a student in this school.
   B: Oh yeah, I remember you. How are you?
   A: Fine, thanks.
   B: Can I help you with something?
   A: Yes, I want to get an application for the TOEFL test.
   B: You mean the one in November? Let's see. They used to be here on this shelf. It looks like they're all gone. I'm sorry, you'll have to wait until they come in next week.
   A: How about sending me one when they come in?
   B: No problem. What's your name and address?

PART 2 Listening to Lectures

Listen

3 Note-Taking Pretest. page 9.

1. Listen to the lecture and take notes in any way you can. Don't worry about doing it the "right" way this first time; just do your best. Use your own paper.

Introduction

Good morning, everyone. My name is Richard Baldwin, and I am the academic advisor here at the English Language Center. If you have any questions about applying to a university, or if you need help with your application, you can come see me in my office.

OK. This morning I want to give you a general introduction to the university system in the United States and Canada. First, I'm going to tell you about three types of university courses . . . three types of university courses. And then my second main topic is course requirements . . . course requirements, which means what you have to *do* in order to pass the course. So I'll talk about those two topics and then you'll have time to ask questions before we take a break. OK?

Part 1

All right, as I said, first I want to tell you about three types of university courses. And I should explain that I'm talking about undergraduate courses now, because the system is different at the graduate level. The most common type of undergraduate course is called a lecture course. Got that? A lecture course. In a lecture course, the professor talks and the students sit and take notes. This is very important . . . I mean it's essential to take notes because the information in a lecture is not the same as the information in your books, and you can expect to have questions on your exams that are based on the lectures. So it isn't enough to just read your textbooks, like it is in some countries; here you have to attend lectures, and during the lecture you can't just sit there and listen, you have to take notes. Then later you use the notes to study for your exams. Is that clear?

Now, as an undergraduate in almost any field or major you'll probably spend four to six hours a week attending lectures. That's four to six hours for each lecture course, all right? And the last thing about lecture courses is that they're often held in very large rooms because undergraduate courses like Introduction to Psychology can have two or three hundred students in them, especially at large universities.

All right. I just told you that a lecture course can have as many as three hundred students in it. And there's no way that one professor can meet with that many students. So, for every lecture course you're taking, you'll also have a second kind of class, which is called a discussion section. This class is smaller, maybe 20 or 30 students, and it meets two or three hours a week. Your discussion section is the place where you can ask questions about the lectures and the readings and go over homework. However, discussion sections are not taught by professors. At large universities they're taught by graduate students called teaching assistants, or TAs.

So far I've told you about lecture courses and discussion sections. The third kind of class I want to mention is especially important for science majors; it's called a lab class. "Lab" is short for laboratory. If your major is chemistry or physics or any other kind of science, you'll have to spend several hours a week in the lab. This is where you do your experiments.

Part 2

Let's move on now to the second major topic I mentioned, which is course requirements. As I told you, "course requirements" means the things you have to do or finish in order to pass a course. First, nearly every class you take will have one or more tests, or exams. Most university courses have at least two big exams: one in the middle of the course, called a midterm, and another big one at the end, called the final exam. You might also have smaller tests from time to time. A small test is called a quiz.

In addition, in many courses you might also have to do something called a term paper or research paper, so let me tell you a little about that. A term paper is a large report that has several steps. First, you choose a topic related to the course. Then you do research on this topic, either in a library or on the Internet. "Do research" means that you read and take notes on the topic. And finally, you use your notes to write a paper in your own words. A research paper can be anything from 5 pages to 25 pages long.

Now, this is a good place for me to introduce you to something called plagiarism. Plagiarism is a serious problem at American universities. First, let me spell it for you; it's P-L-A-G-I-A-R-I-S-M. OK, what is plagiarism? Well, I just said that when you write a term paper, it has to be in your own words. That means you can't copy your paper or even small parts of your paper from another student or a book or the Internet. If you do, if you copy, that's plagiarism. Plagiarism is cheating, and it's absolutely forbidden. If you plagiarize and get caught, the punishment can be very serious. You can fail the course or even get kicked out of the university. As I said, this is a very serious thing and you need to be very careful about it.

OK; does anyone have questions at this point about types of university courses, about course requirements, or about plagiarism? No? Then let's stop here and take a break.

4 **Taking Notes on the Introduction.** page 10. Listen to the lecture introduction again and fill in the blanks.

See Introduction.

5 **Identifying the Three Keys to Writing Effective Lecture Notes.** page 11. Below are sample notes for the first part of the lecture. Look at the notes as you listen again. Notice how the writer used indentation, key words, abbreviations, and symbols.

See Part 1.

6 **Indenting.** page 12. Below are notes for the second part of the lecture. However, the information is not indented correctly. Read the notes as you listen again. Then copy the notes on clean paper with three levels of indentation. Use the notes from Activity 5 as a model.

See Part 2.

PART 3

Focused Listening and Speaking

Getting Meaning from Context

1 **Using Context Clues.** page 15. The following conversations take place on a college campus.

Conversation 1

A: What's wrong?
B: Well, I've got a term paper due in a week, and all the books I need are checked out!
A: I know what you mean. There are a million books in this place, and I can never find what I need.

Question 1: Where are the speakers?
B: Maybe I'll try the other library.

Conversation 2

A: Can I come see you tomorrow?
B: Sure, what's the problem?
A: I am totally confused about this week's chemistry experiment.
B: Didn't you come to the lab yesterday?
A: Yeah, but I had to leave early and I missed part of your demonstration.

Question 2: Who is the student probably talking to?
B: OK, can you come to the TA's office tomorrow at twelve?

Conversation 3

A: What are the requirements for the course?
B: There'll be a quiz every Monday and a final exam. Also, you're required to go to the language lab two hours each week. And of course your attendance and class participation are very important.

Question 3: What class is this?
B: And one more thing. Each student is required to give a short speech in German.

Focused Listening

2 **Listening for Intonation.** page 16. In the items that follow, you will hear the same conversation spoken in two ways. Use the differences in intonation and tone to decide what the speakers are feeling.

Conversation 1A

Kathy: Hello?
Ron: Kathy? Uh, this is Ron, you know, from your history class?
Kathy: Oh, hi!
Ron: Listen, I was wondering . . . um, were you planning to go to Ali's party Saturday?
Kathy: Hmm. I haven't really thought about it yet.
Ron: Well, would you like to go?
Kathy: You mean, with you?
Ron: Yeah.

Question 1: How does the woman feel about the invitation?
Kathy: Well sure, Ron, I'd love to go.

Conversation 1B

Kathy: Hello?
Ron: Kathy? Uh, this is Ron, you know, from your history class?
Kathy: Oh, hi.
Ron: Listen, I was wondering . . . um, were you planning to go to Ali's party Saturday?
Kathy: Hmm. I haven't really thought about it yet.
Ron: Well, would you like to go?
Kathy: You mean, with you?
Ron: Yeah.

Question 2: How does the woman feel about the invitation?
Kathy: Well thanks, Ron, but I just remembered that I'm busy that night.

Conversation 2A

A: Did you hear the news? Professor Bradley had to go out of town suddenly. All his classes are cancelled this week.
B: Cancelled? Oh wow.

Question 3: How do the students feel about the situation?
A: I'm really worried about my score on the last test. Now I'll have to wait until next week to find out.

Conversation 2B

A: Did you hear the news? Professor Bradley had to go out of town suddenly. All his classes are cancelled this week.
B: Cancelled? Oh wow!

Question 4: How do the students feel about the situation?
A: I'm so happy! Now I'll have an extra week to work on my term paper.

PART 4

Listening and Speaking in the Real World

Listen

2 **Pronouncing Expressions of Location.** page 19.

1. Below are expressions for describing locations. Listen and repeat each expression after the speaker. Pay attention to stressed words.
   See student text.

3 **Understanding Expressions of Location in Context.** page 20. Study this map of a college campus. Read the names of the buildings and streets. Then listen to statements about the map. Write T if a statement is true and F if it is false, based on the map. You will hear each statement twice.

1. The Math Building is down the street from Memorial Cafeteria.
2. The Computer Science building is across the street from the theater.
3. The Business Hall is at the intersection of Campus Road and Jones Street.
4. Memorial Cafeteria is in the middle of the block on Bridge Road.
5. There is a park beside the Math Building.
6. The boathouse is between Lakeshore Drive and College Lake.
7. There are buildings on both sides of Bradford Avenue.
8. Smith Library is opposite the Science Hall.

Chapter 2 City Life

PART 1

Listening to Conversations

Listen

3 **Listening for Main Ideas.** page 25. Close your book as you listen to the conversation.

Listen for the answers to these questions.

Nancy: Hello?
Anna: May I speak to Nancy, please?
Nancy: Speaking.
Anna: Uh hi, uh, my name is Anna, and I'm calling about the room for rent. I saw your ad at the campus housing office.
Nancy: Oh, right. OK, uh, are you a student?
Anna: Well, right now I'm just studying English, but I'm planning to start college full-time in March.
Nancy: I see. Where are you living now?
Anna: I've been living in a house with some other students, but I don't like it there.
Nancy: Why? What's the problem?

Anna: Well, first of all, it's really noisy, and it's not very clean. The other people in the house are real slobs. I mean they never lift a finger to clean up after themselves. It really bugs me! I need a place that's cleaner and more private.

Nancy: Well, it's really quiet here. We're not home very much.

Anna: What do you do?

Nancy: I teach English at the college.

Anna: Wait a minute! Didn't we meet yesterday at the placement exam?

Nancy: Oh . . . you're the girl from Italy! What was your name again?

Anna: Anna Maria.

Nancy: Right. What a small world!

Anna: It really is. By the way, who's Jeff? His name is also in the ad.

Nancy: He's my cousin. He's a musician, but he's also taking classes in computer programming. How do you feel about having a male roommate?

Anna: Well, okay, I guess, as long as he's clean and not too noisy.

Nancy: Don't worry. He's really easy to live with.

Anna: OK. Um, is the neighborhood safe?

Nancy: Oh sure. We haven't had any problems, and you can walk to school from here.

Anna: Well, it sounds really nice. When can I come by and see it?

Nancy: Can you make it this evening around five? Then you can meet Jeff too.

Anna: Yeah, 5 o'clock is good. What's the address?

Nancy: It's 3475 Hayworth Avenue. Do you know where that is?

Anna: No, I don't.

Nancy: OK. From University Village you go seven blocks east on Olympic Avenue. At the intersection of Olympic and Alfred there's a stoplight. Turn left, and go up one and a half blocks. Our house is in the middle of the block on the left.

Anna: That sounds easy.

Nancy: Yeah, you can't miss it. Listen, I've got to go. Someone's at the door. See you this evening.

Anna: OK, see you later. Bye.

Nancy: Bye bye.

Stress

4 Listening for Stressed Words. page 26.

1. Now listen to the conversation again. Some of the stressed words are missing. During each pause, repeat the phrase or sentence; then fill in the missing stressed words.
   See conversation.

Reductions

5 Comparing Long and Reduced Forms. page 28. The sentences on the left side are from the conversation. They contain reduced forms. Listen and repeat them after the speaker. Note: You will hear the reduced forms only.

See student text.

6 Listening for Reductions. page 28.

1. Listen to the following conversations. They contain reduced forms. Write the long forms in the blanks.

Conversation 1

Anna: Hey Jeff, where are you going?
Jeff: I want to get a present for Nancy. It's her birthday, you know.
Anna: Yeah, I know. What do you think I should get her?
Jeff: Well, she likes music. How about a CD?

Conversation 2

Nancy: How do you like my new haircut, Anna?
Anna: It's great! Who's your hairstylist?
Nancy: His name's Jose.
Anna: Can you give me his phone number?
Nancy: Sure, but he's always very busy. You can try calling him, but he might not be able to see you until next month.

Conversation 3

Jeff: What do you want to do tonight, Nancy?
Nancy: Nothing special. I've got to stay home and correct my students' compositions.

PART 2

Listening to Lectures

Listen

4 Taking Notes on Statistics. page 33. Listen to sentences from the lecture. Use the abbreviations and symbols from the chart to take notes. You will hear each sentence twice.

1. A year ago there were 54 burglaries in your area; this year it's gone up to 70.
2. The number of car thefts has almost doubled, too.
3. Did you know that in half of all burglaries, 50%, the burglars enter through unlocked doors or windows?

5 Listening for Transitions. page 33.

1. Below is a list of transitions from the lecture. Listen to the lecture. When you hear each transition, write the topic or suggestion that follows it.

Police Officer: Good evening. My name is Officer Michaels, and I'm happy to be here tonight. As you all know, last week someone broke into the Johnsons' house in the middle of the afternoon and took just about everything: uh, stereo, TV, silver, jewelry, money, everything. Now, it's true that there's been very little *violent* crime in your neighborhood, especially compared to other parts of the city. But burglary and car theft are both up in this area. Let me give you some statistics. A year ago there were 54 burglaries in your area; this year it's gone up to 70. Not only that, but the number of car thefts has almost doubled, too. Now, I'm not here to try to scare you. I came here tonight to give you some simple suggestions that will make it harder for burglars to break in to your homes. So let's get started.

First of all, let's talk about lights outside your house. You need to have lights both in the front of your house and in the back. That's because lots of times criminals jump over the back fence and enter your house through the back door. So be sure to turn on your outside lights at night—not just the porch light but also the backyard lights. This is the most important thing you can do to prevent burglaries.

Next, let's talk about lights inside the house. It's a really good idea to put automatic timers on lights; do you know what a timer is? It's like a clock that turns on your lights automatically, so it will look like someone is home even if you're out for the evening.

Woman in Audience: Excuse me, what about apartments? I mean, I live in an apartment building . . .

Police Officer: Good question. If you live in an apartment building, make sure there is good, bright lighting in the garage and hallways. You should report broken lights to your manager immediately. And what I said about automatic timers is also true for apartments. Make it look like you're home even if you're not. OK?

Well, I think I've finished talking about lighting. The next big topic I want to cover is locks. First of all, cheap locks on doors are not safe. Every door in your house should have a deadbolt at least one inch thick. Do you understand what I mean? A deadbolt lock? In addition, there are special locks you can buy for your windows, you know, locks that you can only open with a key. This is especially important if you live on the first floor. I know, I know, it's not very convenient, but believe me, a burglar is going to have a very hard time coming in through a window like that. By the way, that's how they broke into the Johnsons' house—through a window. Did you know that in half of all burglaries, 50 percent, the burglars enter through unlocked doors or windows? I'm telling you, even in a peaceful neighborhood like this, where you know all your neighbors, you have to get into the habit of keeping your windows and doors locked. Are there any questions about that?

Okay, my next suggestions are about valuables like jewelry, silver, and of course, money. First: Do not keep expensive jewelry or large amounts of cash in the house. Put them in the bank where they'll be safe. Second: Mark your big things like televisions, stereos, and expensive cameras with some kind of identification. For example, put your driver's license or passport number on these things so that later the police can identify them and return them to you. That is, if we're lucky enough to find them.

My last piece of advice on what you can do to prevent crime is to form a Neighborhood Watch group, just like you're doing here. As members of Neighborhood Watch, you can do a number of things to help each other. The main thing is that when you go on vacation, ask someone to watch your house for you, to collect your mail, take in your newspaper, stuff like that. Also, if you see something unusual, like a strange van or truck in your neighbor's driveway, or people carrying furniture out, *don't* go out there and try to stop it. Just call the police! And one more thing. Each of you should put this Neighborhood Watch decal—this picture right here of the man in a coat looking over his shoulder—in your front window. This tells criminals that this area has a Neighborhood Watch and that someone might be watching them. OK, are there any questions?

Man in Audience: Yeah, there's something I want to know . . . Do you think it's a good idea to keep a gun in the house?

Police Officer: Well now, that is a very complicated question. I honestly think it's a bad idea to have a gun in your house, especially if you have kids. Thousands of people die in gun accidents each year in this country. In my opinion it is just not worth the risk to have a gun in your house. But of course it is your legal right, if that's what you want. Just make sure you get the proper license and that you take a course in the correct way to use a gun and take care of it. Anything else?

PART 3 Focused Listening and Speaking

Getting Meaning from Context

1 **Using Context Clues.** page 36. The following conversations take place in an apartment building.

Questions 1 through 3 are based on a conversation between a man and a woman.

Manager: Yes? Who is it?
Tenant: It's Donna from 206. I've got a check for you.
Manager: Oh, it's you. Do you know it's the fifth of the month?
Tenant: Yes Mr. Bradley, I'm sorry, I know it was due on the first, but my grandma got sick and I had to go out of town suddenly.

Question 1: Who is the man?

Manager: Look, my job as manager here is to collect the rent on the first. If you're late again next month you'll have to look for another place to live.
Tenant: OK, Mr. Bradley. But look, while I'm here, I need to talk to you about a couple of things.
Manager: Yeah?
Tenant: First, about the cockroaches. They're all over the kitchen again. I'm sick of them!
Manager: Have you used the spray I gave you?
Tenant: It's no good. I need something stronger to kill those horrible bugs once and for all.

Question 2: Who will the manager probably need to call?

Manager: OK, I'll call the exterminator next week.
Tenant: Next week?! Last week you said you'd fix the hole in the ceiling, and you still haven't done that! I'm fed up with waiting for you to fix things around here!

Question 3: What can you guess about Donna's apartment?

Tenant: Why should I pay so much rent for a place in such bad condition?
Manager: Well, you're not the only tenant in this building. If you don't like it, why don't you move out?

Questions 4 and 5 are based on a conversation between two neighbors.

John: Hi, Donna. What do you need this time?
Donna: Hello, John. A couple of eggs. Do you mind?
John: No, come on in.

Question 4: How does John feel about Donna's request?

Donna: Thanks so much, John!
John: You're welcome!

John: Hi, Donna. What do you need this time?
Donna: Hello, John. A couple of eggs. Do you mind?
John: No, come on in.

Question 5: How does John feel about Donna's request?

Donna: Thanks, John.
John: OK, but next time go ask somebody else, all right?

PART 4

Listening and Speaking in the Real World

Listen

2 **Following Directions.** page 40. You will hear directions based on the map. At the end of each item you will hear a question. Write the answer to the question in the spaces. You will hear each item twice.

1. You are at the X. Go two blocks west on 2nd Avenue. Turn left and go down one block. What is on your left?
2. You are at the intersection of Main Street and Third Avenue. Go one block south on Main. Turn left. Go straight for half a block. What is on your left?
3. You have just eaten dinner at the French restaurant at the intersection of 4th and Pine. Go south on Pine Street to 2nd Avenue. Turn right. Go one block west on 2nd. Turn left. Go down Main Street for half a block. What is on your right?
4. You work in the office building at the intersection of 3rd and Main. After work you decide to go shopping. Go one block east on 3rd. Turn left and go one block up Pine Street. Turn right. Go one block east until you reach Oak Street. What is on your right?

Chapter 3 Business and Money

PART 1 Listening to Conversations

Listen

3 **Listening for Main Ideas.** page 45. Close your book as you listen to the conversation.

Listen for the answers to these questions.

Dad: Hello?
Jeff: Hi, Dad.
Dad: Hello, Jeff. How are you?
Jeff: I'm fine, Dad. How's Mom? Did she get over her cold?
Dad: Yes, she's fine now. She went back to work yesterday.
Jeff: That's good. Um, Dad, I need to ask you something.
Dad: Sure, son, what is it?
Jeff: Well, uh, the truth is, I'm broke again. Could you lend me $200 until the end of the month?
Dad: Broke again? Jeff, when you moved in with Nancy, you said you could make ends meet. But this is the third time you've asked me for help!
Jeff: I know, I know, I'm sorry. But my old guitar broke, and I had to buy a new one. I can't play on a broken guitar, right?
Dad: Look Jeff, if you want to play in a band, that's OK with me, but you can't keep asking me to pay for it!
Jeff: OK, OK, you're right. But what do you think I ought to do? Everything costs an arm and a leg.
Dad: Well, first of all, I think you had better go on a budget. Make a list of all your income and all your expenses. And then it's simple. Don't spend more than you earn.
Jeff: But that's exactly the problem! My expenses are always larger than my income. That's why I need to borrow money from you.
Dad: Then maybe you should work more hours at the computer store.
Jeff: Dad! I already work 15 hours a week! How can I study and work and find time to play with my band?
Dad: Come on, Jeff, when I was your age . . .
Jeff: I know, I know. When you were my age you were already married and working and going to school . . .
Dad: That's right. And if I could do it, why can't you?
Jeff: Because I'm not you, Dad, that's why!
Dad: All right, Jeff, calm down. I don't expect you to be like me. But I can't lend you any more money. Your mother and I are on a budget too, you know.
Jeff: Maybe I should just drop out of school, work full-time, and play in the band in the evenings. I can go back to school later.
Dad: I wouldn't do that if I were you . . .
Jeff: Yeah, but you're not me, remember? It's my life!
Dad: All right, Jeff. Let's not argue. Why don't you think about this very carefully and call me back in a few days. And in the meantime, you'd better find a way to pay for that new guitar.

Jeff: Yes, Dad.
Dad: Good-bye, son.
Jeff: Bye.
Jeff: Tightwad . . .

Stress

4 **Listening for Stressed Words.** page 45.

1. Now listen to the conversation again. Some of the stressed words are missing. During each pause, repeat the phrase or sentence; then fill in the missing stressed words.
   See conversation.

Reductions

5 **Comparing Long and Reduced Forms.** page 48. The sentences on the left side are from the conversation. They contain reduced forms. Listen and repeat them after the speaker. Note: You will hear the reduced forms only.

See student text.

6 **Listening for Reductions.** page 48.

1. Listen to the following conversation between a bank teller and a customer. You'll hear reduced forms from Chapters 1, 2, and 3. Write the long forms in the blanks.

Customer: Hi, my name is Chang Lee.
Teller: How can I help you?
Customer: I want to check my balance.
Teller: OK. Can I have your account number, please?
Customer: 381335.
Teller: Your balance is $201.
Customer: OK. And I asked my father to wire me some money. I'd like to know if it's arrived.
Teller: I'm sorry, your account doesn't show any deposits.
Customer: Oh, no. I need to pay my rent tomorrow. What do you think I ought to do?
Teller: Well, the computer's a little slow today. Why don't you come in again tomorrow? Or you can call us. Here's the number.
Customer: OK, thanks.
Teller: You're welcome.

Pronunciation

9 **Pronouncing *Can* and *Can't*.** page 50. Listen and repeat the following pairs of sentences. Place an accent mark over the stressed words. The first one is done for you.

See student text.

10 **Distinguishing between *Can* and *Can't*.** page 50. Listen to the sentences. Decide if they are affirmative or negative. Circle *can* or *can't*.

1. Sue can pay her bills by herself.
2. Jeff can't work and study at the same time.
3. I can't find my checkbook.
4. You can pay with a credit card here.
5. You can't open an account without a social security number.
6. Anna can't work in the United States.
7. I can lend you five dollars.
8. We can't make ends meet.
9. You can apply for a loan at the bank across the street.
10. Jeff can play the guitar very well.

PART 2

Listening to Lectures

Listen

3 **Taking Draft Notes.** page 53. Listen to the lecture and take notes in the best way you can. Use your own paper.

Part 1

How many of you are familiar with the name Jeff Bezos? OK, how about Amazon.com? Have you heard of that? Well, Amazon.com is the world's first and largest Internet bookstore, and Jeff Bezos is the man who started Amazon.com back in 1995. Five years later, Amazon.com was serving millions of customers in 120 different countries. Amazing, right? And this is the reason why, in 1999, Jeff Bezos was selected as *Time* Magazine's Person of the Year, a very great honor.

Now, Jeff Bezos is actually not the topic of my lecture today, but he is a perfect example of my topic, which is entrepreneurs. That's entrepreneurs, spelled E-N-T-R-E-P-R-E-N-E-U-R-S. It's a French word meaning a person who starts a completely new business or industry, um, someone who does something no one else has done before, or who does it in a completely new way, like Jeff Bezos, who started the very first Internet bookstore. Entrepreneurs like Jeff Bezos are very highly respected in American society and, I think, in many other countries too. So in today's lecture I want to talk about three things. First, the characteristics of entrepreneurs, I mean, what kind of people they are. Second, the kind of background they come from. And third, the entrepreneurial process, that is, the steps entrepreneurs follow when they create a new business.

OK, let's begin by looking at the characteristics or, um, the qualities, of entrepreneurs. There are two qualities that I think all entrepreneurs have in common. First, entrepreneurs have vision. I mean that they have the ability to see opportunities that other people simply do not see. Let's look again at the example of Jeff Bezos. One day in 1994, he was surfing the Internet when suddenly he had a brilliant idea: why not use the Internet to sell products? Remember, at that time, no one was using the Internet in that way. After doing some research, Bezos decided that the product he wanted to sell was books. That's how Amazon.com got its start.

The other quality that I think all entrepreneurs possess is that they are not afraid to take risks. I mean they're not afraid to fail. As an example, let me tell you about Frederick Smith, who founded Federal Express, the company that delivers packages anywhere in the United States overnight. Smith first suggested the idea for his company in a college term paper. Do you know what grade he got on it? A "C"! But this didn't stop him, and today his company is worth more than two billion dollars and employs more than 25,000 people.

OK, we've just seen that all entrepreneurs have at least two important qualities in common. But now let's take a look at their backgrounds, and here we'll find lots of differences. First of all, some entrepreneurs are well educated, like Jeff Bezos, who graduated from Princeton University. But others, like Bill Gates, the founder of Microsoft Corporation, never even finished college. Next, some entrepreneurs come from rich families, like Fred Smith, the founder of Federal Express. In contrast, other entrepreneurs come from poor families. You may be interested to know, in addition, that many entrepreneurs are immigrants or the children of immigrants. A great example is Andrew Grove, the former chairman of the Intel computer company, who was born in Hungary and came to America as a refugee after World War II.

OK, the third difference is that although many entrepreneurs start their careers at a young age, lots of others don't get their start until age 40 or later. And finally, I think it's important to remind you that entrepreneurs are not always men. A famous woman entrepreneur, for example, is Debbi Fields, who founded the Mrs. Fields Cookie Company. You can find her shops in malls all over North America and Asia. So, to conclude this section, you can see that entrepreneurs come from many different backgrounds.

Part 2

I want to move on now and take a look at the entrepreneurial process. There are six basic steps that most entrepreneurs follow when they start their businesses. In the first step, they identify a problem; in other words, they see a need or a problem that no one else sees. Then, in the second step, they think of a solution, what needs to be done to solve the problem or meet the need. I think we've already seen several examples today of people who saw a need or an opportunity and then came up with a creative solution to the problem.

Step three is to prepare a business plan. A business plan. This means looking at things like equipment, location, financing, marketing, and so on. There are thousands of details to think about when you start a new business; as a result, this stage can take months or even years.

The next step, the fourth step, is putting together an entrepreneurial team; in other words, hiring the right people to work with the entrepreneur in the new business. After that, the fifth step is something called test marketing. That's test marketing. This involves making and selling a small amount of the product or service. And if customers like the product or service, then, finally, entrepreneurs go to the sixth step, which is raising capital. Now, in this case, capital does not mean a city, it means money. It's another word for money. The entrepreneur has to raise a lot of money in order to produce and sell the product or service in large quantities.

I want to say, in conclusion, that entrepreneurs like Jeff Bezos are among the most respected people in the United States. They are cultural heroes, like movie stars or sports heroes. Why? Because, starting with a dream and working very hard, these people created companies that solved serious, important problems. They provided jobs for millions of people, and in general their companies made life easier and more pleasant for all of us. If you ever order a book from Amazon.com, or eat a Mrs. Fields cookie, say thanks to the remarkable people who created these companies.

4 **Outlining the Lecture.** page 54. Here is a sample outline of the first part of the lecture. Use your notes from Activity 3 to fill in as much information as you can. Remember to use abbreviations and symbols and write key words only. Listen again if necessary.

See Part 1.

5 **Taking Notes on a Process.** page 55. Here is an outline of the second part of the lecture. Listen again and fill in the steps in the entrepreneurial process.

See Part 2.

PART 3

Focused Listening and Speaking

Getting Meaning from Context

2 **Using Context Clues.** page 57. You are going to hear some advertisements about banking services.

Advertisement 1

Every person has valuable possessions that are difficult or impossible to replace, for example, rare stamps, old coins, family photographs, jewelry, a passport, or insurance policies. You should protect these priceless valuables by putting them in a safe place. Lock up your treasures in International Bank's vault and you'll never have to worry about losing your valuables again.

Question 1: The speaker is talking about . . .

The International Bank Safety Deposit Box—safety and protection the easy way!

Advertisement 2

Right now International Bank can lend you money for dozens of projects. For instance, remodeling a kitchen or bathroom can change an old house into an exciting new one. Thinking about solar heating? Need a new roof? International Bank can help you finance them.

Question 2: The speaker is talking about . . .

For any home improvement loan, talk to International Bank first.

Advertisement 3

With an Insta-Teller Card from International Bank, you're close to your money night or day. The Insta-Tellers operate from 6:00 A.M. to midnight, seven days a week, 365 days a year. It's an easy way to get cash, pay your bills, make a deposit, or check your balance even when your bank is closed.

Question 3: The speaker is talking about . . .

Insta-Teller automated banking machines—any transaction, any time.

Advertisement 4

Man: That will be 70 dollars and 59 cents.
Woman: I'm sorry, did you say 17 or 70?
Man: 70.
Woman: Just a minute . . . (aside to husband) I can't find them!
Man: Well, I don't have them either!
Woman: Do you think we lost them? How are we going to pay?

Question 4: What can't the woman find?

Don't worry about losing your traveler's checks. International Bank has branches wherever you go.

Advertisement 5

How would you like to earn 8.5 percent interest and still be able to take out money any time you need it? You can do both with a deposit of $5,000 and a minimum average balance of $500. Come in and ask about our investor's plan.

Question 5: The speaker is talking about . . .

International Bank Investor's Plan—a savings account and more!

Focused Listening

3 **Pronouncing Teens and Tens.** page 58. Listen to the tape and repeat the pairs of numbers after the speaker.

See student text.

4 **Distinguishing between Teens and Tens.** page 58. Listen to the tape and circle the numbers you hear.

1. He paid $40.10 for the bottle of wine.
2. *Woman:* How much does this dictionary cost?
   Man: $16.99.
3. Most credit card companies charge 18 percent interest per month on your outstanding balance.
4. We drove at a speed of 90 miles per hour.
5. I bought my coat in Paris for 630 French francs.
6. The plane from Buenos Aires carried 260 passengers.
7. My dog weighs 14 and a half kilos.
8. The rent on this apartment is $2,215 a month.
9. My aunt lives at 1764 Wilson Avenue.
10. International Bank is located at 1890 West Second Street.

PART 4 Listening and Speaking in the Real World

Listen

3 **Balancing a Checkbook.** page 61. George and Martha Spendthrift have a joint checking account; that is, they share one checking account and both of them can write checks from it. Here is one page from their checkbook record. Listen as they try to balance their checkbook. Fill in the missing information.

George: Let's see here. Check number 200. October 25th. Did you write this check?
Martha: $30.21. Oh, yes. That was last Thursday. ABC Market.
George: Okay, so that leaves a balance of $490.31. Next: number 201. Electric bill. $57.82. So now we have $432.49. Next: October 27th. *Time* magazine. I forgot to enter the amount.
Martha: I remember that. It was $35.00.
George: Okay. So that leaves $397.49. Now what's this $70?
Martha: That was for your sister's birthday present.

George: Oh, yes. Well . . . And here's check 205. When did we pay the dentist?
Martha: The same day I deposited my paycheck. November 1st.
George: Fine. So after the deposit the balance was $1,397.18. And then I made the house payment, check number 206. That's $412, and the VISA payment—that's $155, so now our balance is $830.18.
Martha: You know, George, we should really pay off our VISA balance. The interest is 18% a year.
George: You're right. But we can't afford it right now. Look at this car insurance bill! $305 to Auto Insurance of America. And that's just for four months. And here's another traffic ticket!
Martha: Last month it was you, this month it was me.
George: Oh, well . . . How much was it?
Martha: $68. What's the balance now?
George: $457.18. I guess we're okay for the rest of the month as long as we don't get any more traffic tickets.

Chapter 4 Jobs and Professions

PART 1 Listening to Conversations

Listen

3 **Listening for Main Ideas.** page 67. Close your book as you listen to the conversation.

Listen for the answers to these questions.

Anna: Hey, Jeff, what's going on?
Jeff: Oh, I'm looking at the classified ads. It looks like I have to get a job.
Anna: I thought you had a job, at a computer store or something?
Jeff: Yeah, but that's part-time. I need something full-time.
Anna: Really? But what about school? What about your band? How can you work full-time?
Jeff: Well, to tell you the truth, I'm probably going to drop out of school for a while. I'm just not in the mood for studying these days. I'd rather spend my time playing with my band. But my father won't support me if I'm not in school.
Anna: I see . . . Well, what kind of job do you want to get?
Jeff: I don't really care. I've done lots of different things. I've been a waiter, a taxi driver, a house painter. And I'll never forget my first job; it was in a potato chip factory.
Anna: A potato chip factory? What on earth did you do there?
Jeff: Believe it or not, I was a potato chip inspector. My job was to take out the bad ones before they went into the bags.
Anna: That sounds like a pretty boring job!
Jeff: It was the worst. And I haven't eaten a single potato chip since I quit that job.
Nancy: Hi, what's so funny?
Jeff: Do you remember my job at the potato chip factory?
Nancy: Oh yeah. That was pretty awful. But actually, it doesn't sound so bad to me right now.

Anna: Why, Nancy? What's wrong?
Nancy: Oh, I don't know. Sometimes I think I've been teaching too long. Lately I haven't been as excited about my job as I used to be.
Anna: How long have you been teaching?
Nancy: Twelve years. Maybe it's time to try something else.
Anna: Like what?
Nancy: Well, I've always wanted to be a writer. I could . . .
Jeff: Oh, don't listen to her, Anna. She always talks this way when she's had a bad day at school. At least you have a job, Nancy. Look at me: I'm broke, and Dad won't lend me any more money . . .
Nancy: Oh, stop complaining. If you're so poor, why don't you go back to the potato chip factory?
Anna: Listen you two, stop arguing. Look at me! I can't work at all because I'm an international student.
Jeff: Okay, okay. I'm sorry, Nancy. Tell you what. Let's go out to dinner. I'll pay.
Nancy: But you're broke!
Jeff: All right, *you* pay!

Stress

4 Listening for Stressed Words. page 68.

1. Now listen to the conversation again. Some of the stressed words are missing. During each pause, repeat the phrase or sentence; then fill in the missing stressed words.
   See conversation.

Reductions

5 Comparing Long and Reduced Forms. page 70. The sentences on the left side are from the conversation. They contain reduced forms. Listen and repeat them after the speaker. Note: You will hear the reduced forms only.

See student text.

6 Listening for Reductions. page 70.

1. Listen to the following conversation. It contains reduced forms. Write the long forms in the blanks.

Manager: I'm going to ask you some questions, okay? What kind of jobs have you had?
Applicant: I've had lots of different jobs. I used to work in a plastics factory.
Manager: What did you do there?
Applicant: I used to cut sheets of plastic.
Manager: What do you want to do here?
Applicant: I don't know . . . I'll do anything . . . I'm broke, I have to make some money right away.
Manager: Well, it looks like we're going to have an opening next week. I'll call you.
Applicant: Thanks.

PART 2

Listening to Lectures

Listen

5 **Listening and Taking Notes on Causes and Effects.** page 75. Listen to cause-and-effect statements from the lecture and take notes. You will hear each statement twice.

1. The number of service jobs has increased because of technology.
2. The other reason why there are so many new service jobs is that the American population is changing.
3. Because people are living longer and longer, they need more medical services.
4. Since most married women now work outside the home, there's a much greater need for services such as restaurants and day-care centers.
5. Their salaries are low because they don't have much education or training.

6 **Taking Notes on Statistics.** page 75. The lecture contains many statistics about jobs. Go back to Chapter 2, page 32 and review the section titled Taking Notes on Statistics. Then listen to sentences from the lecture and take notes. You will hear each sentence twice.

1. The percentage of manufacturing jobs has gone down dramatically since the beginning of the 20th century.
2. One hundred years ago, 80% of workers worked in agriculture or manufacturing.
3. Within 20 years, nine out of ten workers in the United States will supply services and not products.
4. Between March 1998 and November 1999, a period of just 20 months, more than half a million U.S. manufacturing jobs were moved to Asia.
5. Thirty percent of the workers in the United States earn less than $8.00 an hour.

7 **Taking Draft Notes.** page 76. Listen to the lecture and take notes in the best way you can. Use your own paper. Listen specifically for the following information:

How has the U.S. job market changed?

Why?

What are some problems connected with today's job market?

Lecturer: If you will be graduating from high school or college in the next year or two, I know you are very concerned about your future. Probably the most important questions on your mind are these: Will you find a good job? and what should you do to make sure that you do? To help you answer these questions, first I am going to describe how the U.S. job market has changed in the last 100 years. After that I will tell you what you can do to prepare yourself for the job market today.

OK, now first of all, to begin, let's talk about the American job market and how it has changed. Without any question, the most important change in the 20th century was the shift, the, uh, change, from a manufacturing economy to a service economy. What do these two terms mean? It's very simple. A manufacturing economy is one that produces a large number of things, or products. People who produce things like cars, furniture, or clothing are working in a manufacturing economy. Have you got that? But on the other hand, a service economy is one in which most workers provide services, I mean that they *do* something instead of *making* something. Some examples of service workers include your doctor, your hairstylist, um . . .

airline pilots, salesclerks, and of course, everybody working in the computer industry. All the people who design and program and service computers, all of them, are part of the service economy.

So again, my point is that the United States has changed from a manufacturing economy to a service economy. You can see this clearly if you take a look at the graph on job restructuring. Let's look at those statistics. You can see that the percentage of manufacturing jobs has gone down dramatically since the beginning of the 20th century, and it will continue to decrease in the 21st century. And what about service jobs? At the same time that the percentage of manufacturing jobs has gone down, there has been a great increase in the percentage of service jobs. Basically, one hundred years ago, 80% of workers worked in agriculture or manufacturing; but today, as we start the 21st century, only about 20% do, while 80% provide services. And you can see that by the year 2020, the percentage of service workers will increase to 90%; in other words, within 20 years, nine out of ten workers in the United States will supply services and not products.

This brings me to my second main point: Why? I mean, what has caused this change in the U.S. economy? First of all, why has the number of manufacturing jobs decreased? Can anyone guess? Yes?

Student 1: Uh, robots? Robots replacing factory workers?

Lecturer: OK, good. Robots or in other words, automation. A lot of the work that our parents and grandparents used to do by hand is now done by machines like computers or computerized robots. Anything else besides automation? Another reason?

Student 2: I would say foreign competition. I mean, most manufacturing is now done outside of the U.S., in China, or Malaysia, you know, countries where the labor costs are cheaper.

Lecturer: That is exactly correct. Most manufacturing these days <u>is</u> being done outside the United States. To give you just one statistic, between March 1998 and November 1999, a period of just 20 months, more than half a million U.S. manufacturing jobs were moved to Asia. But on the other hand, what about service jobs? Why have those increased so much? Well, here again there are two basic causes. First, the number of service jobs has increased because of technology. Think about it. With all the new machines, well, someone has to sell them and install them and fix them when they break, right? None of those jobs existed 25 or 30 years ago.

And the other reason why there are so many new service jobs is that the American population is changing. The population is changing. For example, because people are living longer and longer, they need more medical services, right? So the fastest-growing jobs include things like nursing and home medical workers. Also, another example, since most married women now work outside the home, there's a much greater need for services such as restaurants and day-care centers. Yes?

Student 3: I read somewhere that service jobs in general don't pay very well. I mean, compared to factory jobs, you know, the hourly pay is pretty low.

Lecturer: Yes, that is true, and it is a big problem. Let me explain. You have to remember that there are many different kinds of service jobs. They include everything from a computer engineer earning $70,000 a year to a worker at a fast-food restaurant earning $6 or $7 an hour. Thirty percent—that's three zero percent—of the workers in the United States earn less than $8.00 an hour. Their salaries are low because they don't have much education or training. So low pay is a serious problem.

And there is one other serious problem with service jobs, and that is that a lot of service jobs don't provide benefits like health insurance, vacations, or a retirement plan. You have people working for $8.00 an hour and they don't even get medical insurance. That's the other big problem.

So in conclusion, what does all this mean for future job hunters like you? Well, take a look at the second graph. It lists 25 careers with the fastest growth rate, highest pay, and lowest unemployment in the years between 1996 and 2000. In other words, this is a list of 25 excellent jobs. And the main thing to keep in mind about them is this: of those 25 careers, 18 require at least a bachelor's degree. So, to put it simply: for the best job opportunities with the best pay, go to college. That's the bottom line.

PART 3 Focused Listening and Speaking

Getting Meaning from Context

2 **Using Context Clues.** page 81. The following conversations take place at work.

Conversation 1

Woman: May I see your driver's license, please?
Man: What did I do?
Woman: You ran a red light.
Man: But I'm sure it was yellow.

Question 1: What's the woman's job?
Woman: Are you trying to argue with a police officer?

Conversation 2

Woman: Is this your first visit?
Man: No, I have an appointment every week at this time.
Woman: Oh, I see. Did you bring your insurance form with you?
Man: Here it is.
Woman: The doctor will be with you shortly.

Question 2: What is the woman's job?
Man: You're new here, aren't you? What happened to the other receptionist?

Conversation 3

Man: Do you have a reservation?
Woman: Yes, Jackson, party of four.
Man: Inside or out on the patio?
Woman: Outside. And could we have some coffee right away?

Question 3: What's the man's job?
Man: I'm the host. I'll ask the waiter to bring you some right away.

Conversation 4

Man: I'm sorry, we're just not happy with these plans for the living room.
Woman: Why? You wanted a traditional look, didn't you?
Man: No, uh, really, we'd prefer something more modern.
Woman: Would you like me to draw up another set of blueprints?

Question 4: What's the woman's job?
Man: Actually, we've decided to hire another architect.

Conversation 5

Man: May I help you?
Woman: The sleeves on this jacket are too short. Can you make them longer?
Man: Let me look at it . . . I can do it for twenty dollars.
Woman: That much?

Question 5: What's the man's job?
Man: Well, that's cheap for a good tailor.

Focused Listening

3 **Recognizing the Intonation of Tag Questions.** page 82. Listen to these ten tag questions. Decide if they are "real" questions (if the speaker is really asking for information) or if the speaker is just "making conversation." Put an X in the correct column.

1. We're having a test tomorrow, aren't we?
2. You're the student from Turkey, aren't you?
3. This exercise is easy, isn't it?
4. The teacher is married, isn't she?
5. Smoking is forbidden here, isn't it?
6. That test was really hard, wasn't it?
7. The teacher speaks Arabic, doesn't he?
8. That television program was really boring, wasn't it?
9. Anna speaks beautiful English, doesn't she?
10. We need to write our names on our papers, don't we?

PART 4 Listening and Speaking in the Real World

Listen

4 **Sequencing Events.** page 85. Listen to the woman describe her day. Write numbers under the pictures to show the order in which each activity occurred. If two things happened at the same time, give them the same number. Pay attention to time words ("before," "after," "during," etc.) and verb tenses. (Note: Only *some* of her activities are shown in the pictures.) Then compare answers with a partner.

Do you want to know what I do on a typical day? Well, I'll tell you what I did yesterday as an example. I woke up before my husband and son, and the first thing I did was to come into the kitchen and make the coffee. Then I fixed my son's lunch, you know, to take to school, and after that I started cooking breakfast. I made eggs, oatmeal, and toast because I always want my family to start the day with a full stomach. Then my husband and son came into the kitchen and sat down to eat. While they were eating, I threw a basket of laundry into the washing machine and then I also sat down to eat.

After breakfast I walked my son to the bus stop, and I waited with him until the bus came. I kissed him good-bye and walked home. As soon as I entered the house, the phone rang. It was my mother-in-law. She wanted to know if my husband was still there, but I told her he had just left. So I talked with her for a few more minutes, about the weather and her garden, and then I got off the phone because I had to put the clothes in the dryer. After that, uh, let's see, I spent three hours cleaning the house, and after lunch I went shopping for groceries. By then it was 3 o'clock and it was already time to pick up my son at the bus stop. I helped him with his homework, and then my husband came home. Normally he gets home at about 6 P.M., but yesterday he was a few minutes early. I was so busy all day that I hadn't had time to water the garden, so he did it while I fixed dinner. Finally, after dinner my husband washed the dishes and I just collapsed in front of the TV.

And that was my day. Nothing glamorous—just really busy!

Chapter 5 Lifestyles Around the World

PART 1 Listening to Conversations

Listen

3 **Listening for Main Ideas.** page 91. Close your book as you listen to the conversation.

Listen for the answers to these questions.

Jeff: Who's there?
Margie: It's Margie and Joey!
Jeff: Hi! Come on in. What's happening?
Margie: Can you do me a big favor? I just got a call from the office. They're having a problem with the computer and they want me to look into it right away. Would you mind watching Joey until I get back?
Jeff: Sure, no problem. Is he asleep?
Margie: Yeah, he just fell asleep ten minutes ago. He usually sleeps for a couple of hours at this time of day. But if he wakes up, here's his bottle and some toys.
Anna: Ooh, what a cute baby! He's so little!
Jeff: Anna, this is our neighbor, Margie. And that's her son, Joey. Margie, this is our new roommate, Anna.
Anna: Nice to meet you.
Margie: You too. Listen, I've got to take off. Thanks so much, Jeff, for helping me out.
Jeff and Anna: Bye!
Anna: Hey, Jeff, I didn't know you liked babies.
Jeff: Well, Joey is special. I take care of him from time to time when Margie's busy. And then she does favors for me in return. Like last week she lent me her car, and sometimes she bakes cookies for me.
Anna: What does her husband do?
Jeff: She's not married. I don't think she ever was, actually.

Anna: Never?
Jeff: Nope, never. I think she's happy being a single mother.
Anna: Is that very common in the United States?
Jeff: Well, it's becoming more and more common. Even Nancy's been talking about it.
Nancy: Hi, you two. Uh, what have I been talking about?
Jeff: Having a baby.
Nancy: Oh yeah, I think about it. I sometimes feel like time is running out. What if I never get married?
Anna: Maybe I'm old-fashioned, but I could never bring up a baby by myself. I think it would be so difficult . . .
Nancy: Yeah, but don't forget, I wouldn't have to do it by myself. I have "Uncle Jeff" here to help with babysitting. Right, Jeff?
Jeff: We'll see. Speaking of babysitting, I'd better check up on Joey.

Stress

4 **Listening for Stressed Words.** page 92.

1. Listen to the following sentences from the conversation. They contain two- and three-word verbs. During each pause, repeat the sentence; then fill in the missing stressed words.
    1. Come on in.
    2. They're having a problem with the computer and they want me to look into it right away.
    3. If he wakes up, here's his bottle and some toys.
    4. Listen, I've got to take off.
    5. Thanks so much, Jeff, for helping me out.
    6. I take care of him from time to time when Margie's busy.
    7. I sometimes feel like time is running out.
    8. I could never bring up a baby by myself.
    9. I'd better check up on Joey.
2. Now listen to part of the conversation again. Some of the stressed words are missing. During each pause, repeat the phrase or sentence; then fill in the missing stressed words.

    See conversation.

Reductions

5 **Listening for Reductions.** page 94. Listen to the following sentences from the conversation. Repeat them after the speaker. Draw a slash (/) through any reduced */h/* sounds that are dropped.

See student text.

PART 2

Listening to Lectures

Listen

3 **Taking Notes on Examples.** page 98.

1. Women today are working in professions that were not as open to them 30 or 40 years ago. To give just one example, today more than half of the students in American medical schools are women.
2. This means that most American homes don't have a full-time homemaker anymore, and that creates new problems for families, such as who takes care of babies and old people; who shops, cooks, and cleans; who volunteers at the children's school; etc.
3. In some countries, companies are required by law to give new parents a paid vacation when they have a new baby. Canada, for instance, has a law like that, but the United States does not.

4 **Taking Draft Notes.** page 98.

Have you ever seen an old American television show from the 1950s? If you have, try to picture the typical family that appears in those shows. There's Father, who puts on a suit and goes to work every day. There's Mother, who takes care of the house and children. And there are usually two or three children, and maybe a dog. In those days that was considered to be a typical American family.

But today, the typical American family looks very different. Consider these statistics: in 1965, only 35% of American women worked outside the home. Ten years later, in 1975, it jumped to 55%. And today, close to 80% of American women work outside the home.

Why is that? Well, there are two important reasons why most American women now work. The first one, very simply, is that they need the money. These days the cost of living is so high that most families need two paychecks in order to make ends meet.

The other reason why women are working in larger and larger numbers is that they have more opportunities than they did 30 or 40 years ago. There are laws in the United States that give women the same opportunity as men to go to college and get jobs. As a result, women today are working in professions that were not as open to them 30 or 40 years ago. To give just one example, today more than half of the students in American medical schools are women.

So, to summarize so far, we've seen that the American family has changed dramatically since the days of those old television shows. In the typical family both the father and the mother have jobs. This means that most American homes don't have a full-time homemaker anymore, and that creates new problems for families, such as who takes care of babies and old people; who shops, cooks, and cleans; who volunteers at the children's school; etc.

Now, as the American family has changed, American businesses have changed too. More and more companies understand that people can't do good work if they're worried about their kids or if they're under a lot of stress. As a result, some companies are trying to help their workers with flexible policies and new programs that benefit working families. In the next part of my lecture I want to give you five examples of these policies and programs.

The first policy is paid maternity leave. "Maternity" means mother, and "leave" in this case means "vacation," so what we're talking about is a woman taking a vacation from work when she has a new baby. American law requires companies to give a woman up to 12 weeks of leave when she has a baby, but the problem is that they are not required to pay her during this time. As a result, many women are forced to go back to work much sooner than they want to. What's changing is that some companies, at least the big ones, are voluntarily offering their employees paid maternity leave, so women can stay home with their baby a few weeks longer. By the way, a small percentage of companies now also offer paid paternity leave—that means leave to the father as well. I would like to see a law that requires all companies to give paid leave to both mothers and fathers when they have a new baby. Canada, for instance, already has a law like that.

OK, moving along, here's another example of a policy that helps working families. As you know, big companies like IBM or General Motors often transfer their employees to other cities, right? Well, if a company transfers the husband, for instance, this might create a problem for the wife because now she has to find a new job too. So now there are companies that will help the husband or wife of the transferred worker find a new job.

A third policy that many companies now offer is called "flextime." Here's what that means. In the U.S., a normal workday is from 9 A.M. until 5 P.M., eight hours. With flextime, a worker can choose the hour that she starts work in the morning and can go home after eight hours. So, for instance, a worker who comes in at 7 can leave at 3. Or a worker can come in at 10 and leave at 6. You can imagine how useful this flexibility is for people who have children.

The fourth change I want to describe is called telecommuting. Now, "commute" means to travel back and forth from home to work. And "tele" is like telephone. With telecommuting, people work at home and communicate with their workplace using the phone and computer. It's estimated that about 6% of the U.S. workforce telecommutes now, but the percentage is growing all the time because it saves people time and money if they don't have to travel. And obviously, if a mother or father is allowed to work at home, this solves the problem of who will be with small children.

The fifth program offered by many of the best companies is day care; that is, some companies have day care centers at the office where they take care of the children of their employees. This means the worker comes to work with his or her little kids, leaves them at the center, and can visit them during lunch or whatever. Then the parent and children drive home together at the end of the day. With day care at work, the parent doesn't need to worry about the kids because they're right there.

OK, let me review what I've been talking about. I've given you five examples of company policies and programs designed to make life a little easier for working mothers and fathers. But it's important for me to tell you that only some large companies can afford to help their employees with these kinds of programs. For most people, trying to work and take care of a family at the same time is still very, very difficult. In my opinion, our government and our society need to do a lot more to help working parents and their children.

PART 3 Focused Listening and Speaking

Focused Listening

1 **Pronouncing Linked Phrases.** page 103.

See student text.

2 **Pronouncing Sentences.** page 104.

See student text.

Getting Meaning from Context

3 **Using Context Clues.** page 105. The following conversations are people talking about their lifestyles.

Number 1

Old man: Well, I tell you, things get pretty rough by the end of the month. I don't have any pension—just social security—and that's only $690 a month. Sometimes the check is late, and the rent is due on the first of the month. Do you think the landlord cares?

Question 1: The speaker is a . . .
Old man: Sometimes I think no one cares about retired people in this country.

Number 2

17-year-old girl: Sometimes I feel like I'm in a prison. "Come home by ten." "Don't go there." "Don't do that." "Turn down the music." They treat me like a baby. They have no respect for my privacy.

Question 2: The speaker is talking about . . .
Girl: My parents forget that I'm 17 years old. I'm not a child anymore.

Number 3

Man: My ex-wife and I agreed that the kids would live with me. At first it was hard with all the work and no help. But it's exciting to watch my kids grow up every day.

Question 3: This man . . .
Man: And fortunately, there are organizations to help divorced fathers like me.

Number 4

Young man: I lived with my parents until I was 18, then I left home to go to college and lived with roommates in an apartment near the campus. When I graduated, I got a job with an engineering firm and got my own place. But last year I lost my job and ran out of money, so what could I do? I came back to the nest.

Question 4: This person probably lives . . .
Young man: Boy, it's not easy living with your parents again after all these years.

Number 5

Old woman: After I broke my hip it was too hard to go on living by myself. So I tried living with my son and his family for a while, but their house is small and noisy and I want my privacy, too. So I came here. And it really isn't bad. I have my own doctor, good food, and plenty of friends my own age.

Question 5: This woman is living in . . .
Old woman: This retirement home is really the best place for me.

PART 4 Listening and Speaking in the Real World

Listen

2 Completing Graphs. page 108.

Graph number 1

Graph number one gives statistics on the percentage of American women in the U.S. labor force. In 1960, 37.8% of American women had jobs. By 1980, it had jumped to 51.1%. In 1990, it was 57.5%. And in 1998, 59.8% of American women were working.

Graph number 2

Graph number two shows the divorce rate in the United States between 1960 and 1998. In 1960, the divorce rate was just 2.2 per 1,000 people. In 1970, it rose to 3.5, and in 1980 it jumped to 5.2. However, it declined in 1990 to 4.7, and in 1998 declined even more, to 3.5 per 1,000 people.

Graph number 3

Graph number three presents information on the percentage of people over age 65 who lived alone from 1970 to 1998. You need to make two sets of points here. Use an X for men and an O for women.

In 1970, 35.9% of elderly women lived alone, compared to 10.8% of elderly men. In 1980, the percentage was 31.9 for women and 8.1 for men. In 1990, 51.8% of women lived alone, compared to 21.5% for men. And finally, in 1997, 30% of women and 9% of men were living by themselves.

Chapter 6 Global Connections

PART 1 Listening to Conversations

Listen

3 Listening for Main Ideas. page 116. Close your book as you listen to the conversation.

Listen for the answers to these questions.

Jeff: Come in!
Anna: Am I interrupting?
Jeff: No, I was just checking my e-mail. What's up?
Anna: I need your advice. My composition teacher said that from now on, all our writing has to be typed.
Jeff: So what's the problem?
Anna: Well, you know, I don't own a computer, and I really don't feel like spending all that money just to do word processing.
Jeff: Well, if all you need is word processing, you should just buy a typewriter. But I'd think about getting a computer if I were you. Then you could use e-mail to keep in touch with your family and your friends back in Italy . . .

Anna: I know, I know . . . but to tell you the truth, I'd rather talk to them by phone. It's more personal that way.
Jeff: Yeah, I noticed your phone bill was $160 last month. But seriously, Anna, there are lots of other things you can do with a computer besides word processing and e-mail.
Anna: Yeah? Like what?
Jeff: Well first of all, there's the Internet, of course.
Anna: Yeah, I know, you seem to be online all the time. What do you do, surf the Net?
Jeff: Sometimes. But mostly I use the Internet to get information about things I'm interested in and to talk with people all over the world about music.
Anna: How do you do that?
Jeff: Do you know what a discussion group is?
Anna: No.
Jeff: Well, it's a kind of club, except that it meets online, and uh, anyone who's interested can join the group. If you're a member, you can go online anytime you want and read messages sent in by other members, and of course you can also reply to any message you want. Um, here, look.
Jeff: Here. I belong to a discussion group about hip hop. Remember my friend Hiroshi, the drummer from Japan? Here's a message he posted talking about . . . hip hop in Tokyo.
Anna: Jeff, this is very cool. Are there discussion groups for people learning English?
Jeff: I don't know . . . let's do a quick search . . . OK, look here.
Anna: Wow! So many sites!
Jeff: Look, this one has 25 different discussion groups and live chats. You can communicate with people from all over the world in real time.
Anna: That sounds like fun! And if I had a computer, I could do research at home . . . I wouldn't have to do all my work in the computer lab at school.
Jeff: So what do you think, Anna? Is it worth getting a computer?
Anna: Yeah, I guess it is. Would you mind helping me pick one out?
Jeff: Not at all. Do you have time to go shopping this afternoon?
Anna: Let's go!

Stress

4 **Listening for Stressed Words.** page 116.

1. Now listen to part of the conversation again. Some of the stressed words are missing. During each pause, repeat the phrase or sentence; then fill in the missing stressed words.

   See conversation.

Intonation

5 **Practicing Intonation of Questions.** page 118. Listen to the following items from the conversation and repeat them after the speaker.

See student text.

6 **Identifying Intonation Patterns.** page 118. Listen to the following sentences. Repeat each sentence after the speaker; then circle the rising arrow for rising intonation, and the falling arrow for rising-falling intonation.

1. Are you working on the computer right now?
2. Can you help me?
3. Where do you want me to put this paper?
4. Could you please repeat that?
5. What kind of computer do you have?
6. Did you check your e-mail today?

PART 2

Listening to Lectures

Listen

3 **Taking Notes on Similarities and Differences.** page 123. Listen to sentences with similarities and differences. Complete the notes. You will hear each sentence twice.

1. Americans are quick to use people's first names. In contrast, people in other cultures prefer to be addressed by their family names.
2. In Egypt you should leave some food on your plate at the end of a meal. However, Bolivians expect visitors to eat everything on their plates.
3. Bolivians expect visitors to eat everything on their plate, and Americans also consider a clean plate a sign of satisfaction with the food.
4. Many Japanese people bow when they greet each other, while people from Thailand prefer to hold their hands in a prayer position.
5. In the United States, Canada, and most Western countries, greetings involve some sort of touching.

4 **Taking Draft Notes.** page 123. Listen to the lecture and take notes in the best way you can. Use your own paper. Listen for examples of similarities and differences among people from different cultures.

Lecturer: Good afternoon, class. I want to start my lecture today by telling you a little story. Once there was a young woman from Mexico named Consuela who came to New York to learn English. She got a job at a factory owned by a man from China. One day, as Consuela came to work, her Chinese boss handed her a red envelope. Consuela looked inside and saw 20 dollars. She became very upset and threw the envelope back at her boss. Her boss was shocked. Can you guess why? Well, he had given her the red envelope and the money because it was the Chinese New Year. And on the Chinese New Year it is traditional to give money to young single people for good luck. However, from Consuela's point of view, here was an older man giving her money in an envelope. To her, this meant that he was asking her for sexual favors. Naturally she was very insulted and refused to take the money.

Now, what does this story show us? What is the point? Yes?

Student: It shows that an action can have totally opposite meanings in different cultures. In this case, the boss thought he was being generous, but Consuela was insulted.

Lecturer: Exactly. Every culture has its own rules for what is appropriate and what is not appropriate behavior, and serious misunderstandings can occur if we don't know other people's cultural "rules." And to illustrate my point today I'm going to give examples from four areas. First, the way people greet each other in different cultures. Second, the way they use names and titles. Third, the way people eat. And finally, the way they exchange gifts.

OK, let's start with greeting customs, I mean, how people behave when they say hello. First of all, I'm sure you know that in the United States and in most Western countries, greetings often involve some sort of touching, such as a handshake, a hug, or a kiss if people know each other very well. On the other hand, people from most Asian countries don't usually feel as comfortable touching in public. Although handshakes between businesspeople are common, many Japanese prefer a bow, while people from Thailand normally hold their hands together in a kind of prayer position, like this. So imagine how embarrassing it would be if an American was invited to someone's home in Japan or Thailand and she tried to hug the host! And yet that would be perfectly acceptable in the United States or France or Argentina.

Now, another behavior that differs from culture to culture is the use of names. Have you noticed that Americans are quick to use people's first names, even if they have just met? For instance, visitors to the United States are always surprised to hear employees speak to their bosses using first names. In contrast, people in most other cultures are more formal and prefer to be addressed as "Mr. Martinez" or "Ms. Honda," for example. In addition, in some countries, such as Italy or Korea, people like you to include their title or position with their family names, especially if they're university graduates or owners of a business. For example, Professor Conti or Manager Kim.

The third area I want to look at is eating customs. I'm not talking here about the foods that people like to eat in different countries but rather some of the behaviors that are connected with eating that vary from culture to culture. One of these is the use of utensils. Uh, you probably know that people in many Asian cultures use chopsticks while in the West they usually use forks, knives, and spoons. In parts of India, Ethiopia, and Malaysia, it is customary to eat with your fingers. It's important to be aware of different dining customs, so that your behavior is not seen as rude. Here's another example: In some cultures eating everything on your plate is considered impolite. In Egypt and China, for example, you should leave some food in your dish at the end of the meal. This is to show that your hosts were generous and gave you more than enough to eat. However, Bolivians expect visitors to eat everything on their plates, and Americans also generally consider a clean plate a sign of satisfaction with the food.

Finally, the last area of behavior that I want to mention today is gift giving. Everybody likes to receive gifts, right? So you may think that gift giving is a universal custom and there's not much variation from culture to culture. But actually, the rules of gift giving can be very complicated, and not knowing them can result in great embarrassment. In the United States, if you're invited to someone's home for dinner, bring wine or flowers or a small item as a present. Americans generally don't give gifts in business situations. On the other hand, the Japanese, like many other Asian people, give gifts quite frequently, often to thank someone such as a teacher or doctor for their kindness. In the Japanese culture, the tradition of gift giving is very ancient. There are many detailed rules for everything from the color of the wrapping paper to the time of the gift presentation. Another interesting fact about gift giving is that many cultures have strict rules about gifts you should not give. For example, never give yellow flowers to people from Iran, or they will think you hate them!

I could give you hundreds of additional examples of cultural differences, but let's not forget the main point here: each culture in the world has its own customs and unique ways of doing things.

As the world becomes smaller and we have more opportunities to interact with people from other countries, we should try to learn about these differences to avoid insulting our hosts and embarrassing ourselves. I believe that if all of us could learn to understand our global neighbors better, the world might be a more peaceful place.

PART 3 Focused Listening and Speaking

Focused Listening

1 **Pronouncing Names with Blended Consonants.** page 127.

See student text.

2 **Saying Phrases with Blended Consonants.** page 127.

See student text.

3 **Pronouncing Sentences.** page 127.

See student text.

Getting Meaning from Context

4 **Using Context Clues.** page 128. The following short passages are about customs in different countries.

Number 1

Brazilians are more casual about time than are people from the United States and Canada. For example, in Brazil, it is usual to arrive 10 or 15 minutes late for a business appointment, and university classes almost never start at the appointed hour. In social situations, Brazilians are even more relaxed about time. It is not unusual for people to arrive one or two hours late for dinner or a party.

Question 1: Which statement is probably true about Brazil?

Number 2

For many Americans, patting a child on the head is a sign of love and caring. In contrast, Vietnamese people believe that the soul is contained inside a person's head. Therefore, if another person touches their head, they feel that their soul is in danger.

Question 2: If an American teacher touched the head of a Vietnamese child, the child might feel . . .

Number 3

Americans smile mainly to show friendliness. In Japan, people smile when they are sad, happy, apologetic, angry, or confused. In traditional Korean culture, smiling meant that a person was foolish or thoughtless. On the island of Puerto Rico, a smile can have many positive meanings, including "Please," "Thank you," and "You're welcome."

Question 3: We can conclude from these examples that . . .

Number 4

In the United States, you can sometimes see old shoes attached to the car of a newly married couple. What is the origin of this custom? Some people believe that old shoes can help a couple to have many children. Some people even put old shoes in trees that do not give enough fruit!

Question 4: This passage is mainly about . . .

Number 5

A bribe is an amount of money that is offered to a public official in exchange for some kind of favor or special treatment. In some countries, bribes are a normal part of doing business. However, in the United States, people disapprove of bribery, and it is strictly illegal.

Question 5: If you try to bribe a police officer in the United States, the officer could . . .

PART 4 Listening and Speaking in the Real World

2 **Taking a Trivia Quiz.** page 131.

Kevin: Hi, Georgie, what are you doing? Do you feel like going out for some dinner? Or do you have to study tonight?
Georgie: No, I was just reading the paper. Hey, Kevin, here's another one of those trivia quizzes that you love to take.
Kevin: What's it about?
Georgie: The title is "Global Connections." It's about transportation and communication around the world. Want to try it?
Kevin: Sure, why don't you read it to me?
Georgie: OK, first question. Which country has the largest number of time zones: The United States, Canada, Russia, or China?
Kevin: That's easy. Russia.

Georgie: Right. OK, second question: which country is the most popular tourist destination in the world? Is it France, the United States, Italy, or China?

Kevin: France.

Georgie: Right again. OK, next. Oh, this is hard: Which country has the largest percentage of people who use the Internet: Finland, Japan, Canada, or Mexico?

Kevin: Hmm. Let me think.

Kevin: OK, I guess Finland.

Georgie: Wrong. It's Canada!

Kevin: Canada! Wow, you know it used to be Finland. All the Scandinavian countries—Sweden, Finland, Iceland, Denmark—are in the top 10 for this category. OK, keep going.

Georgie: All right, number 4. Looks like another computer question. Which of the following countries has the largest actual number of computer users? And the choices are: Finland, Japan, the United States, or Brazil?

Kevin: Well, Finland was wrong last time, so I'll say . . . the United States.

Georgie: Yeah, well, you're right this time.

Kevin: [laughs] No kidding. Well, I hope the next question is easier.

Georgie: Let's see. How long does it take to fly from New York to Paris on the Concorde? eight hours? six and a half hours? five hours? or three and a half hours?

Kevin: Well, the Concorde travels faster than the speed of sound . . . It must be three and a half hours.

Georgie: Right. That is so amazing. Sometimes I think it takes me longer than that to get to class!

Kevin: OK, what's next?

Georgie: Which of the following countries has the largest number of daily newspapers: Mexico, Russia, England, or Greece?

Kevin: I'm sure it's England.

Georgie: Wrong! It's Mexico!

Kevin: No kidding! I wonder why . . . OK, next.

Georgie: Number 7 . . . The most frequently used language on the Internet is English. Which language is second: German, Spanish, Japanese, or Chinese?

Kevin: Wow. That's a tricky question. I am going say . . . Chinese.

Georgie: Nope. Japanese.

Kevin: Hmmm. Interesting.

Georgie: Do you want to keep going?

Kevin: Yeah, one more. Then we've got to go.

Georgie: OK, which city has the longest subway system? Moscow, New York, Tokyo, or London?

Kevin: London. For sure.

Georgie: You're right.

Kevin: Yeah, I studied in London last summer and I took the underground everywhere. So what's my score?

Georgie: Five right and three wrong. Not too bad.

Kevin: Yeah, but not too good, either! All right. Let's go eat. I'm starving!

Chapter 7 Language and Communication

PART 1 Listening to Conversations

Listen

3 **Listening for Main Ideas.** page 138. Close your book as you listen to the conversation.

Listen for the answers to these questions.

Anna: Karen! Hi!
Karen: Hi, Anna, how are you?
Anna: Fine, thanks. Um, is anyone sitting here?
Karen: No, have a seat.
Anna: Thanks. Oof, it's so crowded. How're you doing?
Karen: Oh, so busy. I've got school, and work, and I've told you my brother's getting married next month, right?
Anna: Yes, you have.
Karen: Right. Anyway, it's going to be a huge wedding and . . .
Anna: Excuse me for interrupting, Karen; Nancy! Over here!
Nancy: Hi!
Anna: Nancy, this is Karen. She works in the library. Karen, this is my housemate, Nancy. She teaches English here.
Nancy: Nice to meet you, Karen.
Karen: You too.
Anna: Karen's brother is getting married next month, and she was just telling me about the wedding . . .
Karen: Actually, I'm sorry but I've got to go. I have to be at work in ten minutes. I'll see you soon, Anna. We'll go to a movie or something.
Anna: How about Thursday night?
Karen: I have to check my calendar. I'll call you, OK?
Anna: OK, see you.
Anna: I don't understand Americans.
Nancy: Huh?
Anna: Did you hear what she said? "I'll call you, we'll go to a movie." But every time I try to pick a specific day or time, she says she's busy, she has to check her calendar. And then she never calls me.
Nancy: Um hmm . . .
Anna: Why do Americans say things they don't mean? They act so nice, like they always say "How are you," but then they keep on walking and don't even wait for your answer. They're so . . . how do you say it . . . two-faced?
Nancy: I know it seems that way sometimes, Anna. But it's not true. It's just that for Americans, friendliness and friendship aren't always the same thing.
Anna: What do you mean?
Nancy: Well, as you know, Americans can be very open and friendly. For example, they invite you to sit down, they ask you questions, they tell you all about their families. So naturally you think they're trying to make friends with you. But in reality, friendship, real friendship, takes time to build. It doesn't happen overnight.
Anna: So, when people say "How are you," they're just being polite? They don't really care?

Nancy: Not exactly. The thing you have to understand is that "how are you" isn't a real question. It's more of a greeting, a way of saying hello.

Anna: Aha, I get it! And "Have a nice day" is just a friendly way to say good-bye?

Nancy: Exactly. Now you're catching on.

Anna: But I'm still in the dark about Karen. Does she want to be my friend or not?

Nancy: It's hard to say. It sounds like she's pretty stressed out right now. Maybe she'll have more time after the wedding. I guess you'll just have to be patient.

Anna: OK. Thanks for the advice, Nancy.

Stress

4 **Listening for Stressed Words.** page 138.

1. Now listen to part of the conversation again. Some of the stressed words are missing. During each pause, repeat the phrase or sentence; then fill in the missing stressed words.

   See conversation.

Intonation

5 **Understanding Statements with Rising Intonation.** page 140. Listen to the following "statement questions" and rewrite them as "true" questions in the spaces.

1. You're going?
2. You remember my friend Karen?
3. He hasn't done his homework yet?
4. It's at the intersection of First and Main?
5. Jack is Rose's brother?

PART 2 Listening to Lectures

Listen

3 **Classifying Lecture Organization.** page 144. Listen to the introductions from three lectures. Identify the subtopics and write them in the spaces.

Number 1

Personal computers have revolutionized the way people work and communicate. I could talk for hours about the wide use of personal computers, but today we only have time to introduce three major uses of computers: at home, in business, and in education.

Number 2

In today's lecture I plan to provide the most recent information available concerning the growth and characteristics of the U.S. population.

Number 3

You may have guessed by now that my topic for today's lecture is differences between standard American and British English. In particular I want to examine three categories of difference. First, and most obvious, is pronunciation. Second, vocabulary. And third, grammar.

4 **Taking Draft Notes.** page 144. Listen to the lecture and take notes in the best way you can. Use your own paper.

Lecturer: Good afternoon, class. To introduce my topic today, I'd like you to listen to two speech samples, and I'd like you to tell me where the speakers are from. Ready? OK, here's the first one.

Speaker 1: "Today's weather forecast calls for partly cloudy skies in the morning, clearing by mid afternoon with winds up to 15 miles an hour out of the west. The high temperature will be 80 degrees Fahrenheit, and the low will be 64."

Lecturer: OK. Now, where do you think that speaker was from?

Audience: America . . . the United States . . . Canada.

Lecturer: Yes, most of you got it. That was what we call a *standard* American accent, which means the accent that is spoken, with a few small variations, by the majority of people who live in the United States and Canada.

Now, listen to a different speaker reading the same text.

Speaker 2: "Today's weather forecast calls for partly cloudy skies in the morning, clearing by mid afternoon with winds up to 15 miles an hour out of the west. The high temperature will be 80 degrees Fahrenheit, and the low will be 64."

Lecturer: And where is that speaker from?

Audience: England . . . the United Kingdom . . . Great Britain.

Lecturer: Yes, of course. That was British English, specifically, the type of accent known as "RP," which means Received Pronunciation. But did you know that RP English is actually spoken by only about 3% of the British people? That's right! Most British people speak with an accent that is somewhat different from RP. Yet RP is considered the standard because it is the dialect that nearly all the people of Great Britain can understand.

You may have guessed by now that my topic for today's lecture is differences between standard American and British English. In particular I want to examine three categories of difference. First, and most obvious, is pronunciation. Second, vocabulary. And third, grammar.

So to begin, let's go back to the subject of accent, or pronunciation. You had no trouble identifying the American and British accents because each of them has a unique sound. What are the specific features that account for this uniqueness? Well, one obvious difference is in the pronunciation of the sound written with the letter "a." For example, most Americans say */k ænt/,* but the British say */kant/.* Or Americans say "I'd */ræther/* and the British say "I'd */rathuh/.*" The */æ/* sound that is so common in American English, in words like apple, family, and so on, is not very common in British English.

Another noticeable difference between American and British pronunciation is the appearance and disappearance of the */r/* sound in different contexts. As you know, this sound occurs frequently in American English. In British English, however, it is very often dropped. To give some examples, Americans say */kar/* but the British say */ka/.* Americans say */fɤrst/* but British say */fʌst/.* A big American city is "New */yɔrk/* " for Americans, but "New */yok/* " to the British. In the two speech samples you heard at the beginning of this lecture, the American speaker said */forekaest/,* but the British said */fohcast/.* In that single word you can hear the difference both in the "a" vowel and in the pronunciation of */r/.* Listen again: */forkaest/, /fohkast/.*

A third difference between standard American and British pronunciation is the pronunciation of the */t/* sound in the middle of words. In British English it is normally pronounced, but in American English it changes to a */d/* or disappears. For example: a British person will say "little," but an American says *"/liddle/".* You can hear this difference particularly with numbers: Brits say "twenty one, twenty two," and so on, but Americans drop the */t/* and say *"/twenny one, twenny two/",* and so on.

So there you have just three of the differences that give American and British pronunciation their unique sounds. There are many more. But now let's go on to talk about vocabulary.

Some people believe that American and British English are very different in this area, but actually they are not. The English language has more than one million words. Yet there are only a few hundred words and expressions that are different in American and British English, and most of these are words having to do with daily life. You can see a few of them in the chart. So for instance, Americans say "truck" but the Brits say "lorry," and another famous example is "elevator" which is used in the United States but in England people say "lift." Now although the number of vocabulary differences is quite small, funny misunderstandings can occur if English speakers are not aware of them. For instance, if an American says "We have to put the baby down," a British person may be quite shocked because in England, to "put down" means to kill; for example, a sick dog is put down. In contrast, in the United States to put down a baby simply means to put it to sleep.

Vocabulary differences can also create some funny situations in restaurants. If an Englishman traveling in the United States enters a restaurant and orders "bangers and mash," the American waiter would look at him as though he were crazy. The poor Englishman doesn't know that in the United States, these same foods are called sausage and mashed potatoes.

Finally, let's talk a bit about grammar. I've left this category for last because in the area of grammar, standard American and British English are nearly identical. One common difference however, involves the verbs "have" and "got." For example, Americans say "I have a cold" while the British say "I've got a cold." An American might ask, "Have you gotten your grade yet?" whereas a Brit would ask, "Have you got your grade yet?" Americans say, "Do you have a pencil?" but the British say "Have you a pencil?" To give another example, in the United States, some words, like "government," are singular, but in England they are plural. There are also differences in the use of prepositions and two-word verbs, so for instance in the United States it's correct to say that John is different *from* Mary, but the British will say that John is different *than* Mary. But these differences are very small and few in number.

And this brings me to my conclusion, which is this: my focus today has been on differences between American and British English. But the reality is that these two types of English are so similar that speakers from Great Britain and North America have almost no trouble understanding one another. For this reason, we cannot say that American and British English are two different languages. Rather, they are two dialects, two varieties, of the same language, English.

PART 3 # Focused Listening and Speaking

Getting Meaning from Context

1 **Using Context Clues.** page 147. The following conversations are about language.

Conversation 1

A: Have you ever heard of Esperanto?
B: Huh?
A: Esperanto.
B: It sounds like a cigar.
A: No, silly. It's a language.
B: Really? I've never heard of it. Where is it spoken?
A: Lots of places. According to this article it's actually an artificial language; it was invented in 1887 by a man from Poland who was interested in creating a world religion with one language.
B: That's interesting. So who speaks this language now?
A: Well, it says here that there are Esperanto societies in more than 60 countries, and there may be as many as 15 million people who speak Esperanto as a second language.
B: What does "Esperanto" mean, anyway? It doesn't sound like Polish.
A: It's not. The vocabulary of Esperanto comes from lots of different languages. "Esperanto" means "hope" in Latin.
B: Well, I hope I never have to learn it. It's hard enough trying to learn English.

Question 1: What is Esperanto?

Question 2: Where did the woman get her information about Esperanto?

Question 3: Which of the following is probably true about Esperanto?

Conversation 2

A: Look, there's a beehive under the roof.
B: I guess we'd better call an exterminator. I don't want anybody to get stung.
A: Yeah, you're right . . . But I really don't want to kill them. Did you know bees can communicate with one another?
B: Really? How?
A: They use body language to show which direction the food is in, how far away it is, and how much food is available.
B: No kidding . . .
A: Yeah, see that one there? See how she's going around and around in circles, like she's dancing? That means the food is nearby. If the food is farther away, the bee points toward it with her body. And the faster she dances, the more food is available.
B: How do you know so much about bees?
A: I took an entomology class in college. I was a biology major and I thought it would be interesting to learn something about bugs.

Question 4: Why does the man want to call an exterminator?

Question 5: Which information about food is *not* conveyed by the bee's body language?

Question 6: What is entomology?

Conversation 3

A: Hey Carla, what's new?
B: Well, I got a new car.
A: Really? What happened to old Betsy?
B: After 150,000 miles, she finally died.
A: Oh, I'm sorry to hear that. So what kind of car did you get?
B: A Toyota Corolla
A: That's a good little car. Have you ever thought about how cars get their names?
B: Huh-uh, not really.
A: Well think about it. Toyota has a Camry, a Celica, a Corolla, a Corona. They all start with a "c" and sound Italian, but they don't mean anything.
B: And lots of American cars are named after birds or fast animals. There's Mustang, Barracuda, Skylark, Eagle, Cougar . . .
A: Car companies must spend a lot of time and money coming up with these names.
B: Speaking of which, what are you going to call your new car?
A: I don't know yet. Do you have any ideas?

Question 7: In this conversation, Betsy is the name of Carla's ____.

Question 8: What happened to Carla's old car?

Question 9: What is true about American car names?

Focused Listening

2 **Understanding Interjections.** page 148. Listen to the short conversations. Choose the number of the *second* speaker's meaning from the chart, and write the number in the blanks.

Conversation 1

Student: Can we use a dictionary on the test?
Teacher: Uh-huh.

Conversation 2

Mother: Here, let me brush your hair.
Child: Ouch! Not so hard!

Conversation 3

Father: Could you please carry this bag of groceries into the house?
Son: Sure . . . oops!

Conversation 4

A: The computer is down because of a virus that made the hard drive crash.
B: Huh?

Conversation 5

A: I'm expecting an important letter. Has the mail arrived yet?
B: Uh-uh.

Conversation 6

A: Did you remember to buy stamps when you went to the post office?
B: Oh-oh.

PART 4 Listening and Speaking in the Real World

Listen

2 **Identifying Spellings.** page 150. Listen to a spelling bee in an American high school class. The words are taken from a list of commonly misspelled words. As you listen, circle the letter of the spelling you hear, even if it is wrong! During the pause, check whether you think the spelling is right or wrong. Continue listening, and you will hear the correct spelling.

Teacher: Our contestants in today's spelling bee are Jack, Marisa, Yolanda, Evan, and Tony. As you know, I will say the word and then say it in a sentence. Are you ready to begin?
All: Ready, Yes.
Teacher: All right. The first word is for Tony. The word is "tries." "He always tries to do a good job."
Tony: Tries. OK, T-R-I-E-S.
Teacher: Correct. All right. The next word is for Jack. Your word is "choose." "Which flavor ice cream will you choose?"
Jack: Choose. C-H-O-S-E.
Teacher: I'm sorry, but that is wrong. The correct spelling of "choose" is C-H-O-O-S-E. Good try, Jack. OK, the next word goes to Marisa. Your word is "effect." "Jogging has a good effect on our health."
Marisa: Effect. E-F-F-E-C-T.
Teacher: Right! Marisa, you stay in the game. The next word is for Evan. Your word is "quizzes." "We had two grammar quizzes last week."
Evan: OK, quizzes. Uh, Q-U-I-Z-Z-E-S.
Teacher: Yes, that's right. Now, for Yolanda, your word is "succeed." "You must study hard if you want to succeed."
Yolanda: Hmm. Succeed. S-U-C-C-E-D-[pause]-E.
Teacher: I'm sorry, Yolanda, that's wrong. It's S-U-C-C-E-E-D. Good try. OK, let's see who's still in the game: Marisa, Evan, and Tony. Are you ready for the second round?
All: Yes, yeah, let's go.
Teacher: OK, Tony. Your word is "ninety." "The shoes cost ninety dollars."
Tony: N-I-N-E-T-Y. Ninety.
Teacher: You're right! Well done. The next word is for Marisa. "Analyze." "After a test, you should analyze your mistakes."
Marisa: Wow, that's hard. OK: A-N-A-L-I-Z-E. Analyze.
Teacher: Sorry, Marisa. It's A-N-A-L-Y-Z-E. Please sit down. Evan, you're next. Your word is "possibility." "There is a possibility of snow tonight."
Evan: Possibility. OK. P-O-S-S-I-B-I-L-I-T-Y.
Teacher: Great! OK, it's down to Tony and Evan. First Tony. Your word is "mysterious." "During the night we heard mysterious noises."
Tony: Um, M-I-S-T-E-R-I-O-U-S. I think.
Teacher: Oh no, that's not correct. It's M-Y-S-T-E-R-I-O-U-S. You almost got it. Well, that leaves Evan. If you spell this word correctly you'll be the winner today. The last word is "lightning." "We were scared by the thunder and lightning."
Evan: L-I-G-H-T-N-I-N-G. Lightning.
Teacher: Right! Congratulations, Evan! You're our winner today.

Chapter 8 Tastes and Preferences

PART 1 Listening to Conversations

Listen

3 **Listening for Main Ideas.** page 155. Close your book as you listen to the conversation.

Listen for the answers to these questions.

Jeff: Come in!
Dan: Hi.
Anna: Oh, hi, Dan, how are you?
Jeff: Hey, Dan, how ya doin'?
Dan: Great, thanks. Hey, I brought some new CDs for you to listen to.
Jeff: Oh, good. Oh, let me get that. I'll be right back.
Anna,
Dan: Okay.
Dan: So, did you have a good time at the club last night?
Anna: Yeah, it was pretty wild.
Dan: What did you think of our band?
Anna: Well, your music is great for dancing, but to tell you the truth, it was kind of loud. I guess I really prefer jazz.
Dan: Do you go to shows much?
Anna: No, not very often. I can't afford it. They're so expensive here!
Dan: So, what do you like to do for fun?
Anna: Well, I love to eat! And there are so many interesting ethnic restaurants around here!
Dan: What's your favorite kind of food?
Anna: Well, Italian, of course. What about you?
Dan: Believe it or not, I'm not crazy about pasta. But I really like Mexican food.
Anna: Oo, I can't stand beans. Uh . . . What about Indian food?
Dan: I don't care for it. Too spicy. How about American food? You know, hamburgers, hot dogs, french fries . . .
Anna: Disgusting! All that fat and salt and sugar . . . We don't see eye to eye on anything, do we?
Dan: Well, let's see. How do you feel about modern art? There's a wonderful exhibit at the county museum right now.
Anna: To be honest, I don't get the modern stuff. I prefer 19th century art, you know, Monet, Van Gogh, Renoir.
Dan: Hmm. How about sports? Are you interested in football?
Anna: American football? I hate it!
Dan: Baseball?
Anna: It's okay.
Dan: How about tall musicians with curly hair?
Anna: It depends.
Dan: OK, I got it. How about tall musicians with curly hair who invite you to a movie?
Anna: Science fiction?
Dan: Sounds great!
Anna: At least we agree on something!

Stress

4 Listening for Stressed Words. page 156.

1. Now listen to part of the conversation again. Some of the stressed words are missing. During each pause, repeat the phrase or sentence; then fill in the missing stressed words.

   See conversation.

Reductions

5 Listening for Reductions. page 157. Listen to the following short exchanges. Write the full questions instead of the reduced ones.

1. *A:* Do you like Chinese food?
   B: Not really.
   A: Japanese?
2. *A:* Whew! What a day!
   B: Tired?
3. Anybody home?
4. *A:* I guess it's time to go.
   B: Leaving already?
5. *A:* Does he have a wife?
   B: Yes.
   A: Kids?

PART 2 Listening to Lectures

Listen

3 Recognizing Paraphrases. page 162. Listen to the following pairs of sentences. Decide whether their meaning is similar or different and write S or D in the spaces.

1. a. Baby boomers have much more free time than their parents did.
   b. The parents of the baby boomers didn't have a lot of time for leisure activities.
2. a. The biggest expense for people in their 40s is housing.
   b. Americans between the ages of 40 and 50 like to buy expensive houses.
3. a. As they get older, baby boomers are very concerned about staying attractive and healthy.
   b. Most people become fat and sick when they get old.
4. a. Baby boomers would rather spend money than put it in the bank.
   b. Baby boomers like to spend their money instead of saving it.
5. a. From the end of World War II until 1960, there was a huge increase in the birthrate.
   b. The birthrate rose dramatically in the 1940s and the 1950s.

5 **Taking Draft Notes.** page 163. Listen to the interview and take notes in the best way you can. Use your own paper.

Host: Dr. Harris, thank you for joining us today.

Harris: My pleasure.

Host: To begin, could you tell us the meaning of the term "baby boom"?

Harris: Of course. The word "boom" means a sudden, fast increase in something. In this case, we're talking about an increase in the birthrate, in other words, the number of babies born each year. From the end of World War II until the early 1960s, that is, in the 1940s and the 1950s, there was a huge increase in the U.S. birthrate. So this period of 15 years or so is called the "baby boom," and any person born during those years is called a "baby boomer." The baby boomers are the largest age group in the U.S. population. In fact, there are about 76 million of them. Roughly, they are between 40 and 60 years old now.

Host: Is that important?

Harris: Well, yes, it's extremely important, for two reasons. The baby boomers are not only the largest age group in the United States as I just said, but they also spend the most money. As a result of these two things, they have enormous political and economic power in this country, more than any other group.

Host: How are baby boomers different from their parents? I mean, do they spend their money differently from the way their parents did?

Harris: Very differently. You have to remember that the parents of the boomers grew up in the 1920s and 1930s. The years between World War I and World War II were very difficult, especially after the stock market crashed in 1929. Then came the Great Depression. Most people were poor, and there weren't enough jobs. But in contrast to that, the baby boomers were born <u>after</u> World War II, when the U.S. economy was very strong. And it's still strong today, the strongest it's ever been. As a result, first of all, baby boomers like to spend their money instead of putting it in the bank. I mean, they save very little compared to their parents. Second, boomers use a lot of credit; that is to say, they use credit cards instead of paying cash for things. And third, baby boomers have much more free time than their parents did.

Host: OK, so the baby boomers have a very different lifestyle from their parents. They have a lot more money to spend than their parents did. What do they spend it on?

Harris: I'll get you several examples. First, what do you think is the biggest expense for people between the ages of 40 and 55?

Host: Uh . . . housing?

Harris: Right. People in this age group spend between 25 and 40 percent of their income on housing, depending on where they live. In addition, they spend a lot of money on furniture and appliances, you know, refrigerators, dishwashers, washing machines, and so on.

Host: I see. How about another example?

Harris: Baby boomers are crazy about cars. They love foreign cars like BMWs, but also large family cars like station wagons and the latest fad, SUVs, you know, sport utility vehicles like the Jeep Cherokee or Ford Explorer.

Host: Are there products that were created specifically for the baby boom generation?

Harris: There certainly are. First of all, clothes. For example, you can buy Levis jeans especially designed for middle-aged men. Another example would be, uh, expensive electronic gadgets like hand-held computers . . . . And let's not forget the food industry. Think about light beer and all the fat-free products you can buy now. All of these were created because the baby boomers are getting older and they're worried about getting fat.

Host: How about new industries?

Harris: New industries. OK, uh, diet centers, tanning salons, health spas, gyms . . . all these are relatively new. I mean, they didn't even exist 20 years ago. You see, boomers are very concerned about staying attractive and healthy. They spend incredible amounts of money on physical fitness and beauty.

Host: We're just about out of time here . . . uh, Dr. Harris, are you a baby boomer?

Harris: I sure am. I was born in 1953.

Host: And if I may ask you a personal question, what kind of car do you drive?

Harris: A 1998 Toyota Camry. Just what you'd expect from a baby boomer, right?

Host: Right. Dr. Harris, thank you for being with us today.

Harris: You're welcome.

PART 3

Focused Listening and Speaking

Focused Listening

1 **Distinguishing between *Do* and *Did*.** page 167. Listen to pairs of sentences. Circle the *first* item you hear in each pair.

1. Do you have time to eat lunch? / Did you have time to eat lunch?
2. Does he play the piano? / Did he play the piano?
3. Do they need help? / Did they need help?
4. Do I look like my sister? / Did I look like my sister?
5. Does she understand the instructions? / Did she understand the instructions?
6. Did we need to rewrite the composition? / Do we need to rewrite the composition?
7. Do they own a house? / Did they own a house?
8. Did we sound good? / Do we sound good?

2 ***Do* and *Did* in WH-questions.** page 168. Listen to the questions and write the missing words.

1. What did he decide to do?
2. When do we eat?
3. Why do I have to copy my notes?
4. Where did we park our car?
5. Where did I put my keys?
6. Why did she leave class early?
7. Where did you leave your bag?
8. What do they want to do?

Getting Meaning from Context

3 **Using Context Clues.** page 168. The following conversations are about people's tastes and preferences.

Conversation 1

A: You're standing too close. You can't see anything that way.
B: I'm looking for the signature.
A: Don't worry. At that price, it's got to be an original.

Question 1: What are the speakers talking about?
B: Wow, who can afford $15,000 for one painting?

Conversation 2

Woman: You're not thinking about buying that, are you?
Man: Why not? What's wrong with it?
Woman: Well, brown and black don't go together.
Man: Well, what if I wear it with my other suit?

Question 2: What is the man buying?
Woman: You know, the last thing you need is another tie.

Conversation 3

Boy: I'm scared!
Mother: Come on, there's nothing to be afraid of. It's just water.
Boy: But what if I fall in? Won't it hurt?
Mother: Don't worry. We won't go fast.

Question 3: What is the boy afraid to do?
Boy: But I've never been on water skis before!

Conversation 4

Teen girl: You colored your hair.
Teen boy: Yeah, I finally did it.
Girl: You look so . . . different.
Boy: What do you mean, "different"?

Question 4: How does the girl feel about the boy's hair?
Girl: Uh, I'm not sure. I've never seen you with orange hair before.

Conversation 5

Teen girl: You colored your hair!
Teen boy: Yeah, I finally did it.
Girl: You look so different!
Boy: What do you mean, "different"?

Question 5: How does the girl feel about the boy's hair?
Girl: I love it! It's so cool!

PART 4 Listening and Speaking in the Real World

Listen

2 **Comparing People's Qualities.** page 170. Listen as David describes Katherine and Jean. Take notes on their positive and negative qualities.

I don't know what to do. Katherine and Jean are both wonderful women. So how am I supposed to choose between them? Take Katherine. We went to high school and college together, and my parents are crazy about her. Katherine is very intelligent, and she's interesting to talk with; we spend hours discussing art and politics and books.

Jean is also very bright, but she's much quieter than Katherine. It's not as easy to talk to her. But even though she's quiet, she's crazy about sports and has a great sense of humor; I mean, she tells the funniest jokes, and I love the way she laughs. Katherine, on the other hand, is sometimes too sensitive; I mean, she doesn't understand that I'm just joking, so she gets offended.

Another thing I don't like about Katherine is that she's not good at managing money. She has a very good job and a good salary, but somehow she never seems to have any money! It's kind of irresponsible, you know what I mean? Now Jean is great with money and she insists on sharing the cost of our dates.

On the other hand, I want to have children, but Jean says she's not sure. That could be a problem later on. Katherine loves kids, but sometimes she has a bad temper; she gets angry whenever I'm five minutes late! I'm really confused. Katherine and Jean—they're so different and I really like them both. But you know, I don't know if either one is serious about me anyway. What do you think I should do?

Chapter 9 New Frontiers

PART 1 Listening to Conversations

Listen

3 **Listening for Main Ideas.** page 177. Close your book as you listen to the conversation.

Listen for the answers to these questions.

Jeff: Anna! Nancy! Come out to the porch! You've got to see this moon!

Nancy: Wow! Look how big and full it is!

Anna: It looks as if you could reach out and touch it.

Jeff: Do you realize that it's been more than 30 years since the first astronauts walked on the moon? And would you believe their footprints are still there?

Anna: Really? How come?

Jeff: There's no weather on the moon, so there's no wind to blow them away.

Anna: That's fascinating. But you know, I've always wondered why some governments spend so much money on space exploration. I mean, there are so many serious problems on earth, like pollution, hunger, disease . . .

Nancy: Well, you may be surprised to know that the United States spends less than one percent of its annual budget on the space program. And besides, you have to consider the technological and scientific benefits of space exploration.

Anna: Like what?

Jeff: Well, to give just one example, satellites were invented only about 40 years ago, and now they're used for weather prediction, cell phones, satellite TV . . .

Nancy: Also, a lot of medical discoveries have come out of space research. Believe it or not, that's how soft contact lenses were developed. Also, some drugs can be produced more easily and cheaply in space, where there's no gravity.

Jeff: Just imagine—pretty soon we'll be able to buy products labeled "Made in Space" instead of "Made in Indonesia" or "Made in the USA."

Anna: OK, I understand that space research has a lot of benefits. But tell me this: would you like to live in space?

Jeff: That depends. If the living conditions are the same as on earth, then why not?

Nancy: Yeah, all Jeff needs are guitar strings and an ice cream shop and he's perfectly happy. Right Jeff?

Jeff: Yeah . . . Actually, just the other day I read an article on space colonies, and . . .

Anna: Space what?

Jeff: Space colonies. Um, communities of people living in space in big space stations.

Anna: Yeah?

Jeff: The article said that, surprisingly, life in these communities might be even nicer than on earth because they'll be smaller, without the problems we have in big cities today. They'll use solar energy, for instance, so they won't have air pollution.

Nancy: Anyway, Anna, don't you think it would be exciting to be a pioneer?

Anna: What's that?

Nancy: You know, someone who does something first. Like Columbus or Neil Armstrong when he walked on the moon back in 1969.

Anna: You know what? You guys can be the pioneers. I'm going to stay right here on earth and finish college!

Stress

4 Listening for Stressed Words. page 177.

1. Now listen to part of the conversation again. Some of the stressed words are missing. During each pause, repeat the phrase or sentence; then fill in the missing stressed words.

   See conversation.

Pronunciation

6 Pronouncing Voiced and Voiceless */th/*. page 180. Listen to two lists of words. The words in the first list have a voiceless /*th*/ sound. The words in the second list have the voiced sound. Repeat the words after the speaker.

See student text.

7 Distinguishing between Voiced and Voiceless */th/*. page 181. Now listen to the following sentences from the conversation. Repeat them after the speaker. Put a slash (/) through every voiceless /*th*/ you hear. Put a circle around every voiced /*th*/.

See student text.

PART 2

Listening to Lectures

Listen

4 **Taking Notes on a Position and Supporting Evidence.** page 186. Listen to one position about the full moon and three pieces of supporting evidence. Take notes as in the example.

> Dr. Lieber also proposed that the full moon is related to depression. As an example, he states that in 1977, nine people committed suicide during a full moon by jumping off the Golden Gate Bridge in San Francisco. One study published in 1980 showed an increase in the number of people who try to poison themselves on the day of the full moon. And many people who work in mental hospitals complain that patients are more irritable and difficult to handle at the time of the full moon.

5 **Taking Draft Notes.** page 186. Listen to the lecture and take notes in the best way you can. Use your own paper. As you listen and take notes, refer to the two speakers' handouts shown here.

Speaker 1

All of you know that the moon plays an important role in regulating our physical world. For example, the moon regulates the ocean tides, the weather, and the behavior of animals. But what about people? What effect, if any, does the moon, especially the full moon, have on people's behavior? This is the question that we are going to debate today. I will start by arguing that the full moon may be responsible for unusual behavior in some people. Then my classmate Dana will present the opposite point of view.

To begin, I'm sure you've heard stories about people who do strange and unpredictable things during the time of the full moon, which by the way comes once every 29 and a half days. In the English language there is even a word, "loony," which means that someone is crazy. It comes from the Latin word "luna," which means moon.

Now many people are sure that the full moon can cause unpredictable or even violent behavior. Back in 1977, a psychiatrist named Arnold Lieber wrote a book called *The Lunar Effect*, which stated that crime rates seem to increase at the time of the full moon. For example, a woman named Sarah Jane Moore tried to kill then-U.S. President Gerald Ford during a full moon. At least two research studies examined thousands of murders and other violent crimes and showed that they occur more frequently at the time of the full moon. One study involved 11,613 cases of aggravated assault, which is when one person attacks another person with a weapon like a gun or a knife. These attacks took place over a period of five years, and the research showed that they occurred more often around the full moon. Many police officers agree that there is a connection between violent behavior and the occurrence of the full moon.

Dr. Lieber also proposed that the full moon is related to depression. As an example, he states that in 1977, nine people committed suicide during a full moon by jumping off the Golden Gate Bridge in San Francisco. One study published in 1980 showed an increase in the number of people who try to poison themselves on the day of the full moon. And many people who work in mental hospitals complain that patients are more irritable and difficult to handle at the time of the full moon.

Finally, many airline pilots, uh, bartenders, newspaper reporters, and ambulance drivers will also tell you that the full moon has a weird effect on some people, though they can't say why it happens. Here's one possible explanation: the moon is powerful enough to control the ocean tides. In that case, why wouldn't it be strong enough to affect the human body, which, after all, is 90% water?

Speaker 2

After listening to Joshua's presentation, you may believe that the full moon really does cause people, at least some people, to do strange things. But wait. Don't make up your mind yet! The fact is that there is very little scientific support for the hypothesis that the full moon causes people to behave strangely. Moreover, a lot of what Josh told you is just someone's opinion or theory, and that's not the same thing as proof.

OK, first of all, Joshua told you about three studies which showed a relationship between violent behavior and the time of the full moon. However, I was able to locate more than 20 studies that reached exactly the opposite conclusion. These studies found no relation at all between people's behavior and the full moon. I'm going to summarize just a few of them here, and you can look on my handout if you want to see more.

First, in a study of almost 60,000 police arrests over a period of seven years, there was no difference in the number of arrests made during any phase of the moon. In other words, the occurrence of crimes was not related to the moon.

Second, there were seven studies that showed no relationship between the rate of suicide and the time of the full moon. One study reviewed suicides over a period of 58 years and found no relationship! And remember Joshua talked about people who try to poison themselves at the time of the full moon? Well, I discovered a 1986 study of 1,187 cases of self-poisonings in a one-year period in which there was no relationship to the phase of the moon. So again, the results were exactly the opposite of what Josh mentioned.

OK, third, regarding the behavior of patients in mental hospitals, a study in 1998 of 1,289 aggressive incidents showed no significant relationship between the patients' behavior and the phase of the moon. Another study, in 1989, found no link between the phases of the moon and the strange behavior of older people living in nursing homes.

And finally, many studies of people who were admitted to hospital emergency rooms also found no relation between their injuries and the full moon.

In summary, a large number of scientific studies found that there is no relation between the occurrence of the full moon and unusual behavior in humans. Now in addition, Josh told you that many professionals can tell stories about people who did weird or even dangerous things at the time of the full moon. In fact, most cultures have myths or stories about people and animals that do strange or magical things when the moon is full. And who knows, some of these stories may be true; but it's very important to remember that just because two things happen at the same time does not mean that the first one causes the second one. It may just be a coincidence. And that's not the same thing as scientific proof.

PART 3

Focused Listening and Speaking

Getting Meaning from Context

1 **Using Context Clues.** page 190. You are going to hear five short talks about discoveries.

Talk 1

What is the difference between a discovery and an invention? We discover things that were always there. For example, you often hear that Columbus discovered America. In contrast, people invent things that did not exist before. Long ago someone invented ships, for instance. Discovery and invention are often related because many discoveries are made with the help of inventions. As an example, Columbus used ships to discover America.

Question 1: What can we infer from this passage?

Talk 2

The ancient Greeks used the energy of the sun to heat their homes as early as 500 B.C. Later, the Romans followed this example and used solar power to heat baths, houses, and greenhouses. The American Indians were also early users of the sun's energy. Nowadays car manufacturers are developing cars that will run exclusively on solar power.

Question 2: What can we conclude about the use of solar energy?

Talk 3

Five planets were known already at the time of the Roman Empire: Mercury, Venus, Mars, Jupiter, and Saturn. In fact, all five are named after Roman gods. The first planet that was not known in ancient times was Uranus. It was discovered in 1781 by an Englishman named Sir William Herschel.

Question 3: What does the passage imply?

Talk 4

Shang Yeng was the emperor of China almost 5,000 years ago. For health reasons, he ordered his people to boil their water before drinking it. One day Shang Yeng himself was boiling water outside when some leaves from a bush fell into the large open pot. Before he could remove the leaves, they began to cook. The mixture smelled so good that Shang Yeng decided to taste it. In this way tea was discovered.

Question 4: What can we conclude about the discovery of tea?

Talk 5

Rubber is an old discovery. When Columbus arrived in the New World, he saw boys playing with balls made from the hard juice of a tree. Later, in 1736, a Frenchman working in Peru noticed people wearing shoes and clothes made from the same material. In 1770, an English scientist used the material to rub out his writing mistakes. He named the material "rubber."

Question 5: What can we infer from the passage?

Focused Listening

3 **Practicing the Past Tense Endings.** page 191. Listen and repeat the following words after the speaker.

See student text.

4 **Distinguishing between Past Tense Endings.** page 192. Listen to the following past tense verbs and check the pronunciation that you hear. You'll hear each word twice.

1. laughed
2. described
3. rented
4. stopped
5. changed
6. ended
7. helped
8. studied
9. invented
10. danced
11. realized
12. crowded
13. worked
14. listened
15. answered

PART 4 Listening and Speaking in the Real World

Listen

2 **Listening to a Game Show.** page 195. You are going to listen to a game show with questions about explorations, inventions, and discoveries. As you hear each question, you should circle *your* answer in the column below marked Your Answer. Then you will hear the answer given by this week's contestant, Roger Johnson. Finally, the host, Ronnie Perez, will provide the correct answer.

Host: Good evening and welcome to our show! I'm your host, Ronnie Perez. In this game, members of the audience compete with our contestant to answer questions about explorations, inventions, and discoveries. When you hear a question, select your answer from the choices on your answer ballot. Our contestant will do the same. Then we'll see who has the correct answer!

Now let's meet our contestant. He is Roger Johnson from Ottawa, Canada. Roger, as you know, you may continue to play as long as you give correct answers. One wrong answer, however, and the game is over. Are you ready to play?!

Roger: I'm ready, Ronnie.

Host: Then here's our first question. For $1,000, what is the name of the computer company that created the first personal computer? Was it
a. Apple,
b. Microsoft, or
c. Intel?
Members of the audience, select your answer. Is it Apple, Microsoft, or Intel?
OK, audience?

Audience: Apple!

Host: Roger, do you agree?

Roger: Yes I do, Ronnie. It's Apple.

Host: You are right! Well done! Let's go to question number 2. For $2,000: George Mallory, Sir Edmund Hillary, and Tensing Norgay all reached the top of which famous mountain? Was it
a. Mt. Everest in Nepal,
b. Mt. Fuji in Japan, or
c. Mt. Whitney in the United States?
Members of the audience, select your answer.
Audience?

Audience: Everest!

Host: Roger? Your answer?

Roger: Everest. Absolutely.

Host: And that is correct. Good work so far, but as you know, our questions become more difficult as we continue playing. Here's question number 3. Marco Polo, who traveled throughout China at the end of the 13th century, was a native of which country? For $3,000, was it
a. Spain,
b. Portugal, or
c. Italy?
First let's turn to our audience . . .
And what is your answer, audience?

Audience: Spain! Italy!

Host: Roger, is it Spain or Italy? Which did you pick?
Roger: It's Italy, Ronnie.
Host: You sound very confident. Is it Italy . . . Yes! You're on a roll now, Roger. Ready for the next question?
Roger: Yes, sir.
Host: Here we go. This question is for $4,000, and here it is. Who was the first person to land on the shores of North America? Was it
a. Christopher Columbus,
b. Leif Erikkson, or
c. Ferdinand Magellan?
Members of the audience, select your answer.
OK, audience, what do you say?
Audience: Columbus!
Host: And Roger, do you agree with that answer?
Roger: I say it was Leif Erikkson, Ronnie.
Host: Are you sure about that?
Roger: Yes I am, Ronnie.
Host: All right, let's find out. The correct answer is . . . b. Leif Erikkson! Yes, it's true. Leif Erikkson was a Norwegian who came to the shores of North America in the year 1000. Columbus did not arrive until the year 1492. Roger Johnson, you have won another $4,000! Are you ready for the next question?
Roger: Ready, Ronnie.
Host: Here it is. In which country was gunpowder invented? For $5,000, Was it
a. Italy,
b. Egypt, or
c. China?
Choose your answers, please, audience. Gunpowder was invented where?
Audience, what is your answer?
Audience: Egypt! China!
Host: Roger?
Roger: Gosh, this one is difficult. I'm pretty sure it wasn't Italy, but I'm not sure about Egypt or China . . . hmmm . . . OK, I'm going to say China.
Host: Egypt or China? Let's take a look . . . It's China! Well done, Roger! How do you feel now?
Roger: Relieved. I really wasn't sure that time.
Host: Well, let's see if you can do it again, for $6,000 this time. In 1928, Alexander Fleming of Scotland discovered this natural substance, which is still used today to kill bacteria and fight infections. What is the name of this substance? Is it
a. penicillin,
b. aspirin, or
c. ginseng?
Audience members, please choose your answer.
OK, Members of the audience, what do you say? Is it penicillin, aspirin, or ginseng?
Audience: Penicillin!
Host: Do you agree, Roger?
Roger: I sure do, Ronnie. It's penicillin.
Host: Are you right? . . . Yes! The answer is penicillin. Let's see if we can give you something a little more difficult. Are you ready, Roger?
Roger: Yes, sir.

Host: For $7,000, which of the following was *not* invented by the American inventor Thomas Alva Edison. Was it
a. the motion picture,
b. the telephone, or
c. the lightbulb?
Let's give the audience a moment to decide . . .
And what is your answer?

Audience: Telephone! Motion pictures! Lightbulb!

Host: It sounds like the audience is not sure this time. How about you, Roger?

Roger: Oh, I'm very sure. It's the telephone.

Host: Right again! The telephone was invented by Alexander Graham Bell, not Thomas Edison. Now, Roger, so far you have won $28,000, and we've reached the last question of the game. We're going to give you a choice: you can go home right now with $28,000, or you can answer one more question. If you answer it correctly, we'll double your money! Of course if you get it wrong, you go home with nothing. What would you like to do?

Roger: I'll . . . go for the question, Ronnie.

Host: He'll go for the question! Very well. For a chance at taking home $56,000, here it is. Five hundred years ago people believed that the earth was the center of the universe and that the sun revolved around the earth. In the year 1543, a Polish astronomer proved that the opposite is true; that the sun is the center of our solar system, and all the planets go around it. For $56,000, Roger, what was the name of that astronomer? Was it
a. Isaac Newton,
b. Galileo Galilei, or
c. Nicolaus Copernicus?
Members of the audience, what is your answer?
Audience?

Audience: Galileo! Copernicus! Newton!

Host: Hmmm, no agreement there. Roger Johnson, did you pick the right answer? Who is it?

Roger: Well, uh, let me see. Um, Galileo was Italian, and I'm pretty sure Newton was English. So that leaves Copernicus.

Host: Is that your final answer?

Roger: Yes, it is.

Host: Is he right? For $56,000, the correct answer is . . . Copernicus! Roger Johnson, you have won it all! Congratulations! And that concludes our show for this evening. Please join us next week . . .

Chapter 10 Medicine, Myths, and Magic

PART 1 Listening to Conversations

Listen

3 **Listening for Main Ideas.** page 201. Close your book as you listen to the conversation. Listen for the answers to these questions.

Nancy: Jeff?
Anna: Anybody home?
Nancy: Jeff, what are you doing at home in the middle of the afternoon? Too much partying last night?
Jeff: I've got the flu. My head aches, I've got a temperature of 102, my nose won't stop running, everything hurts. I feel like I'm going to die.
Nancy: Cheer up, you're not going to die. But you sound terrible. Tell you what, I'll go make you some hot herbal tea. Meanwhile, let's get some air in this room. It's awfully hot in here.
Anna: Wait! My grandmother always said you should sweat when you have the flu to reduce the fever. Maybe you shouldn't open the window.
Nancy: Oh that's an old wives' tale.
Anna: An old what?
Nancy: An old wives' tale. You know, a superstition, uh, a folk remedy. Like wearing garlic around your neck to prevent colds, or wearing a copper bracelet if you have rheumatism, or . . .
Jeff: Or hot herbal tea?
Nancy: Oh, no. That really works! There are scientific studies that prove it!
Anna: Herbal Tea? Well, I guess that makes sense. When I was sick as a child, my mother used to give me hot water with lemon. And for a cough, a spoonful of honey.
Nancy: That reminds me of our grandmother's cure for a cough. Talk about an old wives' tale! She came from a small village in Russia, and in the old days, people used to have these special glass cups. They'd heat them and put them on the sick person's chest. That was supposed to get rid of a cough. Can you believe it?
Anna: Why not? You know, lots of times I think home remedies really work because people believe in them. We say they're superstitious, because we think everything has to be scientific. But there are lots of things that science can't explain. Sometimes the best doctor is faith, don't you agree?
Nancy: Yes, I do. So what do you say, Jeff? Do you want to try the cups?
Jeff: Give me a break. Why don't you just bring me some orange juice? And could you help me find the TV remote?
TV Announcer: Cold-Aid contains five times more of the pain reliever doctors recommend most. Next time you have a cold or the flu, try Cold-Aid—the new advanced formula cold medicine that really works.
Jeff: Forget the herbal tea, Nancy! Just bring me some Cold-Aid!

Stress

4 **Listening for Stressed Words.** page 202.

1. Now listen to part of the conversation again. Some of the stressed words are missing. During each pause, repeat the phrase or sentence; then fill in the missing stressed words.
   See conversation.

5 **Pronouncing Compound Phrases.** page 203. Listen to examples of compound nouns from the conversation. Notice which syllables are stressed as you repeat each phrase after the speaker.

See student text.

6 **Predicting Stress in Adjective + Noun Combinations.** page 203. The following table contains both compound phrases and adjective + noun combinations. Following the rules you have just learned, mark the stressed word(s) in each item. Then listen to the tape to check your answers.

See student text.

PART 2 Listening to Lectures

Listen

4 **Recognizing Digressions.** page 207. Listen to information on one type of sleep disorder. Listen carefully for the place where the speaker goes off and then returns to the topic. Remember that you do not need to take notes on digressions.

> The second sleep disorder that I want to describe today is called narcolepsy. That's spelled N-A-R-C-O-L-E-P-S-Y. Perhaps you've seen a movie in which people are sitting at a table, eating and talking, and suddenly one person just falls over; perhaps his face falls into his soup. It's funny in a movie, but in reality this could be a symptom of narcolepsy. Narcoleptic persons get sudden attacks of sleep, in the middle of the day, any time, any place. They can't control it; they simply fall asleep for brief periods of time. By the way, this disorder appears to be particularly frequent among students enrolled in 8 A.M. classes. But seriously, narcolepsy can be quite scary. The cause is high levels of certain chemicals in the part of the brain that regulates sleep. Once narcolepsy is diagnosed, it's usually treated successfully with medication.

5 **Taking Draft Notes.** page 207. Listen to the lecture and take notes in the best way you can. Use your own paper.

Speaker: So, is everyone awake? I guess that's a good question at the start of an early-morning lecture about sleep. Seriously, how many of you feel you didn't get enough sleep last night? Raise your hands. Hmm. About a third of you. That's interesting, because it shows that you're not so different from the population in general. About 30% of adults say they frequently don't feel rested when they wake up in the morning. And why is that? Well, in most cases it's because they stayed up too late partying or watching TV. But in a small percentage of cases, they could be suffering from a sleep disorder, er . . . a condition that interferes with a person's ability to sleep normally. There are many different kinds of sleep disorders but the three that I want to describe today are called sleep apnea, narcolepsy, and insomnia.

OK, the first disorder I listed is sleep apnea. That's A-P-N-E-A. People with sleep apnea stop breathing, sometimes for 10 seconds or longer. And not just once; it can happen several hundred times a night! Each time this happens, they wake up and go right back to sleep, so their sleep is constantly interrupted, but in the morning they don't remember waking up. They just feel tired and sleepy. Yes?

Student 1: So how do you know if you have this problem?

Speaker: I was just getting to that. The usual symptoms are heavy breathing and snoring, combined with feeling tired all the time.

Student 2: What's the cause?

Speaker: The cause of this problem is that air can't go into and out of the nose or mouth, usually because the throat is too relaxed. Consequently, the treatment is fairly simple: the person wears a soft mask attached to a machine that helps to regulate his or her breathing throughout the night. In extreme cases of apnea, surgery may be necessary. You know, a friend of mine waited for 30 years before his sleep apnea was finally diagnosed properly! Now he is happier than ever! So if your roommate or a family member snores a lot and appears to be sleepy all the time, they may have sleep apnea and you might want to send them to a sleep specialist.

The second sleep disorder that I want to describe today is called narcolepsy. That's spelled N-A-R-C-O-L-E-P-S-Y. Perhaps you've seen a movie in which people are sitting at a table, eating and talking, and suddenly one person just falls over; perhaps his face falls into his soup. It's funny in a movie, but in reality this could be a symptom of narcolepsy. Narcoleptic persons get sudden attacks of sleep, in the middle of the day, any time, any place. They can't control it; they simply fall asleep for brief periods of time. By the way, this disorder appears to be particularly frequent among students enrolled in 8 A.M. classes. But seriously, narcolepsy can be quite scary. The cause is high levels of certain chemicals in the part of the brain that regulates sleep. Once narcolepsy is diagnosed, it's usually treated successfully with medication.

Sleep apnea and narcolepsy are serious problems, but they are rare conditions. In contrast, the third sleep disorder I want to discuss, insomnia, is quite common. Insomnia means difficulty either falling asleep or staying asleep. Almost everybody has insomnia once in a while. But I want to talk about chronic insomnia, which is when sleeping becomes difficult for weeks, months, or years at a time. The cause could be either psychological or physical. Most often, it's psychological; that is, it's caused by stress—you know, worrying about problems at work or at home and so on. Or the cause could be physical, such as too much caffeine or nicotine in the body. Both of these chemicals are stimulants that can keep you from sleeping.

Student 3: Excuse me for interrupting, but what are stimulants?

Speaker: Stimulants are substances that make you feel awake and energetic. As I said, coffee and cigarettes are both stimulants.

Now, that brings us to treatments for insomnia.

Obviously, if you have trouble sleeping the first thing you should do is avoid coffee, tea, and cigarettes in the evening. You should also avoid alcohol. Many people say that a glass of beer or wine helps them sleep, and that may be true once in a while. But drinking alcohol every night is dangerous because after a while it stops working and, as everyone knows, alcohol is addictive. You should also avoid sleeping pills for the same reason, because they are addictive. These are the things you *shouldn't* do if you have insomnia. Now, what *should* you do?

Some methods that doctors recommend are, first, listening to relaxation tapes or soft music. Second, you can try self-hypnosis, which is easy to learn. Then there's always TV; many people like to watch TV when they can't sleep. And reading a boring book can also be very effective. That reminds me, your textbooks finally arrived in the bookstore. No, really, please buy them as soon as possible because we'll start using the book next Monday. Anyway, where was I? Oh yes. Treatments for insomnia. What really works for chronic insomnia is taking care of the cause. What I mean is, if stress is the cause of a person's insomnia, it's important to find out where that stress is coming from and to work on lowering the stress. In many cultures people do this with the help of a professional therapist. If therapy doesn't work, medication may be the answer, and luckily there are some wonderful new drugs on the market that aren't addictive.

So, in summary, the thing I want you to remember is that everyone suffers from occasional sleeping problems, but a large number of people suffer from serious sleep disorders such as insomnia, apnea, and narcolepsy. As you've just heard, these disorders have distinct symptoms, causes, and treatments. Thanks to a lot of research in this area in the last few decades, doctors are now able to send patients to special sleep disorders clinics for specialized treatment. Since human beings spend one-third of their lives sleeping, we should all be glad that medical science is now able to help people with sleeping problems.

PART 3 Focused Listening and Speaking

Getting Meaning from Context

1 **Using Context Clues.** page 209. You are going to hear five short conversations.

Conversation 1

Man: All right, now let's talk about prenatal care.
Woman: Well, I know I shouldn't smoke . . .
Man: That's right. Not only that, but you also shouldn't drink alcohol or coffee, especially during the first three months.
Woman: OK, what special things should I eat?
Man: Just eat a balanced diet, but don't overeat. You don't want to gain too much weight, do you? And make sure to take the vitamins I gave you.

Question 1: What is this woman's condition?
Man: Congratulations on your pregnancy. I know you're going to be a fine mother.

Conversation 2

Woman: I just read a book about magic tricks, and I was wondering where the word "magic" came from.

Man: Well, the word "magic" has a very long history. It goes back through Middle English, Middle French, Latin, and ancient Greek, all the way to the old Persian word *mogush*. *Mogush* meant magician, and several languages still use a form of the word *mogush* to mean magic or magician.

Question 2: Who is the speaker, probably?

Woman: Thank you, Professor Bailey. You are better than a dictionary!

Conversation 3

Child: Mama! Guess what! It fell out!

Mother: Let me see. Yes, well, do you know what we're going to do with it?

Child: What?

Mother: Tonight when you go to sleep we're going to put it under your pillow. And while you're asleep, the tooth fairy will come, and she'll leave you some money. Don't forget to check under your pillow in the morning.

Question 3: What has just happened to the child?

Child: Will the tooth fairy come every time I lose a tooth?

Conversation 4

Woman: Oh, no! I've got the hiccups again!

Old man: Did you try holding your breath?

Woman: Yes, but it didn't work.

Old man: All right dear, here's what my grandmother used to do. Take your right hand, put it over your head, and hold your left ear like this. Now take a glass of water in your left hand and drink exactly nine gulps without breathing in between. I don't know why, but it works every time.

Question 4: This man is probably . . .

Woman: Oh Daddy, you're kidding, right?

Conversation 5

Young woman: You're not going to eat that huge piece of pie, are you?

Young man: Why not?

Young woman: You've just had a huge dinner! How can you eat so much? That isn't good for you.

Young man: Come on Christina, give me a break. I just have a big appetite.

Question 5: Why is the girl worried?

Young woman: Still, I think that's too much food at one time!

Focused Listening

2 **Recognizing the Meaning of Negative Tag Questions.** page 210. Listen to negative tag questions and decide the speaker's meaning.

1. Maria didn't call, did she? (rising)
2. There's no homework today, is there? (falling)
3. It's not going to rain today, is it? (rising)
4. You're not going out tonight, are you? (rising)
5. That comedian isn't very funny, is he? (falling)
6. You didn't finish all the ice cream, did you? (rising)
7. You didn't invite James for dinner, did you? (falling)
8. The bus hasn't arrived yet, has it? (rising)

PART 4 Listening and Speaking in the Real World

Listen

3 **Identifying the Steps in Rescue Breathing.** page 214. Listen as a first aid instructor explains the steps in rescue breathing. Write numbers under the pictures to show the correct order. Note: one of the steps is performed twice.

Instructor: Good evening everybody. In this session we're going to go over the basic steps involved in rescue breathing, which is what you do when someone stops breathing in an accident or in a medical emergency. First we're going to look at a slide presentation of the entire procedure and then we'll break into teams to practice.

OK, to begin, if you think someone may have stopped breathing, the first thing you should do is check to see if the person is conscious. To do this touch the person or shake gently and ask, "Are you OK?"

If the person doesn't move or answer, shout for help. Get the attention of other people, who can call an ambulance and help you.

Then, working quickly, move the victim onto his or her back if necessary. Make sure to support the head.

OK, the next step is very important. You need to open the victim's airway so that air can get into his or her lungs. To do this, tilt back the head with one hand and lift the chin with the other. You see how the neck is stretched? That's the way to do it.

Now, check to see if the victim is breathing. Look for the chest to rise and fall; listen for breathing, and feel for air coming out of the victim's nose and mouth. Do this for about five seconds.

If you see that the victim is not breathing, it's up to you to start breathing for him or her. Keep the head tilted back, close off the nose, take a deep breath, and put your mouth tightly over the victim's mouth. Breathe into the victim's lungs. Check for the chest to rise, which means the air is getting through. Then remove your mouth and see if the chest falls. Start by giving two full breaths for about 1 or 1.5 seconds each.

After that, check to see if the person's heart is beating by putting your fingers on the side of his or her neck. If you feel a pulse, then continue rescue breathing. Give one breath every five seconds for an adult. Keep going until the victim starts breathing or until help arrives.

Chapter 11 The Media

PART 1 Listening to Conversations

Listen

3 **Listening for Main Ideas.** page 220. Close your book as you listen to the conversation. Listen for the answers to these questions.

Jeff: Hi, guys. Want some coffee?
Dan: Thanks, that'd be great.
Anna: Yes, thank you.
Dan: Anna? You've been really quiet since we left the theater. What's the matter? Didn't you like the movie?
Anna: No, to tell you the truth I didn't. All that blood and people killing each other. I just don't see the point of such violent movies. And I don't think they should be shown.
Dan: Hold on! You saw how full the theater was. Obviously a lot of people want to see movies like that. And you have no right to tell them they can't. If you think it's offensive, you should just stay home.
Anna: You may be right, but I didn't know it was going to be so violent!
Dan: Come on, Anna, life is violent! And movies are just a reflection of real life. If you don't like a movie you're free to walk out.
Jeff: Here's the coffee. What are you arguing about?
Dan: The movie.
Jeff: What about it? Was it good?
Dan: I liked it but Anna's upset about the violence. She thinks violent movies shouldn't be shown.
Jeff: Hmmm. Well, I don't believe in total censorship, especially not for adults. But just the other day I was reading that there may be a connection between watching violent films and acting violently.
Dan: For some people that may be true, but not for ordinary people. I mean, we just saw the film and we're not about to do anything violent, are we?
Anna: No, but what if some disturbed person in the audience saw it and got some strange ideas from it?
Dan: I think that sooner or later, a person like that is probably going to do something strange or violent anyway. Seeing a movie doesn't cause people to go off the deep end unless there is something wrong with them in the first place.
Anna: Maybe you're right. But what about those teenagers in the audience? That was an R-rated movie, so what were they doing there?
Dan: OK, you've got a point there. I agree that kids shouldn't be allowed to see violent films. I think parents need to supervise their kids better, and theaters should be stricter about enforcing the ratings. But that's different from total censorship, which is what you were talking about before, Anna.
Anna: OK, Dan, you win. But next time, can we please see a comedy?

Stress

4 **Listening for Stressed Words.** page 220.

1. Now listen to part of the conversation again. Some of the stressed words are missing. During each pause, repeat the phrase or sentence; then fill in the missing stressed words.

   See conversation.

PART 2

Listening to Lectures

Listen

3 **Taking Notes on Advantages and Disadvantages.** page 224. Here are abbreviated notes from one part of the lecture. Listen to the passage and rewrite the notes in two forms:

1. an outline
2. two columns, with advantages on one side and disadvantages on the other

Teacher: Let's start with the print media in other words, newspapers and magazines. Both of these have advantages and disadvantages for an advertiser. First, newspapers. If you were an advertiser, why would you choose to advertise in a newspaper?

Student 1: Everyone reads newspapers.

Teacher: Correct. And that's important because it means the ads reach large numbers of people. OK. What else?

Student 2: It's cheap?

Teacher: Yes, relatively speaking. I mean, it's cheaper than a magazine ad, for example. And there are two more advantages: newspapers are published every day, so ads can be repeated. And finally, newspapers are usually local. This is an advantage because it allows advertisers to advertise directly to their customers. For example, let's say I own a bakery in a small town; in that case I will choose to advertise in my town's local newspaper because that's where my customers are. Understand?

OK. Now, on the other hand, there is a disadvantage to advertising in newspapers, and that is that most newspapers don't have color, so they're not very exciting or memorable. I mean most of us throw away the newspaper at the end of the day, right? This is why you usually don't find ads for expensive cars like, oh, Mercedes Benz in newspapers.

4 **Taking Draft Notes.** page 224. Listen to the whole lecture and take notes in the form of an outline, a two-column chart, or a combination of the two. Use your own paper.

Teacher: Let's say that a car company like Mitsubishi, or BMW, or General Motors has just come out with a new car. Naturally the company wants to sell lots of cars and make lots of money, right? But before anyone will buy this new car, the company has to inform the public about its new product. How does the company do that? By advertising, of course. No company can hope to make a profit on a product unless it advertises it first. That's why, for example, U.S. companies spend more than $180 *billion* a year on advertising. Japan, by the way, spends almost 50 billion, and other Asian countries spend more than 10 billion.

Now, the most important decision that a company has to make regarding advertising is *where* to advertise. Basically an advertiser can choose from three categories of media: print, broadcast, and direct. Again, those categories are print, broadcast, and direct. All the media that you're familiar with, you know, radio, newspapers, uh, billboards, and so on, fit into one of these categories. So, in today's lecture we're going to look at the most common types of media used in advertising and learn about their advantages and disadvantages for advertisers.

Let's start with the print media, in other words, newspapers and magazines. Both of these have advantages and disadvantages for an advertiser. First, newspapers. If you were an advertiser, why would you choose to advertise in a newspaper?

Student 1: Everyone reads newspapers.

Teacher: Correct. And that's important because it means the ads reach large numbers of people. What else?

Student 2: It's cheap?

Teacher: Yes, relatively speaking. I mean, it's cheaper than a magazine ad, for example. And there are two more advantages: newspapers are published every day, so ads can be repeated. And finally, newspapers are usually local. This is an advantage because it allows advertisers to advertise directly to their customers. For example, let's say I own a bakery in a small town; in that case I will choose to advertise in my town's local newspaper because that's where my customers are. Understand?

Now, on the other hand, there is a disadvantage to advertising in newspapers, and that is that most newspapers don't have color, so the ads aren't very exciting or memorable. Also, most of us throw away the newspaper at the end of the day, right? This is why you usually don't find ads for expensive cars like, oh, Mercedes Benz in newspapers. Instead, you find those ads in the second type of print media, in magazines.

Again, with magazines there are both advantages and disadvantages. The first advantage of magazine advertising is, of course, the color and the nice paper, so magazine ads are more exciting than newspaper ads, and people tend to keep them for a while instead of throwing them out. Second, most magazines have specialized groups of readers. Let me explain this. There are special magazines for . . . sports, magazines for car lovers, magazines about politics, and so on. So let's say you're an advertiser, and your product is . . . a kind of tea that helps people lose weight. Where would you choose to advertise?

Student 3: In a health magazine.

Student 4: In a magazine about herbs.

Teacher: Good. And you wouldn't advertise in a political magazine because it would not be the best way to spend money. People who read magazines about politics are probably not going to pay as much attention to an ad about losing weight as people who read magazines about health. So again, the advantage of advertising in magazines is it allows a business to direct, or send, its ads to specialized groups of people who are most interested in the product. You got that? OK. In contrast, the disadvantage of magazine ads is that they can be very expensive, especially in popular magazines like *Newsweek* or *People*.

OK, let's move on now and talk about the second category, the broadcast media, by which we mean radio and television. These also have both advantages and disadvantages. First, radio, uh, radio is similar to newspapers in that everybody listens to it, so radio ads reach lots of people. Also, radio is usually local. The disadvantage is that radio ads are not permanent in the way printed ads are, so . . . Yes?

Student 1: I'm sorry, I'm not really clear on what you mean by "local."

Teacher: OK, let's say you live in . . . Toronto, in Canada. A local newspaper would be a paper that's written and published in Toronto and not in London or New York. So it would tend to focus on news and information that the people of Toronto are interested in. Does that make sense?

Student 1: Yes, thanks.

Teacher: OK, I was about to start talking about television advertising. But first I want to ask you a question: how many people here have a favorite newspaper ad? Nobody? OK, how about a favorite magazine ad? Nobody again. A favorite radio ad? Still nobody. Well, how about a favorite television ad?

Class: I like the Nike ads with Michael Jordan. Coca-Cola: "It's the real thing . . ."

Teacher: Now why is it that many of you have a favorite TV ad? What is it about TV that's so memorable?

Student 2: The sound and the movement.

Student 3: The ads tell a story.

Student 4: The color.

Teacher: Well, there you have the advantages of TV advertising. With sound, movement, and color, TV ads are the easiest to remember. Another advantage of TV is that everybody watches it, so it's the easiest way to reach people all over the world, like during the Olympic Games, for example. On the other hand, I'm sure you can guess the big disadvantage with TV ads.

Student 2: The cost.

Teacher: Yes. TV advertising is enormously expensive. In the United States, for example, a 30-second ad on an evening TV show costs more than half a million dollars. Clearly, only large, successful companies can afford to advertise on television.

Hmmm. It's time for a break. After that we'll talk about the direct media and also about advertising on the World Wide Web.

PART 3 Focused Listening and Speaking

Getting Meaning from Context

2 **Using Context Clues.** page 227. Listen as a man reads selections from the newspaper out loud. Decide which part of the newspaper the selections probably appeared in. Write the letters in the blanks.

Number 1

Mission Impossible 2, Tom Cruise's action-packed sequel, took in almost $93 million in its first six days, far more than the original film, which grossed $75 million in the same time period in 1996. The new film, with its relatively bloodless slow-motion ballets of kicks, punches, gunplay, and car crashes, is nevertheless far too violent for children.

Number 2

Forecasters at the National Hurricane Center are watching Hurricane Aletta, which was upgraded from a tropical storm Wednesday morning. As of Thursday morning, Aletta's top winds were 105 miles per hour with higher gusts as it progressed west at 8 miles per hour. The hurricane is expected to continue strengthening over the next few days as it slowly moves west.

Number 3

The Olympic flame crossed into the southern hemisphere today for the first time since 1956, landing in the Pacific island nation of Nauru, the world's smallest republic. Next Friday the flame will travel to the Solomon Islands for the next stop in its journey to Australia for the Sydney Olympic Games that start Sept. 15.

Number 4

Surveys have proven that talking on a car phone while driving isn't safe. A study published in *The New England Journal of Medicine* in 1997 concluded that the risk of collision is four times higher for those with phones in hand. Yet this activity is permitted in most states. Concerned citizens need to get involved and help put an end to this dangerous conduct. I urge you to write or call your state representatives and tell them what you think. But don't call from your car!

Number 5

Attendance at Disney World, the world's No. 1 travel destination, has jumped nearly 50 percent since 1995. Yet it's not an easy trip—prices are soaring, and the number of things to see has grown so much that vacationers no longer can do it all in one trip. Therefore, planning is essential.

Number 6

A judge ordered the breakup Wednesday of Microsoft Corporation, the world's largest maker of PC software, into two parts after finding that the company had engaged in unfair business practices. Bill Gates, founder and president of Microsoft, contested the finding and vowed to appeal the judge's decision.

Number 7

The Mexican peso strengthened somewhat Friday, closing at 9.89 to the dollar, but it still stood near its weakest level in 15 months after a long period of relative stability. On Thursday, the peso slipped as low as 10 to the dollar before closing at 9.94, a rate not seen since March 1999. As recently as May 31, a dollar cost just 9.50 pesos.

Focused Listening

3 **Pronouncing Noun/Verb Pairs.** page 227.

1. Listen to and repeat the noun/verb pairs in the chart.
   See student text.

4 **Discriminating between Nouns and Verbs Spelled Alike.** page 228. Listen to sentences containing the following words. Place a mark above the stressed syllable you hear.

1. Our teacher does not permit us to eat or drink during the lesson.
2. Coffee is the chief export of Brazil.
3. Susanna received an expensive birthday present from her boyfriend.
4. My country produces cars and electronic equipment.
5. During the war, many families were forced to desert their homes.
6. In some countries, it is an insult to show someone the bottom of your shoe.
7. The price of gasoline has increased lately.
8. John interviewed three people and recorded their answers.
9. There are many contrasts between the American and Japanese cultures.
10. Some countries import all their oil.

PART 4

Listening and Speaking in the Real World

Listen

2 **Listening to a Telephone Survey.** page 230. Before listening to the phone survey, look at the questionnaire. What do you think the purpose of the survey is? As you listen, take the role of the caller and complete the form based on the information you hear.

Woman: Hello.
Man: This is Jim Evers from Market Research Corporation. We're conducting a nationwide survey of people's reading habits. Would you have five minutes to answer a few questions?
Woman: Oh, I suppose.
Man: First of all, do you read any newspapers and, if so, which ones?
Woman: I read the *New York Times* and the *Wall Street Journal.*
Man: Approximately how many hours per week do you spend reading a newspaper?
Woman: Oh, let's see. About an hour a day, so I'd say at least seven hours a week.
Man: Okay. Now, do you subscribe to these newspapers?
Woman: I subscribe to the *Times,* but I get the *Wall Street Journal* at the office.
Man: I see. What about magazines? Do you subscribe to any?
Woman: Oh, yeah. I get *Fortune* and *People.* And my husband gets *Sports Illustrated,* so I read that too, sometimes.
Man: About how many hours a week do you read magazines then?
Woman: Oh, maybe two or three.
Man: All right. Now, do you read books regularly and, if so, what type?
Woman: Well, novels are my favorite kind but, to tell you the truth, I haven't read one in quite a while. I'm taking a class at night, so the only books I've been reading lately are textbooks.
Man: I take it then that you don't belong to a book club?
Woman: No, I don't.
Man: And about how much time do you spend a week reading textbooks?
Woman: Not enough. I guess a couple of hours.
Man: Okay. Besides textbooks, about how much money do you spend a year on books?
Woman: Very little. I prefer going to the library.
Man: About how many hours of television do you watch a week?
Woman: Television? Who's got the time? We have two sets, but I only watch once in a while—no more than an hour a week.
Man: Well, we're just about done. I just have a few personal questions, if you don't mind answering them.
Woman: That depends.
Man: I need your approximate age. Are you between 25 and 35, 36 and 45, 46 and 55, 56 and above?
Woman: I'm 49.
Man: And what is your occupation, ma'am?
Woman: I'm a stockbroker.
Man: Is your yearly income between 15 and 20 thousand, between 21 and 30 thousand . . .?
Woman: I'd rather not answer that.
Man: OK. That's the last question. Thank you very much for your time.
Woman: You're welcome. Bye.

Chapter 12 With Liberty and Justice for All

PART 1 Listening to Conversations

Listen

3 **Listening for Main Ideas.** page 236. Close your book as you listen to the conversation. Listen for the answers to these questions.

Manager: Mr. Evans, on your application you list your current occupation as "musician." Would you mind telling me why you're applying for a job in an office?

Jeff: Well, you know, it's pretty hard to make a living as a musician. I mean, most musicians work at other jobs during the daytime.

Manager: Yes, I know. But, uh, I'm a little concerned that your music may interfere with your responsibilities in the office.

Jeff: I don't think there will be any problem. It's true that I work nights a lot, but this job doesn't start until 10 A.M., right?

Manager: Yes. Well, uh, let's talk about your experience. Your last job was at a computer store.

Jeff: Right.

Manager: And I see that you've worked in a doctor's office before. What did you . . . I mean, what were your responsibilities there?

Jeff: I had to answer the phones, make appointments, type letters, and take care of the billing.

Manager: I see. Look, Mr. Evans, you're obviously qualified for the job. The only thing is, well, you'd be the only man working in an office full of women. How do you feel about that?

Jeff: I live with two women, my cousin and one of her students. It's no big deal to me.

Manager: Well, okay, Mr. Evans. I think that will be all. You'll be hearing from us in a day or two.

Jeff: All right. Thanks for your time.

Manager: Good-bye.

Jeff: Bye.

Jeff: Hi, Nancy.

Nancy: Hi. How did your interview go?

Jeff: I blew it, Nancy. The office manager and I didn't hit it off very well. First of all, she seemed very uptight when I told her I was a musician. And you should have seen her face when I told her I lived with two women! Maybe if I'd been a woman I would have had a chance, but I really think it's a long shot.

Nancy: That's not fair. It's illegal to discriminate against people because of their sex. If you're the best person for the job, she has to hire you.

Jeff: I know, but . . .

Jeff: Hello?

Manager: Can I speak to Jeff Evans, please?

Jeff: Speaking.

Manager: This is Marla Graham from Dr. Erickson's office. I'm calling to tell you that if you're still interested in working for us, well, we'd be happy to have you.

Jeff: You're kidding. I got the job?
Manager: Yes, Mr. Evans, you got it. You've got a good head on your shoulders. Besides, we decided that we need a male touch around this office. Can you start on Monday at 1:00?
Jeff: I'll be there.
Manager: Okay. See you then.
Jeff: Great. Bye. I don't believe it! I got the job!
Nancy: Congratulations! Break a leg!

Stress

4 **Listening for Stressed Words.** page 236.

1. Now listen to part of the conversation again. Some of the stressed words are missing. During each pause, repeat the phrase or sentence; then fill in the missing stressed words.

   See conversation.

Reductions

5 **Comparing Long and Reduced Forms.** page 237. The sentences on the left side contain reduced forms. Listen and repeat them after the speaker. Note: you will hear the reduced forms only.

See student text.

6 **Listening for Reductions.** page 238.

1. Listen to the following conversation. It contains reduced forms. Write the long forms in the blanks.

   A: What's wrong?
   B: I'm sure I flunked my test in Chinese history.
   A: Didn't you study?
   B: Yeah, but I guess I should have studied more. I shouldn't have watched that basketball game on TV last night. Then maybe I would have done better.
   A: The test must have been really hard.
   B: Yeah, and it was too long. There wasn't enough time to answer all the questions.

PART 2 Listening to Lectures

Listen

3 **Taking Draft Notes.** page 242. Listen to the lecture and take notes in the best way you can. Use your own paper.

Speaker: Does the date December 10, 1948, have any special meaning to you? Probably not. You weren't born yet; in fact, most of your parents weren't even born. Yet on this date, something happened that changed history. On December 10, 1948, all the members of the United Nations passed the Universal Declaration of Human Rights. The Declaration is a document that outlined, for the first time in history, the basic rights, or freedoms, that *all* people have, simply because they are human. Many people feel that December 10, 1948, was the beginning of the modern human rights movement, and since that date, the world has observed December 10 as Human Rights Day.

So, in this lecture I want to tell you something about the Universal Declaration of Human Rights. First of all, what does this document say?

Well, the Universal Declaration of Human Rights contains 30 articles, or sections, in four categories of human rights: first, civil and political rights; second, economic rights; third, social rights; and fourth, cultural rights. We don't have time to examine all 30 articles, but let me give you some examples of the rights that are included in each of these areas.

To begin, more than half of the Declaration deals with civil or political rights. Um . . . yes?

Student 1: I have heard the phrase "civil rights" many times, but I don't really know what it means.

Speaker: Well, that's a good question. "Civil rights" means the basic freedoms that all the citizens of a country have. For example, uh, what country do you come from?

Student 1: Spain.

Speaker: OK, now in Spain, if you don't like something the president did, and you write a letter to the newspaper about it, will you be arrested?

Student: Of course not.

Speaker: That's because you have freedom of speech. That is one of your civil rights. Now here's another example. Suppose you live in one city, and you decide to accept a job in another city. Do you need the government's permission to move?

Student 1: No . . .

Teacher: Well, freedom of movement is also a civil right. So now do you understand what "civil rights" means?

Student 1: Yes, thanks.

Speaker: OK, as I was saying, the Universal Declaration of Human Rights contains a detailed list of people's civil rights. Article 1, for example, says that all human beings are born free and equal. In addition, the Declaration states that every person should have freedom of movement, freedom of speech, and freedom of religion. Furthermore, the Declaration prohibits slavery and torture, and it also prohibits discrimination against minority groups.

The second group of articles deals with economic rights. Article 23, for instance, states that everyone has a right to work and to be paid for work, and furthermore, that everyone has the right to equal pay for equal work; in other words, if men and women are doing the same work, they should be paid at the same level.

The next category, social rights, mainly deals with education. The Declaration states that everyone has a right to education and that parents have a right to choose the kind of education they want for their children.

Finally, in the area of cultural rights, the Declaration states that people have the right to participate in the cultural, artistic, and scientific life of their communities. This means that countries like Cuba that control literature and art aren't respecting their people's human rights, according to the Declaration.

Now that I've described the Declaration, let's talk about the significance of this document. Why was this document so important? Because, for the first time in history, there was a written document that contained universal standards, um, definitions or descriptions of right and wrong. To put it simply, the Declaration established rules for how nations should treat their citizens. And in cases where countries or the leaders of countries mistreated their people, the Declaration gave United Nations the power to force them to change or to be punished for their behavior. Understand?

It has been more than 50 years since the Universal Declaration of Human Rights was passed. In that time, we have seen improvements in human rights in many countries. Uh, can you think of any countries where this is true?

Student 2: South Africa.

Speaker: Very good. In 1991, South Africa abolished the practice of apartheid. Under apartheid, black people were separated from white people and were forced to obey the laws of the white government. By the way, for most of its history, the United States also allowed discrimination against black people. Did you know that during the 1950s, black Americans had separate schools, separate churches, even separate swimming pools? It wasn't until 1964 that discrimination became illegal in the United States.

So, there is no doubt that there has been a lot of progress in human rights in the last 50 years. But I don't have to tell you that there's still a lot of work to do. Millions of people are still living in conditions that violate their human rights. Here are some facts that, in my opinion, are quite shocking:

- Today more than a billion people are living in poverty.
- More than 16 million people are homeless refugees.
- At least 30 wars are being fought at this very moment.
- Many war criminals are walking around free.
- Torture of prisoners is still common in many places.
- And, believe it or not, there are still countries in which children and women are being sold as slaves.

It may be difficult for you to imagine the lives of unfortunate people far away. But let me conclude by reminding you that human rights violations don't just happen far away. There is discrimination and violence, especially against women, children, and minority groups everywhere. Human rights violations happen in both developing nations and industrialized nations. Let's face it: we live in an imperfect world where many people are suffering. But the Universal Declaration of Human Rights provides us with a hope, a vision of a world where every human being is free and equal.

PART 3 Focused Listening and Speaking

Focused Listening

1 **Pronouncing Word Families.** page 244. Listen and repeat the following word families. Place a mark over the stressed syllable in each word.

See student text.

2 **Predicting Stress.** page 244. In the following word families, the stress is marked for the first word. Predict where the stress will fall on the other words. Then listen to the tape and check your answers.

See student text.

Getting Meaning from Context

3 **Using Context Clues.** page 245. You are going to hear five short talks.

Talk 1

Most people think freedom of speech is a basic human right. However, not everybody agrees. For example, should you have freedom of speech when using e-mail? In the United States, about 40% of companies don't think so. They read their workers' e-mail because they are concerned that workers use company computers during work hours to send personal messages. They are also concerned about the words or the language used in e-mail messages. The question is, what is more important, the right to privacy and free speech or the right of the employer to control company equipment and time?

Question 1: What can we guess?

Talk 2

Capital punishment is the execution, or legal killing, of a person for committing a serious crime. Many people are against capital punishment. They say it is a violation of human rights. Other people believe that death is the right punishment for certain crimes. They also believe that capital punishment helps prevent crime. By the year 2000, 108 countries had discontinued the practice of capital punishment. However, it was still legal in 87 countries, including the United States.

Question 2: Which statement is true, based on the information in the passage?

Talk 3

Did you know that about 120 million children in the world work full-time? Many of these children work in dangerous conditions for very low pay. Most of them—61%—work in Asia, but child labor also exists in industrialized countries. These children are usually employed in clothing factories and agriculture. Fortunately, over the past ten years the world has become more concerned about the cruelty of child labor. In addition, globalization is improving the economic conditions of many countries. As economies improve, the need to employ children will decrease.

Question 3: Which of the following will probably happen in the future?

Talk 4

People from different cultures have different ideas about the treatment of animals. Some are very concerned about this issue, while others may not think about it at all. For example, many American people are strongly opposed to violence against animals. Some people believe that animals have rights just as humans do. Therefore, they do not eat meat or hunt, and some of them will not wear clothes made from the skin of animals. They may also be against testing chemicals on animals. At the end of an American movie it's common to see an announcement like this: "No animals were hurt during the production of this movie."

Question 4: What can we conclude?

Talk 5

In 1990, the United States passed a new law to stop discrimination against people with disabilities. The law helps these people find jobs, and it also makes their lives easier and more comfortable. For example, according to this law, public buildings must have special doors and seats for people in wheelchairs. The law protects not only people with physical disabilities like blindness and deafness, but also those with diseases like cancer, AIDS, or heart disease. About 50 million Americans are protected by this law, which is called the Americans with Disabilities Act.

Question 5: Which of the following is probably true in the United States?

PART 4 Listening and Speaking in the Real World

Listen

2 **Completing Graphs.** page 247. Listen to the tape and complete the following graphs.

Graph 1

According to the International Labor Organization, one half of all the workers in the world are women. Yet women are paid less than men for the same kind of work in every country in the world. Let's look at a few examples. Place a mark in the correct place when you hear the numbers. In Turkey, women are paid 93 cents for every dollar that men earn. In Australia, it is 90 cents. In the United States, 82 cents. In France, 81 cents. In Germany, 74. In Hong Kong, 63. And in Japan, women earn only 51 cents for every dollar that men are paid.

http://www.essential.org/ilo/press_releases/ilo1.html

Graph 2

This bar graph shows differences in education among four ethnic groups in the United States. Write the percentages you hear next to the matching bars. First let's talk about high school achievement. 85% of Asian Americans graduated from high school in 1997. This compared with 83 percent of whites, 75% of blacks, and about 55% of Hispanics, which means people with a Spanish-speaking background. Now, if we look at college graduation rates, we see even larger differences among the groups. Asian Americans are the most educated group, with 42% receiving bachelor's degrees. The next group is whites. 25% of whites graduated from college. The third group is blacks, with 13%. And last came Hispanics, with only 10% graduating from college.

http://www.infoplease.com/ipa/A0112596.html

Graph 3

More than 11 million people worldwide are refugees, meaning that they have been forced to leave their homes because of wars, natural disasters, or economic problems. There are refugees on every continent. Write the percentages you hear on the continents on the map. By the end of 1998, the largest number of refugees, 41%, was found in Asia. Next was Africa, with 28%. Europe was third, with 23%. After that came North America, with 6%, then South America, with 1%, and Oceania, which includes Australia and the island countries near it, also with 1%. By the way, at the end of 1998, the largest refugee population in one country was found in Afghanistan, where 2.6 million persons were displaced.

http://www.unhcr.ch/statist/98oview/ch1.htm

Photo Credits

Page 1 ©Bob Kramer/Stock Boston; ***Page 8*** ©Bob Krist/Corbis; ***Page 23*** ©Jack K. Clark/The Image Works; ***Page 31*** ©Nance Trueworthy; ***Page 32*** ©Jim Whitmer/Stock Boston; ***Page 35*** ©Joel Gordon Photography; ***Page 36*** ©Nance Trueworthy; ***Page 43*** ©Allan Tannenbaum/The Image Works; ***Page 52*** http://www.time.com; ***Page 54 (left)*** ©Bettman/Corbis, ***(middle)*** Courtesy, Mrs. Fields Cookies, ***(right)*** ©J. Sulley/The Image Works; ***Page 56*** ©John Fung; ***Page 65*** ©Mark Richards/Photo Edit; ***Page 80 (top left)*** ©Esbin Anderson/The Image Works, ***(top right)*** ©Spencer Grant/Photo Edit, ***(remainder of photos on this page)*** ©Joel Gordon Photography; ***Page 89*** Photo courtesy of Annie Sullivan; ***Page 96*** ©Photofest; ***Page 99*** ©Lawrence Migdale/Photo Researchers Inc.; ***Page 102*** ©Blair Seitz/Photo Researchers Inc.; ***Page 113*** ©Bill Bachmann/Stock Boston; ***Page 121 (top left)*** ©Fujifotos/The Image Works, ***(top right)*** ©John Fung, ***(bottom left)*** ©Amy C. Etra/Photo Edit, ***(bottom right)*** ©Nance Trueworthy; ***Page 125*** ©Patrick Giardino/Corbis; ***Page 129*** ©J. Sohm/The Image Works; ***Page 130*** ©Robert Brenner/Photo Edit; ***Page 132 (top left)*** ©J. Griffin/The Image Works, ***(top right)*** ©Jeff Greenberg/Photo Edit, ***(middle left)*** ©Tom Bean/Corbis, ***(middle right)*** ©Lichtenstein/The Image Works, ***(bottom left)*** ©Jeremy Homer/Corbis, ***(bottom right)*** ©Susan Van Etten/Photo Edit; ***Page 135*** ©Owen Franken/Stock Boston; ***Page 147*** ©Gilbert L. Twest/Visuals Unlimited; ***Page 150*** ©Syracuse Newspapers/The Image Works; ***Page 151*** ©Nance Trueworthy; ***Page 153*** ©Walter Gilardetti; ***Page 161 (left)*** ©Bettman/Corbis; ***Page 165*** ©Joel Gordon Photography; ***Page 175*** ©Maslowski/Visuals Unlimited; ***Page 184*** ©Roy C. Bishop/Stock Boston; ***Page 194*** ©Photofest; ***Page 199*** ©A. Ramey/Photo Edit; ***Page 206*** ©Russell D. Curtis/Photo Researchers Inc.; ***Page 217*** ©Reuters/Bettmann; ***Page 226*** ©Joel Gordon Photography; ***Page 233*** ©Gary Donner/Photo Edit; ***Page 241*** ©Mark Ludak/The Image Works; ***Page 249 (left)*** ©Reuters/Dylan Martinez/Hulton Archive, ***(top right)*** ©AFP/Corbis, ***(bottom)*** ©Reuters/New Media/Corbis; ***Page 250 (top left)*** ©AFP/Corbis, ***(top right)*** ©Douglan Engle/AP Wideworld Photos, ***(middle left)*** ©AFP/Corbis, ***(middle)*** ©Reuters New Media/Corbis, ***(middle right)*** ©Miki Kratsman/Corbis, ***(bottom left)*** ©Louise Gubb/The Image Works, ***(bottom middle)*** ©Alison Wright/The Image Works, ***(bottom right)*** ©David & Peter Tumley/Corbis. ***Page 129*** from "This is the typical day of a relatively typical soul . . . " by Pico Lyer, TIME, December 29, 1993, ©Time, Inc., reprinted by permission.